The Essence of Humanism

The Essence of Humanism

Free Thought Versus Religious Belief

Glenn M. Hardie

Copyright © 2004 by Glenn M. Hardie.

ISBN: Softcover   1-4134-5113-6

All rights reserved. No part of this book may be reproduced or transmitted in any form or by any means, electronic or mechanical, including photocopying, recording, or by any information storage and retrieval system, without permission in writing from the copyright owner.

This book was printed in the United States of America.

To order additional copies of this book, contact:
Xlibris Corporation
1-888-795-4274
www.Xlibris.com
Orders@Xlibris.com
24384

Contents

FOREWORD 9
ACKNOWLEDGMENTS 11
RATIONALE 13

PROLOGUE 15

PART ONE
Humanism and Freethought

CHAPTER 1.1: THE ELEMENTS OF HUMANISM 27
CHAPTER 1.2: THE HUMANIST OBSERVED 49
CHAPTER 1.3: MORALITY 77
CHAPTER 1.4: APOSTASY 94
CHAPTER 1.5: THE ESSENTIALS OF HUMANISM 102

PART TWO
Religion and Mysticism

CHAPTER 2.1: THE HUMAN CONDITION 115
CHAPTER 2.2: BELIEF SYSTEMS 132
CHAPTER 2.3: THEISTIC SYSTEMS 166
CHAPTER 2.4: NON-THEISTIC SYSTEMS 190
CHAPTER 2.5: OTHER SYSTEMS 199

EPILOGUE 219

Appendices and Bibliography

APPENDICES 233
BIBLIOGRAPHIES 247
INDEX 257

"The fact that a believer is happier than a skeptic is no more to the point than the fact that a drunk man is happier than a sober one"

George Bernard Shaw

FOREWORD

This book has been written as a kind of primer in humanistic thought for the benefit of others who, like myself, are not profound scholars of philosophy or religion. All of the information in this book came from readily available sources, such as public lectures, libraries, and bookstores. It is directed towards ordinary people who have to work at other things for a living, and who thus may not have the time, money, facility, or inclination to permit extensive and detailed study of matters pertaining to humanism.

The book is also directed towards that vast and rapidly increasing number of humans who do not subscribe to any particular religion, and who may find in this book the expression of their own latent humanism. Many people are simply not aware of the lengthy existence and growing significance of the Humanist Movement. They may be relieved to discover, as I was, that they are not alone, and to know that a channel exists into which they may direct their thoughts, energies, and support, if they should so choose to assist in improving the only world in which we all have to live.

It has often been said that it is wrong to criticize religion, because religion makes people virtuous and lets them feel comfortable. While one might debate why anyone would want to choose comfort over reason, there is not much evidence anywhere in the world that so-called religious people are more virtuous than non-religious people. In fact, some recent psychological studies have shown that there is no significant difference between religious and non-religious people in tests involving conscience and morality. Some data show that students raised in strict religious denominational schools subsequently have a higher crime rate when compared to populations in general. Indeed, it may further be said that religious people are often more hypocritical than non-religious people, because they literally do not practice what they preach. Virtuous sentiments, such as "love thy neighbor" and "give to the poor" are viewed as having an essentially theoretical value for many religious protagonists; they are certainly not always acted upon in real life.

However, this essay is not intended as an attack on anything or anybody. It is presented rather as a positive and hopefully constructive argument for abandoning ancient, superstitious, and harmful religious beliefs in favor of a more cogent set of modern, scientific, and kindly precepts for the conduct of human affairs.

Glenn M. Hardie
Vancouver, B.C.
Spring 2004

ACKNOWLEDGMENTS

Although virtually every person we encounter on our way through life has some effect on our thoughts and outlook, it is considered appropriate to acknowledge the more direct contributions to the present work of a small number of specific individuals personally known to the author from the distant and more recent past. They are listed in terms of their approximate chronological involvement in the experiences that led to this present work.

Leslie Rosin, a Jewish friend, who showed me that, although most religious dogmas are incompatible one with another, humans beings of good will can live in harmony with each other.

Keith Collier, a Christian friend, who introduced me to the works of several theologians and who engaged me in constructive philosophical polemic whenever it seemed justified.

Gordon Rodgers, a Humanist friend, who specifically showed me humanism in action in ordinary life, and who generally gave direction to the efforts of myself and many other humanists.

Lorraine Hardie, my wife and closest friend, who listened to my ideas, offered suggestions for inclusion or exclusion, and gave me the space, time, and encouragement to complete the project.

I also acknowledge the thoughtful contributions of **Paul Pfalzner** (Past President of the Humanist Association of Canada),

Theo Meijer (Past President of the British Columbia Humanist Association), **Pat Duffy Hutcheon** (Canadian Humanist of the Year 2002), and **Ernest Poser** (one of the founders of modern humanism in Canada), all of whom suggested improvements to the manuscript; of many friends and colleagues encountered over many years in the humanist movement who sharpened my focus on humanism; and of faculty members in the **Philosophy Department** at the University of British Columbia, from whom I learned a great deal about the world of ideas, and a little about myself.

As noted in the Foreword, it is appropriate to reiterate that most of the ideas to be found in this book came from other authorities. The intention for the book is to be a reference work. No claim is made by the author regarding the generation of original philosophical ideas, policy formulations, formal statements, or informal commentary. Wherever possible and appropriate, credit is given to other authors or sources for their direct or indirect contributions to this current work. If omissions are noted or are of concern, please contact the publisher for correction in future editions.

RATIONALE

The concept for this book arose primarily from three sources, one major and two relatively minor: The *major* source was my own life experiences, such as family upbringing, conversations with friends and relations, and various readings I had undertaken from time to time as I matured in my thoughts and behaviors. I resolved to try to organize and articulate my thoughts and feelings in connection with these general themes.

The first *minor* source arose at a meeting of local humanists, when, during an oral presentation on the basic tenets of humanism, I asked the members of the audience how many of them could name at least one humanist "hero." The results astonished me. Apart from a few academics in the group (who were away ahead of me), about 15% of the remainder of the people present could not identify one single name of importance to the Humanist Movement. They had never heard of *Robert Ingersoll*, or *Charles Bradlaugh*, or even *Bertrand Russell.* They were either unaware of, or could not identify, the humanist inclinations of people like *Isaac Asimov*, the well known science fiction author and former President of the American Humanist Association, *Carl Sagan* of "Cosmos" fame, and *Gene Roddenberry,* the creator of "Star Trek," to name just a few. They had never heard of the various editions of the Humanist Manifesto, and had never read any of the works of influential and published humanists, such as *Paul Kurtz* and *Corliss Lamont.* I wondered just how such people could consider themselves to be humanists, if they were so lacking in what seemed to me to be basic knowledge of the movement in general, and I resolved to do something to fill this apparent vacuum. This book is the result.

The second *minor* source arose from casual conversations I have had with a number of humanist colleagues, in which I happened to mention the names of a couple of the lesser known religions, such as Jainism or Shintoism, and some mystical pursuits, such as astrology or feng shui, in order to compare them to the rational basis of humanism. As these conversations developed, it became clear to me that many of my colleagues not only did not know about these admittedly esoteric life stances, they were quite unclear on the basis of and differences between some of the more mainline religions, such as Islam and Hinduism. It seemed to me that it is not enough just to absorb the principles of humanism and adopt its practices; it is also desirable to have at least some rudimentary knowledge of at least the larger of the thousands of competing religious denominations to be found throughout the world and against which humanism can be fairly compared. This is not to say that humanists should be *against* religion, or anything else, for that matter; they should be *for* education and the acquisition of useful knowledge in order to be in a position to make informed judgements.

Thus, following a short **Prologue** outlining some life experiences, **Part One** deals with humanism and free-thought. **Part Two** deals with religions, both theistic and non-theistic, as well as a variety of selected mystical beliefs. The book ends with an **Epilogue**, containing personal opinion about the general content. There are a number of (hopefully) useful appendices included in the volume, as well as a fully detailed bibliography and an index to facilitate pin-pointing specific issues.

PROLOGUE

P.1 INTRODUCTION

It was felt appropriate to place this book into context with the life experiences of the author, as it is out of those experiences that the content emerged. This introduction therefore starts with a short outline of the moral and philosophical development of the author. Readers who do not wish to review these personal reminiscences can skip to Part One with no loss of continuity or clarity in understanding of the principles of humanism.

While the sum total of life experiences of each individual is unique, it is possible that many activities or events described by the author have occurred in parallel or similar parts of the lives of many readers. It is intended and hoped that to discover them in the life of another person may strike a responsive chord of understanding and empathy, and occasionally sympathy, in the mind of the reader. It is a fact that the great majority of people hold the same religious, political, and societal beliefs as their parents and their extended families, and moreover, hold these beliefs in a relatively unquestioning atmosphere. In other words, just as most people in any one communal group learn to speak the same language, they learn to hold or essentially similar views on many topics, constantly reinforced, with only minor procedural differences and with virtually no critical discussion, so that the possibility for young people to speak languages or to hold views other than those of their parents and close friends is limited if indeed possible at all, at first. However, things can and do change from time to time, and my life is proof of that fact, as the rest of this prologue (and indeed the remainder of the entire book) will show.

I was born in 1930 in Glasgow, Scotland, into a family which practiced one of the many forms of the Christian Faith, specifically Scottish Presbyterianism, which is a relatively mild form of religious neurosis. Because of this so-called "accident" of birth, I was raised as a Christian for the first few years of my life, without choice or opinion. My parents had me baptized at birth because according to their views it was the thing to do, living as they did in fear of their God and their church, and more likely of the neighbors and the opinion of society. In any event, at the time of my baptism, I was only a couple of weeks old, and could not even speak, let alone protest! I hold no grudge against them for having done it. They viewed baptism as a form of spiritual insurance, just like a vaccination is a form of medical insurance, and a fire-and-theft policy is a form of financial insurance. These insurances were devised by allegedly greater minds than those of my parents, and they therefore accepted all such medical, financial, and spiritual guidance on authority in their attempts to be on the safe side of life.

My parents were both off-spring of well-intentioned but relatively uneducated Scottish stock, and they were simply carrying on in the tradition of their own people. Like many of their friends, my parents did not make much distinction or separation between moral behavior and religious belief. They led reasonably good lives, partly because of their religion, but mostly because of their innate sense of decency and fairness. In spite of the subsequent divergence of our views on religious matters, I loved and was loved by both my parents, and I have held them in high regard all my life. They were good, kindly, sincere, and considerate people, and they were especially kind and good to me, although at times I must have sorely tried them and their God.

P.2 PHILOSOPHICAL AWAKENING

When I was about 3 or 4 years old, my parents started sending me to a Sunday School operated by their church to coincide with the services for adults. I continued with that formal though sporadic instruction until I was about 9 or 10 years of age.

The Sunday School served two purposes: it was an opportunity for the church to spread the gospel to uncritical young minds, and it prevented parents using children as an excuse not to attend the services for adults. I did not much enjoy Sunday School, not because of any religious conflicts (I knew of none at that age), but because the teacher I had for most of my time there was a somewhat eccentric spinster who set such high moral standards that we children could not hope to attain and mostly did not even try. I cannot pin-point the exact moment when I began to feel some uncertainty that all was not quite as suggested, but it stemmed from some early experiences in that Sunday School and the astonishing revelations of that unhappy woman.

When I was about 7 or 8, I discovered that Santa Claus and the Tooth Fairy were just amusements created by adults to divert children and their parents from having to deal with realities and to avoid having to think about or explain the way life actually operates. I did not then find such diversions to be very amusing; I found them to be quite frightening, and I now consider them to be dishonest. As a result of these revelations, I began to think that the religious spirits described by the Sunday School teacher were probably in the same category as Santa and the Fairies.

We did not live in a virulently religious atmosphere in either our home or our neighborhood. Religion was a sort of social sport to be practiced only in church on Sunday mornings, and during baptisms, marriages, funerals, or other special events, such as Remembrance Day (Memorial Day) or at Christmas. Whatever my mother or father inwardly thought about it, religion did not have much significance in our daily lives. For example, grace was never said before our meals, except on very special occasions, such as when guests were present. I do not remember much, if any, discussion of religious issues in our house, even when the local preacher would come to call. As my father was a deacon (that is, a member of the board which ran the church as a business) the preacher's visits seemed to be mostly concerned with the financial side of church affairs and the problems of maintaining membership and interest, topics not unknown to humanist organizations.

I certainly did not go around my childhood world seeking answers to troublesome existential questions; I gave the whole subject almost no thought whatsoever, until I was well into my teenage years. As it did not seem to me at the time to be either harmful or especially uncomfortable, I never particularly objected to going to the church, although I would never have thought of going of my own volition. I put going-to-church in the same category as going-to-school or going-to-stores or going-to-lavatories; it was just one more thing that children tolerate in their parents. However, the unexpected death of my brother from pneumonia at 21 years of age when I was 16, caused me to consider the purpose of life more closely.

The Scottish Presbyterian church services were fairly simple affairs. They sang a few songs, heard a few readings from the Bible, enjoyed some fine organ music, and received a rousing fire-and-brimstone sermon from the minister in exchange for cash donations in the collection plate. I also liked the sermons, not because of their content, but because my mother used to feed the family large round white peppermint candies which were calculated to prevent us from fidgeting while the sermon progressed to its usually dramatic conclusion. I did not like having to dress up on Sundays in special clean clothes, nor having my face wiped with a damp handkerchief by my mother to remove microscopic spots of dirt which appeared to her likely to offend the preacher or the Lord. I thought God would understand that a young boy can't keep still or clean, but my mother didn't, and she did not take any chances with such important matters.

P.3 SOCIAL EXPERIENCES

When I was in my early teens, I became involved with an organization called the *Boys Brigade*, popularly known as the "BB." The BB was established in Scotland around 1880 by a man called William Smith, for young males between the ages of 12 and 18, and having primarily two objectives: to give these young people something constructive, disciplined, and interesting to do with their spare time, and to promote Christianity among its members. Its membership rose rapidly to number several thousands of young boys and men all over Britain, and indeed some other commonwealth countries. I joined it when I was about 11 years of age, not because I was all that interested in (or even much aware of) its objectives, but because my parents wanted me to join, and most of my friends were already either members of the BB or its rival organization, the Boy Scouts.

The BB was run along para-military lines, with divisions, battalions, companies, and so on. There was a junior wing called the Life Boys (similar to the Cub Scouts) for younger boys between the ages of about 8 to 12, which I first joined before transferring to the older group. There was a simple uniform consisting of a belt, a hat, and an arm band onto which badges of merit or rank could be attached. In 1943, I joined the 120th Glasgow BB Company which met every Friday evening during the winter months. Most evenings had a similar pattern: some drill formations, prayers and announcements, individual activities (working for merit badges in band, first aid, fire fighting, signaling, and so on), group tasks such as rehearsals for plays or public parades, and always some physical exercises, such as swinging clubs, pushing bar-bells, or doing simple gymnastics. If a disaster occurred which called for first aid skills and signaling with a bit of bugle music thrown in, I could probably have been of some assistance.

As a result of my association with the BB which operated in a local church hall, I became involved at age 16 as a Sunday School teacher in that church. One day, the Sunday School superintendent noted that my classes were twice as large as any of the other teachers' classes, and so she asked me if I would reveal my secret. I explained that each Sunday morning I asked the kids what they would like to do, and the rest of the time was taken up either talking about what they liked to do, or actually doing it, if that was possible. The super replied that the children and I were not there to enjoy ourselves, we were there to learn about the Lord. I asked if these two things were not compatible, and she seemed to think that they were not. So I quit, somewhat disillusioned and downcast, as I had thought that religion was generally supposed to bring happiness, and yet here I was officially banned from spreading that very desirable commodity.

About the same time, I realized that one of my closest friends could not join the Boys Brigade, not because he didn't want to, but because he came from a Jewish family. Jews of course were not welcome in a Christian organization in the part of Glasgow where I lived at that time. I found this conflict to be troublesome, as I knew my friend and his family well, and could not imagine what harm could come from his enjoying himself with both his and my other friends. As mentioned earlier, it was also around this time that my brother died, having a profound effect on me and my beliefs.

P.4 SUBSEQUENT DEVELOPMENTS

It was about this time that my long-held but still vague thoughts that religion had some problems associated with it began to crystallize, and I resolved to think it all over in greater detail, when I could find the time. I also had the already weak basis of my religious beliefs further shaken by associating with the ordinary girls and boys of our neighborhood, few of whom were any more or less convinced of the truth or worth of it all than I was. To all of us, except the Catholic kids, it was just a colossal game, played for the benefit of our parents. To the Catholics, who were in the minority, it was a colossal embarrassment, as the rest of us took it out on them in many cruel ways known only to children.

During the Korean War, I was drafted into the Army for two years. The bulk of my time was spent in learning and practicing the so-called "military arts" of how to kill people singly or in large numbers. I never warmed to the subject matter. From time to time, the unit to which I was attached would arrange a church parade. I find it hard to understand that, in war, each side calls on presumably the same God for guidance and deliverance. I guess we were fortunate to be fighting "godless commies" as it made the theological equation seem less balanced and the enemy seem less human.

The conclusion that I drew from all this religious instruction, practiced in the home, in church, in school, in the army and elsewhere, was that it raises far more questions than it answers, and therefore the doubts in my mind gradually took precedence over the beliefs, over a period of about 8 or 9 years during my late youth and early manhood. The doubts, and the shaky beliefs on which they were based, have long since vanished in the light of later knowledge and experience. I knew from my own observation, which I think was pretty typical, that what people *thought* about religion, and what they *said and did* about religion, were not necessarily the same thing. So I became an apostate from Protestant Christianity. I had not yet heard about humanism.

Following my military service and during my post-secondary school years, I had neither time nor inclination to reflect upon or research philosophical or religious matters. I was busy working on my technical education in construction economics, trying to earn a living, entertaining a succession of girl-friends, tinkering with an old car which I had bought, and arranging my move from Scotland to Canada. However, I was becoming more interested in general philosophical issues, such as the meaning of life, truth, value, and so on, and began to spend some time thinking and talking about such topics with friends.

The first winter in which I had time available occurred after I had moved to Vancouver in 1958. I enrolled in a non-credit university evening extension course entitled *Comparative Religion*. On the first evening of that course, the professor, Dr. Barnard Savary, stated that no doubt many of the participants had come seeking answers, but that he was only going to pose some questions. About half of the participants left at that point! During the next few weeks, the professor gave the remainder of us a very good review of the world's major religions. Dr. Savary also encouraged us to look at some of the world's great atheists, agnostics, humanists, and so-called heretics, and the advances in attitude and knowledge which they had contributed to civilization. As a result of that introduction, I began to read some of the authorities which he had recommended, such as John Dewey, Henry James, Thomas Paine, and Bertrand Russell, as well as taking a look at Buddhism, Communism, Hinduism, Jainism, Judaism and several other "isms."

In addition to reading technical publications connected with my professional career in the construction industry, I also took some time to read other contemporary authors, such as Carlos Castenada, Pierre Teilhard, Buckminster Fuller, Julian Huxley, A. S. Neill, Robert Pirsig, Carl Rogers, and Alan Watts. There was no particular pattern to this reading selection; I just read books as I came across them, and then discussed them with friends in mostly social settings.

The results of this informal study led me to believe that my intuitive hunches or feelings were in fact correct. First, there is no reliable evidence nor irrefutable argument to support claims for the existence of God or gods outside of the human mind. Secondly, that life does not have any cosmic meaning or purpose except that which we humans wish (or are able) to attach to it; and thirdly, that human problems have to be solved by human actions, primarily involving love for and understanding of our fellow humans, and certainly without any kind of superstitious or divine intervention. There is a saying attributed to Voltaire: "If God did not exist, he would have had to have been invented by man." That statement should be modified to read: "As God does not exist, he has been invented by man."

All of this activity finally led me to make contact with the *Humanist Association of Canada* about 1980, curiously enough through the simple act of picking up a copy of its quarterly magazine in the Vancouver Public Library. I immediately noticed that the general philosophical stance of this Association was virtually identical to my own views on most of this broad subject matter, but much more clearly and forcefully articulated, and so I wrote to their head office in Ottawa for more information. I joined the national Association at that time and some months later, I helped to establish and became a member of the Vancouver Chapter of the Association, in concert with some other like-minded colleagues in 1982. The Chapter later developed in 1984 into an autonomous group called the *Humanist Association of Greater Vancouver*, of which I was one of several founding members. In 1990, its name was changed to the *British Columbia Humanist Association.*

Although I considered myself to be an amateur humanist at that time (in the 1980s), I began to realize that many of the other members (and the public) had even less understanding of humanism than I did. I resolved first, to educate myself on the main principles of humanism, and secondly, to try to spread the ideas of rationality, knowledge, and toleration that are at the core of humanist thought. To the extent that this book serves that purpose, the year spent in its production will have been worthwhile.

PART ONE

Humanism and Freethought

CHAPTER 1.1

THE ELEMENTS OF HUMANISM

1.1.1 INTRODUCTION

The underlying precept of Humanism is simple. It can be approximately expressed in the single concept: "Do unto others as you would have them do unto you." Now it will be observed that this is not a particularly original thought, nor of particularly recent invention. Many philosophies and most religions, all of which have been invented by humans, have a similar notion at their root. The main distinction between humanism and these many other world-views is twofold: first, humanists do not clutter their thoughts by attributing this sentiment to non-existent deities, and secondly, humanists practice what they preach.

Humanist philosophy has two primary components: *knowledge* and *love*; These are elaborated in this section. The Philosophy is further developed into a 5-point statement of principles and a 10-point topical definition in the next section of this chapter.

With respect to *knowledge*, one should willingly acquire as much as possible, using experience and intelligence in the process. No subject area should be proscribed or censored. With adequate knowledge, one is more likely to act reasonably and appropriately in any given circumstance. While it is acknowledged that no one can know everything, each person can learn enough about the general ways that society operates and the particular ways that each person can fit into and become an appropriate and useful part of that society.

With respect to *love*, one should willingly practice acceptance, tolerance and caring towards others, again using experience and intelligence in the process. There are those who are clearly worthy of unrestrained love and affection, while others require a different degree of understanding and acceptance. While emotions or feelings of distaste for certain unacceptable situations or antagonistic behaviors are natural, bigotry and intolerance should have no permanent place in the true humanist mind. This is not to say that humanists should accept any and all forms of anti-social behavior; they can certainly speak out and act against activity which is detrimental to good relationships within families, among friends, and throughout society in general. To understand humanist philosophy more clearly, one should understand both what it is and what it is not.

1. What Humanism Is

The philosophy of humanism involves the notions that nature is the totality of being, that humans are evolutionary products, that people are responsible for their actions and that they can solve problems through science and its technological applications, that morality is based on human needs and experience, and that the purpose or general objective of humankind (insofar as one exists) is essentially the pursuit of happiness and well-being for each person, among other criteria. Humanism is essentially agnostic with respect to knowledge of and belief in any of the alleged supernatural forces of the universe.

Humanism is a life-stance or a way of being, involving positive attitudes towards oneself and one's fellow human beings. Humanism is a movement; that means people with ideas on the move. The movement is open to all who see merit in its ideas; it welcomes involvement at any level by anyone who is interested in its aims. It particularly welcomes those who are prepared to physically, psychologically, financially or otherwise support its objectives in any practical manner, and extends the hand of friendship to others who simply wish to be inactive fellow travelers.

Individual humanism is an attitude to life, a way of action, a method of being. As stated, its central foundations are knowledge and love, combined with awareness, tolerance, and kindliness. Organized humanism is a general association of individuals having no specific single objective but rather some general aims regarding the universal adoption of positive policies which will improve life for everyone, and not just for members of one sect, clan, class, church, nation, or group, to the detriment of others.

Humanism views the political process as a means to an end, the end being the process of continued improvement for all humankind everywhere in the world. Humanism considers that all political and economic systems should be valued by the benefits which they offer to all humankind, and not by the rhetoric which continues the present division of the people of the world on the basis of alleged superiority of any specific nationalism, capitalism, communism, or any other "ism," including humanism if it were to be used for such purposes. The slogan "My Country, Right or Wrong" has no place in the humanist frame. In the humanist view, the true function of the state is to let each individual fully develop his or her true worth and to permit and encourage the fullest participation by all people in all aspects of life. People must come first, before decalogues, creeds, regulations, oaths, and similar constraints and repression. Many (though not all) humanists recommend that sovereign national power should be abolished, and that all political and military power should be vested in one United Nations Congress, with that body being elected by and accountable to all the peoples of the world, and operating under an iron-clad guarantee (backed by policing power) of universal individual human rights and freedoms. Economic, social, and regional development should be delegated on a rational basis to local authorities directly accountable to the United Nations Congress.

Humanism is also concerned with the development in all people of a proper and balanced feeling of well-being about their different racial, ethnic, cultural, and regional backgrounds. There is nothing wrong with (and a lot of good in) some diversity in this regard. The best elements of the twin social concepts of the *"melting-pot"* and the *"cultural mosaic"* should be reviewed for adoption. In humanism, the importance of individual self-reliance, cooperation between individuals, the use of reason, and the application of planning based on a good knowledge of probabilities is generally understood and accepted. This is what gives humanism its internal strength, because normal people seldom let themselves down, and when they cooperate, the results of the whole society can usually be seen to be greater than the sum of its parts. Informed human beings can reason properly, and therefore they can make plans with some certainty of the outcome.

Humanists are inextricably involved with their peers and others in seeking ways to better conditions of all kinds for all people of the world. Their value systems are completely interwoven with the secular aspirations of much of the religious remainder of humankind, such as the desire for adequate food and shelter, access to appropriate health care and education, sustaining the environment, and suitable job opportunities (to mention some issues). A review of the basic principles of humanism enunciated at the beginning of this chapter should make this point crystal clear.

To conclude, the *purpose* of humanism is to bring about the greatest good and happiness for the greatest number of people in their own lifetime. The *method* of humanism is to seek true knowledge about nature and its ways and to practice kindliness and caring towards all people, animals, and things affected by human thought and action. The *technique* of humanism is to have humanists band together in ever-larger and more-numerous groups in all regions and with world-wide connections and communications, thus creating a rising ground swell of rational opinion in the minds of a growing number of educated, powerful, and influential groups of citizens of this planet Earth, which is our only home.

2. What Humanism Is Not

Humanism is not a religion, although it does subscribe to a number of beliefs, such as the worth of the individual human being. Humanism has no metaphysical content involving creeds, deities, faith, miracles, or the like. It is not a pure philosophy, although it has adopted some philosophical positions which require a defense. True humanism is not a cult having narrow fixed notions, and it does not have sects; sectarianism would terminate humanism. It is not a political party although it does have some aspirations to bring about humanistic solutions to social problems through legitimate political channels. It does not intend to be instrumental in securing military means to humanistic ends. It is non-threatening, non-violent, non-mystical, and non-exclusive, although some people in humanist organizations who continue to harbor religious or spiritual beliefs may be challenged to justify them.

Petitionary prayers to imaginary gods are not necessary in the humanist scheme of things. Human beings can accomplish as much on their own without references to deities as any group of believers can accomplish with appeals for supernatural aid, and furthermore, they can do so at a faster rate as they do not waste time in prayer. No matter how long people spend on their knees in prayer, sooner or later, they have to get up on their feet and go and do something if they wish to accomplish anything. Humanists simply cut out the middle man in this equation between wishful thinking and successful action.

There are no requirements to join humanist clubs, no *compulsory* tithes to pay to humanist leaders (although *voluntary* financial support is necessary as in any organization), no secret handshakes for humanist members, no funny clothes or hats for its leaders to wear, no dietary rules (except for reasons of health and those of moderation related to general human well-being), no religious holidays to observe (although ways of publicly recognizing humanist values could replace some current dates), and no ideological nonsense to debase human beings. In contrast to most religions, in which there is almost always a hierarchy of priests, there are no charismatic humanist leaders. That is not to say that there are no humanists having both charisma and a prominent public profile, but rather that each humanist has to come to his or her own understanding about what humanism means, through reading, discussion, and observing other humanists. There are many scholars and authors who have written books or articles (or have produced audio or video tapes) about the origins, development, and practices of humanism, and many of these works are worthy of study and debate. There are some praise-worthy people who have been recognized for practicing genuinely humanist principles in their public or private lives, and in some ways, such people might be considered by some to be humanist leaders or heroes. There are also individuals who undertake paid or voluntary administrative work on behalf of humanist organizations, but these positions do not involve leadership in the sense of directing the thoughts of members. Their role is to focus proposed humanist activities (such as monthly meetings, publications, or specific social actions) in such a way as to bring about results beneficial both to the movement and to the public.

1.1.2 PRINCIPLES AND DEFINITIONS

Although it is customary to define a word before exemplifying its use in context, it will become clear from reading the next two parts of this section that a review of the general principles of humanism will lead to a better understanding of the complex specific definitions that follow.

1. General Principles

The basic humanist concepts are represented by five fundamental principles formulated at the inaugural International Congress on Ethics and Humanism (IHEU), held at the Hague in Holland in 1952, as follows:

1. Humanism is *democratic*; it aims at the fullest development of every human being.
2. Humanism is *ethical*; it affirms the dignity of humans and the right of the individual to the greatest possible freedom of development compatible with the rights of others.
3. Humanism insists that *personal liberty* is an end that must be combined with social responsibility in order that it shall not be sacrificed to the improvement of material conditions.
4. Humanism is a way of life, aiming at the maximum possible *fulfillment*, through the cultivation of ethical and creative living.
5. Humanism seeks to use *science* creatively, not destructively.

Paraphrasing the foregoing, humanism is Democratic, Ethical, Egalitarian, Developmental, and Scientific. To use a *mnemonic* device to assist with remembering these five precepts, an acronym (which is a word made up of the first letters of other words, like "*NASA*" is made from "National Aeronautics and Space Administration") can be developed from these five words. Thus it might be said that Humanism is *"DEEDS"* in action.

These principles were later incorporated by the IHEU into a more general definition, as follows: "Humanism is a democratic and ethical life stance which affirms that human beings have the right and the responsibility to give meaning and shape to their own lives. It stands for the building of a more humane society through an ethics based on human and other natural values in a spirit of reason and free inquiry through human capabilities. It is not theistic, and does not accept supernatural views of reality." An expanded version was issued in 2002.

2. Specific Definitions

The general *DEEDS* of Humanism are set out more fully below in a 10-point definition, extracted from *The Philosophy of Humanism* written by a former president of the American Humanist Association [Lamont 1982]. Readers are urged to take a more extensive look at this particular book and at other humanist literature, to judge for themselves the worth of its claims. Before discussing the 10-point definition, readers are advised that the words "belief" and "believe" are used in a colloquial sense and not necessarily in their literal sense. Humanist beliefs are held on the basis of knowledge and experience, and not on faith or unverifiable opinion.

The 10 points are as follows. The first 5 are defining principles; the remainder might be more correctly viewed as humanist aspirations:

1. Humanists regard Nature as the totality of being.
2. Humanists believe that "Man" is an evolutionary product of nature, with mind indivisibly a part of body.
3. Humanists believe that humans can solve their problems through reason and applications of the scientific method.
4. Humanists question all theories of universal determinism, fatalism, or predestination, and they support freedom of choice in all matters, consistent with the rights of others.
5. Humanists believe in an ethics or morality that grounds all human values in this-earthly experience, with the goal of highest levels of this-earthly happiness, freedom, and progress.
6. Humanists believe that the good life consists of an harmonious combination of personal satisfaction, significant work, constructive self-development, and worthwhile contributions to community welfare.
7. Humanists believe in the development of art and the awareness of the beauty of Nature, so that aesthetic experience becomes a normal reality of life.
8. Humanists believe in a worldwide social program of democracy, peace, and a high standard of living for all.
9. Humanists believe in the complete implementation of reason and the scientific method in all social procedures and government, with full freedom of expression and civil liberties.

10. Humanists believe in an unending questioning of basic assumptions and convictions, including its own. Humanism is a developing philosophy open to testing, accommodation of new facts, and rigorous reasoning.

These ten points are further elaborated in the various Humanist Manifestos, discussed later in this book [see Chapter 1.5]. Other authors at other times have also produced other definitions of the "DEEDS" of humanism, of which the following are but a very brief selection:

1. **Tom Flynn**, editor of *Free Inquiry*: "Humanism is a comprehensive nonreligious life stance that incorporates a naturalistic philosophy, a cosmic outlook rooted in science, and a consequentialist ethical system." (*Free Inquiry*, Fall 2002, Vol. 22, No. 4, p.42)
2. **Sidney Hook**, philosopher, author, humanist activist: "An ethical humanist is one who relies on the arts of intelligence to defend, enlarge, and enhance the areas of human freedom in the world." (*The Best of Humanism*, p.47)
3. **Paul Kurtz**, philosopher, author, founder of the *Council for Secular Humanism*: "Secular humanism, as distinct from all other forms (of humanism), emphasizes the use of science and critical intelligence in solving human problems. It has confidence in (human) ability to apply science and technology for the betterment lf human life. It is skeptical about the existence of occult, paranormal, or transcendent realities. Although it is the modern-day expression of classical atheism in what it rejects, it also expresses a normative concern for developing constructive ethical values appropriate to the present situation of (humans) on this planet. It is uncompromising in its commitment to democracy, and it considers human freedom the highest value." (*Encyclopedia of Unbelief*, p.332)

4. **Bertrand Russell**, mathematician, pacifist, agnostic: "The good life is one inspired by love and guided by knowledge." ("What I Believe" in *Why I am Not a Christian*, p.56)
5. **Webster's** *College Dictionary*: "Any system or mode of thought or action in which human interests, values, and dignity predominate, and especially an ethical theory that often rejects the importance of a belief in God" (*Random House*, 1991, p.653)

The attention of readers is also directed to various humanist and freethought associations, such as the American Humanist Association, the Humanist Association of Canada, the British Humanist Association, and the Freedom from Religion Foundation, all of which have from time to time developed definitions (or *Statements of Principle*) of varying lengths and qualities for the edification of their memberships. Addresses for organizations noted above are given in Appendix A.2; titles of books cited are given in Appendix B.

1.1.3 SOME DISTINCTIONS

Before examining selected aspects of humanism in more detail, it may assist readers to more clearly understand the points of view expressed if the following distinctions are made between the four words *atheism, agnosticism, humanism* and *skepticism*.

1. Atheism

The word "atheism" stems from two Greek words: a root "theos" which means god (or of god) and a prefix "a" which means not or none; when these two parts of the word are put together they literally mean no god. The word atheism may be held by some to mean a denial of the existence of God, but in this context it more properly and simply means no god. Atheists simply do not believe in the existence of God or gods; they are therefore not necessarily against the idea of God or belief in gods in general, although some undoubtedly are. Atheists say that the idea or belief that a God or gods exist does not necessarily make it so.

There are at least four major categories of atheists:

1. There are many thousands, possibly millions of people who have simply never heard about gods of any kind. Apart from people who might grow up in social isolation, or who might develop in atheistic circumstances, it could be said that every newborn child starts out in life as an atheist (though some might prefer *agnostic*) because babies can have no internal concept or belief in any God (despite religious claims about souls) until some semblance of reason and understanding is internally developed in the brain. Then external influences and experiences, such as pedagogical processes, may induce impressions, leading to beliefs of one type or another.
2. There are many millions of people who believe in one particular God but not in another God; although they would not consider themselves to be atheists, they may be (and often are) considered to be atheists by those who believe in these other Gods. Jesus Christ himself (if such existed) fell into this category. He was considered to be an atheist by some of his Roman prosecutors as he did not believe in the gods in which they believed. So there are at least two points of view to consider in this regard: the view which you have of yourself, and the view which others may have of you.
3. There are atheists who have (at one time or another) considered the possibility of God and for whom theology in general and theistic doctrine in particular may have been more or less meaningful but who find that the positive evidence is insufficient to sustain belief while the negative evidence leads to rejection of belief. Increasing numbers of former priests, ministers, rabbis, and other ex-believers fall into this category; such people are called apostates (for more detail, see Section 1.4.0 *Apostasy*).

4. There are atheists for whom theology and related doctrine is not meaningful and they assert that at best it is only a symbolic rendering of human hopes, fears, and ideals, and at worst, that it can and should be rejected as incomprehensible rubbish.

In some respects, atheism or adamant non-belief in God as a viable intellectual position suffers from the same weaknesses as theism or adamant belief in God. There is no absolutely conclusive evidence or ultimate proof *one way or the other* that gods do or do not exist—the best one can hope for is to be convinced of the correctness of one's position, based on the strength of one's argument.

Believers naturally attempt to paint the bleakest possible picture of atheism. They contrast what they say is the atheist's gloomy and negative view of life with their own imaginary rosy and positive view. They say that atheism renders the fate of atheists to be victims of a purposeless and pointless existence, living in pain and anxiety and dying in hopelessness and misery, with no promise of salvation. They seem oblivious to the statistical fact that although there are more believers than non-believers, many millions more of these believers already live such ghastly and hopeless lives than all of the non-believers put together.

The atheist counters by saying that every week, billions of believers of all faiths individually and collectively raise their voices all over the world in ineffectual prayers and praise to non-existent gods, with few significant or scientifically demonstrable results. They assert that such actions debase the human condition, degrade the human intellect, raise false hopes, and in general are fripperies that divert attention and energy from the real issues of the world to be dealt with here and now. It also ignores the fact that atheists as a group are generally better educated and thus for the most part enjoy a standard of living above the average levels, two factors which contribute to a generally happier and more pleasant life, compared to the more miserable lot of the average believer.

Atheists say that they do not have to prove that God does *not* exist; they say that it is up to the theists to prove that God does exist, in some more compelling and convincing way than merely by making assertions and statements about voluntarily adopted faith. If the theists cannot finally and conclusively prove God's existence, then the atheist's position is logically the correct one.

Many claims have been made about the sasquatch (or bigfoot) animal, abominable snowmen, Loch Ness monsters and so on, but normal people usually reserve judgement in such things, remaining as non-believers until actual proof of existence is reliably and independently determined. Yet there is more physical, photographic and experiential reason and evidence to believe in the sasquatch than in God. Some day, someone may actually produce incontrovertible evidence of a real sasquatch, in the form of artifacts, photos, film, or even a body (preferably live). Then faith in the sasquatch will be easily converted to knowledge, and we will have to turn our attentions to the Loch Ness monster. Granted, little is known about the sasquatch but it is thought that, if they do exist, they are very much more powerful than men. If in fact God exists and is in fact more powerful than any earthly creature, as is claimed by theists, then one would think that it would be easier, and not more difficult, to prove his existence as compared to the sasquatch, for which there is some evidence.

To say that God is ineffable, and therefore not demonstrable, is simply a cop out. Those who say that it is as necessary for atheists as it is for theists to prove their case are ignoring the experiential facts of scientific life, namely that the burden of proof is always on those who make the claim, and not on those who deny it. Atheists do not have to prove that gods do not exist, any more than those who do not believe in the sasquatch have to prove it. So the atheists rest their case. Until definite proof of apparently non-existent immaterial things is available, and the manner in which they can affect us in our material existence can be reliably and repeatedly demonstrated, it makes more sense to believe that they do not exist [Smith 1989].

True atheists are usually highly individualistic types of people, and by virtue of their belief (or lack of it), feel little need to congregate with their fellow humans to further their own ends in this regard. They often have feelings of non-involvement in and even isolation from general human affairs. That is not to say that they are anti-social, or do not belong to clubs, associations, committees, boards, or other human enterprises in concert with their fellow humans. Far from it; they just do not feel a need nor see a purpose to congregate together for what can best be called emotional support of their cosmic feelings and attitudes. As a result, there is no wide-spread truly, purely, or exclusively atheistic movement to be found anywhere in the world today, although there are several political systems (such as communism) having atheism as one of their tenets. There is also a number of separate and discrete atheist associations having members in various parts of the world. One of the largest of these is located at Vijayawada in India [see Appendix A.2 *Humanist Associations*]. It was founded by Gora, who considered himself to be a humanist, and is run by his son Lavanan and other family members.

For further reading, the following titles are suggested:

1. *Atheism—a Philosophical Justification* [Martin 1990].
2. *Atheism—the Case against God* [Smith 1989]

2. Agnosticism

The word "agnostic" stems from two ancient Greek words: a root "gnostos" meaning to know or to have knowledge, and a prefix "a" which means not or none; when these two parts are put together, they can mean no knowledge or insufficient knowledge. The word was coined by T.H. Huxley, a noted free-thinker in 19th century England.

In ordinary usage, this word simply refers to a person who claims no knowledge of some topic. In modern philosophical and theological usage, it is usually held to mean a person who claims that there is not enough reliable knowledge to permit a firm and total conclusion to be reached by any of the many claims or arguments made about the existence or non-existence of God or other supernatural powers in the universe. The agnostic says that reason cannot go beyond experience. The word can also mean a person who has not experienced an internal mental religious revelation sufficient to convince him or her of the existence of God or another supernatural power.

To say the same thing in more colloquial terms, the agnostic says that the jury is still out, because all the evidence is not yet in. Furthermore, most agnostics would say that the evidence which so far has been presented regarding claims about the existence of God is in itself unreliable, incomplete, and inconclusive. They would say that all metaphysical belief depends on faith alone, and that this is simply not convincing enough. As a consequence, the agnostic says it makes more sense and is better to reserve judgement and thus continue to doubt the existence of gods than to accept such poor evidence on faith as a basis for belief. Needless to say, believers say the opposite: they say it is better (and safer) to believe, even though the evidence is incomplete, until there is conclusive reason not to do so. They say that there is nothing to lose by believing, and something to be gained, namely everlasting heavenly life beyond the present earthly life. This argument is often referred to as "Pascal's Wager" as it was first articulated by Blaise Pascal, a 17th Century theologian and mathematician. The agnostic counters that such a claim cannot be verified and therefore cannot be known to be true. If is turns out to be true, the believer and agnostic alike will benefit; if it turns out to be untrue, then the believers are in for some serious short-changing by their God. As one noted 19th century American humanist, Robert Ingersoll, observed: "In this matter, it is better to ignorantly hope, than to dishonestly affirm."

However, nobody really knows; not ministers, not priests, not gurus, not rabbis, not even the Pope himself. All one can do is speculate on these and similar related issues, and then form an opinion. The agnostic also feels it is more prudent for individuals and society as a whole to focus attention on this-earthly present-day problems than to waste time and energy worrying about the possibility of some indistinct type of life in the imaginary hereafter.

It may be appropriate to introduce a related concept at this point. Rationally, one can say that there is only one choice: either one believes in the existence of God or one does not. If one does, one is classified as being a theist; if one does not, then one is classified as being non-theist. The second classification admits of two categories: unconditional atheism as discussed in the preceding section, or agnosticism which is a form of conditional atheism as described in this section. The point is that agnostics are not sitting on the fence halfway between believers and non-believers; they are clearly on the non-believing side of the fence. Agnostics are not hedging their bets, so to speak; they are simply and wisely and sometimes uncomfortably reserving their judgement. But then it always has been more difficult to take a path against the mainstream of society, however intellectually rational and emotionally rewarding that course may be. However, one waggish agnostic was quoted as saying that the only reason he did not become an atheist was because they had no national holidays. At the moment, neither do the agnostics, and there have been some efforts to ask governments to reconsider the practice of declaring parochial religious celebrations, such as Christmas and Easter, to be national paid holidays.

For further reading, the following titles are suggested:

1. *The Humanist Frame* [Huxley 1962]
2. *Agnosticism is also Faith* [Strem 1986]

3. Humanism

The word "humanism" has several meanings, other than that used in the general context of this book. For example, one of these alternative meanings relates to what are generally known as the humanities or classical studies in literature, culture, and anthropological subject matter. Because of the all the positive aspects comprising humanism as this word is being used in this book, it is not uncommon to hear believers or members of many of the world's religions claiming to be religious humanists. Thus one hears, for example, of self-described Christian Humanists or Judaic Humanists, people who want to have their cake and eat it too. To be a true humanist, one cannot be a theist; it is a fundamental tenet of true humanism that it eschews or rejects all supernatural belief and religious dogma. Having said that, one can also say that some humanists prefer to call themselves *secular* humanists, as the word "secular" has Latin roots for *worldly* or *temporal*.

In the previous sections of this chapter, some concepts relative to atheism and agnosticism were presented. There is however another position that can be taken, which is slightly different from either that of the true atheist or the true agnostic. Theists believe in the existence of God or gods; atheists assert their non-belief in such existence. Agnostics assert that one cannot say for certain, because the evidence is too incomplete to sustain belief either way. It is also possible to introduce a third possibility, by stating that the word "God" itself is so entirely incomprehensible that no meaningful discussion, either pro or con, can be sustained. God is presented by believers as being on the one hand a definable entity (albeit of superlative qualities and characteristics) and yet on the other hand, an immaterial spirit (ineffable, indescribable, immanent, unknowable, mysterious, disembodied). Not only can believers not have it both ways, it appears certain that they cannot have it either way. There is absolutely no evidence to support the contention that God has an anthropomorphic (or bodily) basis, nor that this spirit (if such exists) has any demonstrable effect on the so-called real world. One group of philosophers, the logical positivists, go so far as to say that as the existence of God is unverifiable, the word is therefore meaningless. The only reason we can apparently talk meaningfully about God is because there has been so much "God-talk" in our Judaic-Christian (and increasingly Islamic) society that we are deluded into thinking that this term actually means something intelligible. For further study, two branches of philosophy that concern such issues are called *epistemology* (theories of knowledge) and *metaphysics* (mind and body relationships).

While humanism may be classified as a religion by some people and according to some dictionary definitions, in that it does appear to have a number of beliefs, it is clearly not a religion according to others. Humanism is not a religion in the sense that one is required to make a leap of faith at some point. In humanism, nothing is taken on faith; everything is open for questioning. There is no dogma or divinity in humanism; no creed, no preachers, no churches, no charismatic leaders, no nonsense. It therefore appeals to the rational mind, although it might be admitted that there is not much appeal in humanism to the undeveloped emotional mind. This deficiency may partly account for its lack of popular support from the general public, which likes a bit of passion and mysticism in its beliefs. The most likely cause for this lack of support, though, probably has more to do with the teaching of traditional religions to young children before they attain maturity. The result is a reluctance to question the shibboleths of society and a genuine disinterest in and fear of following any course that might lead to the discovery of uncomfortable truths.

It might be observed that, although there might be some social, political, economic or other benefit to be gained by hypocritically professing to be religious when one is not, there is absolutely no justifiable reason for people to say they are humanists if they are not. It would also be unethical and immoral and regrettably (as yet in present western society) pointless to do so. Denial of the existence of God is not necessarily linked to or excluded from any system of morality or values (see Chapter 1.4 Morals). The relatively static or limited situation of true atheism can be contrasted to the rapidly-growing world-wide humanist movement, as evidenced by the development of secular associations such as the International Humanist and Ethical Union and the United Nations Organization.

For further reading, the following titles are suggested:

1. *Humanism* [Smoker 1984]
2. *In Defense of Secular Humanism* [Kurtz 1983]

4. Skepticism

The words *skeptic* and *skepticism* are derived from a Greek word *skeptikos* which means to *consider* or to *examine*. In more colloquial terms, it means to *inquire*, but it has in recent times taken on a more popular though less correct meaning of to *doubt*. Skeptics are therefore people who doubt various claims made by others and who are inclined or prepared to inquire into such claims to determine if there is any substance to them. Most atheists, agnostics, and humanists are thus by definition skeptics. As with many other life-stances, there are at least four discrete degrees or distinctions of skepticism observable in society, as shown in a recent work* on the topic.

1. *Nihilism:* Some skeptics totally reject all claims to certainty, truth, or knowledge. They simply doubt everything and everyone. They say that for every argument there is an effective counter-argument. They assert that the senses by which we experience the world are unreliable and the criteria by which we judge claims or situations are themselves dubious. For example, they claim no normative basis for morality apart from cultural custom. One contradictory weakness in their position is that, in making their claim that absolutely certain knowledge is not possible, they are in fact asserting that their cosmic view is the only acceptable one. Such extreme and negative skepticism is undoubtedly at odds with many of the everyday facts of life, and in general is not a satisfactory philosophical position for a rational person to hold.
2. *Neutrality:* Some skeptics adopt a more neutral or agnostic position, in which they will neither affirm nor deny any

claim made by others. They do not deny certainty, truth or knowledge; they simply suspend their judgements on the grounds that they have no grounds to take a stand. One benefit of this neutral skepticism over nihilism is that it is better able to accept the ordinary occurrences in life.

3. *Mitigation:* The development of this form of skepticism is attributed to the 18th century Scottish philosopher David Hume who, in noticing the limitations of the more extreme forms, introduced the notion of probabilities into the equation. The advocates of this modified form of skepticism held the view that, although the ultimate philosophical basis of knowledge, values, truths, reality, and so on may indeed forever be beyond us, we still have a great deal of reliable historical experience, gained through our senses, about the world in which we live to permit us to lead adequate if not perfect lives. They also took the view that morality is related more to contemporary social custom that to unprovable and allegedly eternal truths.

4. *Inquiry*: This fourth and final form of skepticism is in one sense a modern amalgam of portions of the other forms, but it is also a return to the roots of the word *skepticism* itself. It conjoins *pragmatism* in daily life with the critical *examination* of claims of every sort. Rather than being negative and nihilistic, it is positive and constructive. The key to this new form of skepticism is methodology in the process of inquiry. It is based on scientific observations, empirical testing, and logical standards. It does not utilize a broad scatter-gun approach, but can be limited to particular topics. It embraces a more surgical delicacy in addressing specific elements or components, considered within their contexts and with findings based upon evidence and reason. It accepts the limitations of the human biological and metaphysical framework, but does not let such awareness detract from the process or the usefulness of achieving results within our ability to do so.

It is not a perfectly evolved system, but then, neither are human beings.

For further reading, the following titles are suggested:

1. *The New Skepticism** [Kurtz 1992]
2. *An Enquiry Concerning Morals* [Hume 1995]

1.1.4 HUMANIST SYMBOLISM

In many of the world's religions, adroit use is made of symbolism in the form of icons, music, and other sensory stimuli; perhaps one of the minor errors of humanism has been to discount this apparently important aspect of human need. To take a simple example, most people are aware that the word "father" is attached to the word "god" in many religions, while the words "brother" and "sister" are used to refer to monks and nuns respectively. One hears of the "Mother" church, and every Roman Catholic adherent refers to his or her priest as "Father." This choice of words cannot be considered as coincidental or accidental. It is indicative of the deliberate attempt by religious protagonists to convey direct feelings of both subjectiveness and belonging to their converts through the use of emotionally charged words.

Humanism, while clearly defendable on rational grounds, as yet lacks the necessary emotional appeal to give it wide-spread acceptance. Perhaps the development of new but significant symbols might give humanism a more publicly palatable form. For instance, bodies of symbolic but secular literature, music, and art could be identified. Inspiring secular words could be distributed to be sung to well-known tunes at time of public gatherings. Poems extolling humanist values could be composed for use in secular ceremonies. Art and sculpture could show the physical, moral, and emotional strengths of ordinary human beings engaged in worthy enterprises. If, as religious protagonists claim, knowledge is of two types (observed and revealed), then humanists should be at some pains to reveal their own knowledge of secular life to the public at large, to counterbalance the large mass of incorrect and misleading religious propaganda. This revelation of the humanist frame of mind should be focused at the very source of being, with up-to-date information about the latest in scientific discoveries and all coupled to easily recognized symbols.

What is the direct symbol of humanism? Well, just as Judaism has its Star, Islam its Sword, and Christianity its Cross, so Humanism has its "Happy Human" logo, shown on the title page of this book. The logo was designed by Dennis Barrington in London, England, in 1965. It was the winner of 150 entries in a competition sponsored by the British Humanist Association.

What are the indirect symbols of humanism? Altruism? Aspiration? Democracy? Love? Morality? Rationality? Scientific Method? Secularity? All of these are certainly symbolic of humanism, but many of them are also to be found in other systems of belief. What is it that truly sets humanism apart from religion? The essence of humanism is *knowledge* coupled to *caring* as distinct from *belief* coupled to *hope*. The symbols of the humanist essence are the *pursuit* of knowledge of nature in all its varied aspects and the *practice* of love of humankind in all of its many forms. Such an essence is indeed a heady mixture.

CHAPTER 1.2

THE HUMANIST OBSERVED

1.2.1 INTRODUCTION

There are many aspects of life, such as morality, politics, spirituality, and so on, about which some sort of opinion is or has to be formed by the individual person who wishes to take his or her accepted place in society. For those who subscribe to any one of the many religious faiths, much of that opinion is prescribed by authority for acceptance without question. For atheists, agnostics, humanists, and other free thinkers, opinions on such matters have to be formed out of real-life experiences and observations. In this chapter, a humanist view-point on some of the basic aspects of social life is presented in outline form.

Each person should form his or her own views about the topics listed, as well as others, by further study, debate, and reflection beyond the confines of this book. Although it is safe to say that not all humanists will agree with all of the observations made, it is hoped that the ideas expressed in the following paragraphs generally reflect the ways in which most humanists view these selected aspects of life.

1.2.2 SELECTED TOPICS

The comments contained in each of the following numbered

paragraphs may assist the undecided or open-minded person with the formation of humanist opinion on a number of selected facets of being. The topics are not listed in any particular order of priority, and the ideas presented under each topic heading are quite rudimentary and incomplete. This approach has been deliberately adopted, to enable readers to add something from their own life experiences.

1. Life

For humanists, the fact of life is not a problem. That is not to say that some humanists do not have problems with the so-called "facts of life," about which more will be said later, or that other humanists do not have trouble with a number of so-far unanswered questions about the origin, nature, and continuity of life. Before proceeding, it may be appropriate to differentiate two meanings of the word "life." In one sense, Life (with an upper-case L) means the larger universal aspects of the on-going animate life force, whereas life (with a lower-case l) refers to that short period of time between conception and death that permits some activity by individual animals and plants. It may be said that in general most humanists consider *Life* to be a fundamental, continuous, and universal force, and *life* to be an opportunity to make something of oneself.

If one accepts the practical and likely proposition that the universe always has existed and always will exist, then one can accept the equally likely proposition that Life has also always existed and always will, being as it is a part of the universe. In a very broad sense, Life is the universe, and the universe is Life. Life does not start with each new born baby or newly seeded plant; each new baby or plant is simply one more confirmation of the continuity of a universally pervasive Life force, just as each living cell is also confirmation of the life force pervading individual animal or vegetable tissues. If Life is considered to be as broad, long, and deep as the Universe itself, the question of the origin of Life need not arise.

If, on the other hand, one adheres to the Big-Bang theory of the universe, then Life commenced simultaneously with the beginning of the universe. No one living today knows with absolute certainty the answer to the questions about the origins of Life and of the Universe, no matter what claims they may make to the contrary. Religious protagonists claim that their Gods created everything, including life, and that there is therefore no need to consider the matter further. More knowledgeable scientists have speculated that life on the planet we now call Earth was probably started by influences external to the planet several billion years ago in the so-called primordial soup, at a point in the development of the planet when the appropriate physical, chemical, electrical, and organic characteristics were in a suitable confluence. It is now known, for example, that the tail of Halley's comet harbors living bacteria that contaminate the atmosphere of this planet, and it is therefore possible that the original impetus that triggered the advent of life on earth came from just such a contaminating source. It is also possible that this hypothesis is just a piece of nonsense, but it is certainly less nonsensical than to hypothesize non-existent Gods working miracles in space to create something out of nothing. The evidence is very much better for the scientific hypothesis, as we do get visits from Halley's comet every 75 years; we have yet to see any God.

Speaking broadly, one might say that the chances of a general Life force being introduced to earth is analogous to a specific life force being conceived in the womb: the odds are small, but they are not impossible. However small the chance, if conditions are right, Life (and life) did, does, and will result. The evidence is before our eyes to see, and there is no need to attribute this to the workings of imaginary gods.

2. Death

For humanists, the fact of death is not a problem. Humanists understand and accept that death is simply the end of life for the individual person, animal or plant. Death may be sad, it may involve pain for the dying, and it may cause emotional, economic, or other problems for those who remain alive. All reasonable steps should be taken to defer its occurrence; but as it is inevitable, it is appropriate for humans to come to grips with the concept.

There is far too much energy expended by much of society in wishful thinking, intended to deny the fact of death. Death is real, but it is not to be feared, as it can be well enough understood to be accepted. In one respect, death is a part of life; the cycle of nature clearly shows the relationship. To deny death is to denigrate life, and those who claim to *know* (as distinct from *believe*) about any possible life after death for individual persons can best be described as misguided. People may hope or believe that some such form of after-life exists, but they do not and cannot have actual knowledge of such life. And the weight of evidence is clearly against such speculation.

There are of course some people who have had close encounters with death (sometimes referred to as near-death experiences or NDEs). They have then recovered to tell of their experiences of passing through various ethereal realms or tunnels, of floating out of their bodies, of seeing bright lights, and of marvelous meetings with imaginary gods and angels in beautiful shining palaces. Humanists do not question that some individuals have had such experiences; what is open to question is their correct interpretation. The fact remains that, as these people are still alive to talk about it; they therefore have not been truly dead. The simple absence of the customary signs of life, such as pulse or breath, do not signify death. There are cases where people are completely anaesthetized, with few or no vital signs, yet they are not dead. Many eastern mystics and yogi have mastered control of aspects of bodily function, and can appear to be dead or at least in some state of suspended animation. There are absolutely no independent data to confirm such tales of recovery from death; they cannot be proven, and there is no credible medical evidence to sustain such beliefs. There is, however, some scientific data to show that what is experienced is what is to be expected. To some extent, it is because of this realistic attitude towards death that humanists have fairly liberal attitudes towards suicide and euthanasia, involving voluntary death (but not to capital punishment which involves involuntary death). However, this does not mean to suggest that humanists propose to open the floodgates for private slaughter and public bloodshed—far from it.

With respect to *suicide*, humanists do not encourage adoption of procedures by emotionally disturbed people that lead to the premature death of an otherwise physically healthy human being. However, they do believe that individuals should have control over the basic decisions regarding the continuation of one's own life, provided consideration is given to the effects that such decisions might have on others who may be affected by their outcome. Timely counseling, appropriate treatment of mental illness, and proper education will do far more to reduce the number of suicides than any amount of preventive legislation.

With regard to *euthanasia*, which is the act of deliberately causing premature death in patients suffering from unbearable pain or incurable illness, legalization of an appropriate process, such as that recently instituted in the Netherlands, could improve the quality of life for many troubled individuals and their families and friends, who otherwise have to wait and watch their loved ones decline past the point of no return. There are two primary forms of euthanasia: *active* (involving direct intervention by others leading to the death of a patient, i.e. making one die) and *passive* (with no direct involvement of others, i.e. letting one die). Without specifying the precise elements of the processes involved, because of the enormous number of factors to be taken into account (most beyond the scope of this short book), it can be said that humanists are generally in favor of taking a positive stance in favor of passive euthanasia.

With regard to *capital punishment*, humanists are generally opposed to the deliberate taking of life of any citizen of any state by that state on the pretext of punishment. There are four main reasons for this stance: the sentence is *irreversible*; the executed criminal cannot be *rehabilitated*; the remainder of society is not much *deterred* by the execution of guilty criminals; and the process (which to some extent involves the notion of revenge) is *debasing* to civilized society. It could be argued (though weakly) that it is a failure of society that permits individuals to develop such anti-social attitudes in the first place, and there is thus a communal obligation to assist such unfortunates so that they will not commit capital crimes. It is acknowledged, though, that there are a few persons who act with such incredible depravity, ferocity, and callousness towards their fellow creatures that some form of *ultimate* sanction may be always necessary to preserve the general interests of society. Just what that *ultimate* form should be is for society as a whole to decide, but Canada and many of the United States have already banned capital punishment. To the extent that one differentiates between euthanasia (which is *mercy* killing) and capital punishment (which is *a* form of *vengeful* killing), the case has been presented for terminating the lives of hopelessly deranged humans found without any doubt guilty of particularly heinous crimes, demonstrably incurable of their actions, and clearly incapable of release into normal society at any future time. But it is a thin line to walk; consideration and concern for one's fellow humans, however troubled, would counsel the humanist towards moderation, toleration, and medical or psychiatric treatment in such cases, regardless of the nature of the transgression.

3. Abortion

Humanists know that the human body sheds or aborts thousands of living cells every day, every single one of which has the potential for full development. We know that every period of menstruation by every normal woman results in the formation of eggs and their subsequent expulsion if unfertilized. We know that every episode of ejaculation by every normal male results in the expulsion of millions of spermatozoa, only one of which may result in the fertilization of an egg. The rest of the sperm are aborted.

Most normal women ovulate every month from their mid-teen years to their mid-forties over about 30 years. Approximately 12 times per year, each normal woman produces about 400 ova or egg cells, any one of which has the potential to become a human being if fertilized. It is interesting to consider that science has now given us the means of fertilizing all of these eggs, using in-vitro or out-of-womb techniques. However, if any one of these eggs is fertilized in the body, then no more eggs will be produced by that body for about a year. So although it may be theoretically possible for each woman to produce (30 x 12 x 400) 144,000 potential human beings over the course of her child-bearing years, the practical upper limit would appear to be closer to 30, or one per year during that period.

But how many women have ever had 30 babies during their life? Even 50% of that number is unusual, and more common figures are found to be around 10% or three children per mother. Even with such low factors, the world is still experiencing overpopulation problems, and in some countries, such as China, married couples were encouraged to have only one child for life. Without digressing into the fascinating topic of the effects that such a one-child policy will have on a population which then grows up without brothers or sisters and with generally fewer relatives, the point to note here is that all the other eggs cells and spermatozoa are simply aborted, accidentally or deliberately by either natural or artificial means. One can therefore conclude that unfertilized cell abortion is a very common and widespread phenomenon in nature and in society.

The early abortion of a fertilized ovum (called a zygote) is no different in principle to the abortion of any other body cell or tissue as described, although the DNA of the fetus is arguably distinct from that of the mother. There does comes a point where such tissue begins to take on the potential for a viable separate life, and society should agree as to when that point is achieved in the course of a normal pregnancy, with abortion being permitted prior to the point, and not afterwards, with allowance being made for exceptional medical circumstances.

The abortion issue is really one of human rights, as much as one of medical ethics. All women should have the political right to decide whether they should become pregnant in the first place. Secondly, upon becoming pregnant, women should have the right to decide if they wish to remain pregnant, for a definite period of time, say during the first 3 months of the 9 month pregnancy. During that time, the rights of the potential mother should supercede the rights of the developing fetus. After that time has elapsed, the rights of the fetus should supercede the mother, and abortion should not be permitted except on clearly legislated medical grounds relative to the health of either the mother or fetus.

Ideally, the people of the world are now able to (and therefore should) establish the correct size of population that the resources of the world can adequately sustain in acceptable conditions in terms of energy expended and consumed. People should be encouraged and rewarded to try to achieve that optimum birth rate. The methods of family planning and birth control necessary to achieve such stability are now well understood and should be widely disseminated throughout the population of the world on a major scale.

While humanists, male and female, do not endorse or advocate casual abortion of fertilized ova as a means of general birth control, they certainly view it as a viable option to solve certain social problems that may occur as the result of an unwanted pregnancy, until improvements in contraception, medication, education and living standards for all can reduce the need for abortions arising from such causes. Humanists realize that women do not lightly resort to abortion as a means of birth control; rather, women do so because they find themselves in intolerable situations because of an unplanned pregnancy. Regard for life, common decency, and kindly attitudes towards our fellow human beings in trouble suggest that the liberal approach to abortion advocated by humanists is the correct approach for an enlightened society to adopt.

The humanist position is: abortion if necessary, but not necessarily abortion. Consideration should be given to prospects for a successful, rewarding, and happy life, for the mother, the father, the child, and all other affected family members, in such matters. However, the final decision and choice to abort or not should, as a matter of principle, ultimately rest with the mother who has to bear the fetus and raise the child; it should not rest with some outside agency, sanctioned by state or church, that is itself unwilling or unable to take responsibility for the outcome of the pregnancy. Humanists are not swayed nor misled by incorrect, biased, and emotionally charged rhetoric spread by the anti-abortion movement. That movement, funded primarily by the churches, seems concerned only with the quantity of life, and not with quality of life for the as-yet unborn. The fetus, in its early stages, is best viewed as no more than body tissue; the removal of such tissue by natural or artificial means cannot by any stretch of the imagination be compared to the murder of a fully developed human being, despite exaggerated, incorrect, dramatic, misleading, and colorful claims by noisy, vociferous, at times violent and (lately) murderous members of the anti-abortion movement, determined to enforce their conservative religious values and erroneous medical views on the rest of society. In most of North America, freedom of choice is a matter of legal fact as well as a constitutional right.

4. Sexuality

Humanists understand that the primary function of sex is continuity (not "procreation") of the species, whether of the animal or vegetable category. They also recognize that the sex drives of normal people are natural. As most sexual activity is also pleasurable, humanists see no reason not to enjoy it, provided no physical, psychological, economic, or other harm is done to either party involved with sexual activities.

Humanists see nothing intrinsically wrong with eroticism, being the depiction of aspects of love in a sexual form, but they can and do make a distinction between artistic eroticism and tasteless pornography, which is the use of sex to degrade the person. Humanists do not advocate censorship of pornography;

instead, they argue that a population properly educated in sexual matters would have little use for pornographic material, and the problem would therefore resolve itself as the market for it would diminish. To be realistic, though, it will probably never completely disappear as such education will probably never become universal and there will always be a certain proportion of deviants in every society. Humanists do not condone promiscuity nor any other form of exploitive, violent, or degrading sexual practices in which there are real or apparent victims of any type, race, age, class, or gender.

As a group, humanists are neither for nor against homosexuality. Such relationships between consenting adults should be in whatever form the partners mutually agree upon, always provided that nobody inside or outside the homosexual grouping is harmed or imposed upon against their will. Humanists advocate the fullest education of children at appropriate ages in every aspect of sexuality, birth control, venereal disease, and the reproductive process, to enable children to develop into mature, knowledgeable, responsible and guilt-free adults. When asked what should one tell children about sexual matters, the answer is to tell them what they want to know, in a manner that they can understand. Mature adults can surely edit information to prepare answers sufficient to satisfy childish curiosity.

5. Morality

Humanists realize that the experience of men and women, and not the alleged pronouncements of gods, are at the core of moral behavior, and model their standards accordingly. Humanists are ethical beings; their morality springs directly from altruism, which is concern for their fellow human beings. To be treated properly, one has to learn how to conduct oneself properly and how to treat others properly. Any voluntary action contemplated by any individual should be capable of universal application by all individuals. In philosophical terms, this is often referred to as *utilitarianism* (the greatest good for the greatest number). The morality of humanists also springs from knowledge of the principles of moral behavior, involving the elements of rationality, impartiality, and prescription. This topic is further elaborated in Chapter1.3 *Morality*.

6. Science

Humanists believe in and endorse the scientific method of experimentation and testing of hypotheses for the acquisition of reliable and useful knowledge. Science has provided many correct answers to problems faced by civilized communities, although many more questions remain to be formulated and answered. Science has also provided many incorrect answers, but these are usually corrected, modified, or abandoned in the light of better knowledge. Nevertheless, it is because of science (and scientists) that humanists do not believe that earthquakes, floods, lightning, disease, disasters, or comets are examples of the wrath of gods; they literally know better.

Humanists support unfettered scientific exploration, although they do have some reservations about the indiscriminate application of many scientific discoveries, such as cloning and organ transplants. Humanists acknowledge that there are many ethical, legal, and social problems raised by scientific discoveries that society has yet to resolve satisfactorily. Nevertheless, *Science* and its partner *Technology* offer the best hope for humans to find solutions to many problems that confront society. Some of these problems are of course the *result* of science and technology, reminding us that technical feasibility does not necessarily imply broad societal acceptance. The benefits to the planet as a whole must be considered.

7. Reason

Humanists are rationalists and pragmatists; they consider that reason and human intelligence are the most effective devices or instruments available for the solution of life's many problems. They also accept that the human mind and body have some limitations, and that the frontiers of knowledge and ability are constantly being examined and extended by human wit and wisdom.

Humanists can live with considerable uncertainty, as they realize that many questions posed by humans cannot yet be answered. Some questions may indeed have no answers, and other questions may need to be rephrased. Such adjustments do not disturb the humanist; he or she simply accepts the new or modified circumstances. There is no underlying fundamental body of so-called revealed truth in the minds of humanists that has to be reconciled with the new findings. When reason is applied to solve a problem, humanists are prepared to accept the outcome; their minds are not blocked by pre-conceived notions that may conflict with the results of rational thought processes.

8. Belief

Humanists are free thinkers; they decide for themselves what to think about the great issues of birth, life, death, and relationships. They have no creed, no dogmatic beliefs, no rote quotations of predigested principles prepared by other people, whether of church or party, to save individuals from having to think for themselves. Humanists are generally (small—l) liberal in political affairs and believe in informed democratic choice in all matters of public policy. They are adamantly opposed to most forms of censorship, except where deemed necessary to shield immature children from unnecessary concerns arising from issues that they may not as yet properly comprehend. It is for the reasons given above that humanists are opposed to compulsory prayers in schools. It is simply wrong to impose the religious beliefs of one group, no matter how large in number, on the minds and lives of other groups. This is not democracy; it is the tyranny of the majority, trampling on the constitutional rights of minorities. As all children between certain ages are required by law to attend school, the same laws should equally protect the interests of all children. If there are those who wish or feel that they must recite prayers to their various gods during school hours, let *them* be the ones to leave the classroom, so that the remainder can continue to progress with their more useful secular studies.

To paraphrase a light-hearted opinion, it may be all right to worship a god in the classroom, but first we should all have to agree on which particular god it should be [Rooney 1982]. And as we were reminded by the lyrics for a famous song on racial intolerance from the Rodgers and Hammerstein musical play "South Pacific," one has got to be carefully taught to become a bigot. It is the same with religious intolerance; it has got to be drummed into children from the earliest of ages. You have got to be taught to hate and fear the people, things, and ideas that your parents were taught to hate and fear; it does not come naturally to the open mind. It would be just as easy (or difficult) to teach understanding and tolerance for the beliefs of others, but it is not in the interests of the promoters of the religious status quo to do so. Apart from any constitutional issue, the recitation in schools of petitionary prayers to any one of a large number of imaginary gods is not only mindless and useless; it is divisive. It sets children apart from each other for purely ideological reasons, and that cannot be beneficial for any of them.

Humanists would prefer to see an end to compulsory lip service to the beliefs of any one religion in any school in the world, and the introduction of courses of compulsory instruction covering all the major systems of religious and non-religious beliefs of the world, so that children would learn about the many good (and not-so-good) elements of all such systems. A good place to start would be to put a copy of the book titled "In God We Trust—But Which One?"[Hayes 1996] in every school library. Children would then be able to decide for themselves the particular set of values to which they might adhere, just as they can now choose a particular career they might follow, based on their demonstrated ability or interest in certain academic or technical subject areas. Given such an informed base, it is doubtful that many children would elect to adopt a sectarian religious outlook as a significant element in their lives.

9. Spirituality

Humanists are materialists and monists, in that they do not believe that there is such a separate thing as a spirit, human or otherwise, sometimes referred to as the so-called Cartesian Mind, after the work of Rene Descartes, a noted 17th century French dualist philosopher. They believe that body and mind (i.e. the active brain) are inseparable. The mind is a function or aspect of the brain; when the brain dies, the mind dies with it. The mind and the thoughts it generates are no more than brain states, in essence, neural patterns. Although humanists enjoy the so-called creature comforts of life, such as good food, clothing, and shelter, humanists are not necessarily materialists in the sense that this word means to crave ownership of increasing quantities of property or material possessions for their own sake. Such ownership often brings with it difficulties and hardships that many humanists simply shun.

There is no problem with the concept of the soul for humanists; they do not believe that such an entity exists. To believe in souls, one has also to believe in supernatural gods; not to believe in souls or gods is to dispense with two unnecessary thoughts and all the odd questions associated with them. For example, what evidence is there for the existence of souls, where do they come from, how and when (and why) are they transmitted to new persons, where do they go after death, and how do they occupy themselves throughout all eternity? As the population of the world is increasing, are enough new souls of the right type being manufactured? The reader can invent additional nonsense.

At the same time, humanists recognize a human trait or attribute that can best be described using the word "élan" to signify a lively or enthusiastic approach to and awareness of life and its several opportunities and problems. This quality is something that stems from within the brain of each individual; it is not imposed or implanted by some external divinity, although it is certainly influenced by external life experiences. Also, this quality is more highly developed in some people than in others, and it dies with the death of the person with whom it was associated. The memory of it may linger in the minds of those who live on, though, either through direct personal contact before death or through the writings, art, music, or other recorded expressions of activity left by the deceased person. No one living today has ever met Aristotle, the ancient Greek philosopher, yet most of us have heard of his name and all of us have been affected by his teachings. In this sense, the spirit of Aristotle lives on in our beliefs and behaviors. Recent medical research into what is being called neuro-biology is also shedding new light on parts of the brain that appear to have a great deal to do with the extent to which individuals have religious experiences.

10. Evolution

Humanists are evolutionaries, and not revolutionaries, in that they know that nature exhibits an evolutionary trend. As non-believers, humanists do not believe the Bible stories about creation of the universe by a God a few thousand years ago; reliable scientific evidence now available is overwhelmingly opposed to and in conflict with such archaic notions. Humanists also do not confuse the apparently progressive *trend* of evolution with so-called *purpose*; while individual human beings can have purposes, nature as a whole does not appear to have any general purpose. Humanists believe that the inherent progress of nature can be positively and beneficially influenced by intelligent intervention by human action. As part of nature, humanists do not believe in letting the rest of nature simply take its own untrammeled course, if it is not to the benefit of humankind to let it do so, and if it is within the power of humankind to intervene in a beneficial manner.

At the same time, humanists grant that many mistakes have been made by human intervention in many areas of economy, ecology, science, sociology, biology, and so on. Humanists also observe that, because the majority of human beings profess to have religious beliefs, the majority of these mistakes are logically attributable to the same majority of believers. These believers seem to have had precious little help from their assorted gods in the avoidance of mistakes, despite billions of man-hours wasted in praise, prayer, sacrifice, and requests for help, spread over thousands of years. Perhaps it is time for society to listen to the non-believers.

Undue emphasis has been placed historically by people on the relative importance of the position of Planet Earth and Humankind in the cosmos. We are not at the center of the universe (if there is indeed such a location), except perhaps in the minds of some deluded people. The universe consists of all time, space, and matter; the earth is but one of a group of tiny planets in orbit near an insignificant star in a minor galaxy in a region relatively remote from the center of the *known* astronomical universe. The chances of what happened chemically, physically, and electrically to our planet, giving rise to life, is likely to be typical of similar events throughout the cosmos. The amount of matter comprising all animal and vegetable life on earth compared only to the total amount of matter comprising our planet is itself of very tiny proportions; and that an even smaller amount of that matter comprises humankind. In fact, the amount of matter observable in the universe is now reckoned to be only about one-third of the total amount. The other two-thirds consist of dark matter, about which practically nothing is as yet known. In view of the foregoing facts, the rational mind has to question the view that the human race is of any real significance to any entity other than ourselves, and perhaps to the so-called lower forms of life with whom we share the planet and on whom we usually have adverse effects. It is a scientific fact that sooner or later, our Sun will fade and die, and with it will go life as we know it on planet Earth.

11. Ceremony

Most (but not all) humanists consider that the great events of life (birth, graduation, marriage, and death) should be marked with joyous or somber celebration appropriate to the occasion, much as they have been for centuries. Many human achievements are worthy of official or public recognition, and individuals and society in general need and should have the opportunity to be recognized or to express their compliments or condolences as circumstances require. When children are born to humanist parents, these parents are as proud and happy as any other parents, and usually invite their friends and relations to share in the joy by arranging a suitable party to recognize the event. The freedom and worth of the child are recognized by the absence of any imposed religious ritual attending such birthday celebrations, and the focus of attention is placed on the birth of the new child and not on the formal ceremony (see endnote 1 below). When young adults achieve suitable academic distinction, such as their graduation from high school, college, or university, they are worthy of public recognition by appropriate commencement or convocation exercises.

Such ceremonies can be entirely secular; they do not require to have any religious component to be profoundly meaningful. For example, in Norway, a secular ceremony of confirmation has been developed for teenagers to recognize the passage from the freedoms of youth to the responsibilities of adulthood; the ceremony is preceded by a year of instruction in life-skills, and it is marked by a happy gathering of friends and relatives in a public place (such as the city hall) to witness the event.

When humanists decide to get married, they recognize that society requires legal registration of the fact, to protect the rights of the partners and their children. Such legal recognition is all that is needed to establish the fact of marriage; there is no need for any religious ceremony of any kind, although there is a definite need for friends and relations to have an opportunity to get together to share in the joy of the the newly wed couple, and to give them a positive start to their married life. Most humanist marriages include a significant and dignified contractual exchange between the parties, usually followed by a joyful wedding reception. There is no evidence to show that the divorce rate among humanists is higher the national average, which includes a majority of marriages performed with strong religious components. Several publications suggest outlines for suitable ceremonies for secular weddings (endnotes 2 & 3).

When humanists die, it is recognized that there is a need for survivors to be able to express and share their grief through mourning, as well as a need to remember the virtues and achievements of the deceased person in a public or private ceremony, keeping in mind the wishes of the deceased in this matter. Humanist funeral services therefore focus on the deceased and his or her positive contributions to the lives of others around them. They include descriptions of the main lifework of the deceased, and often include excerpts from the works of some of the deceased person's favorite authors and composers, but nothing in the ceremony distracts the attention of the mourners from the reasons for the gathering, which are two-fold: *remembrances* of the deceased; and *condolences* for the living. Humanists do not use phrases like "passed away" or "taken from us." Furthermore, few humanist funerals involve the macabre spectacle of open caskets in heated churches and closed burials in cold graveyards. Humanists tend to favor private and immediate cremation of the deceased person's corpse, after all serviceable body parts and organs have been removed for use by others, and before any remembrance ceremony occurs. Several publications suggest suitable ceremonies for secular remembrance services (endnotes 4 & 5).

Although the opening of a new bridge, or the launching of a new ship, or the inauguration of any other significant enterprise or project brought into being by human ingenuity, effort, money, and social conscience should be marked by suitable ceremony, there is absolutely no need to invoke the intervention of imaginary gods in such events. The blessings of God are often called for on such occasions, but how many bridges so blessed have collapsed, how many ships so blessed have sunk, and how many other enterprises so blessed have failed? Such blessings seem to have no effect on subsequent events. Should a ship sink, or bridge collapse, or enterprise fail, God is seldom blamed for his failure to protect them. Yet such failures are often described as Acts of God, even though they are often found to be attributable to human error or shortcoming or some natural cause. It is a curious paradox, difficult to understand except for believers who are of course used to such conundrums.

For humanists, simple formal ceremonies have been developed to cover all the normal private passages of life, for those who wish to use them. For other more public ceremonies, humanists suggest that the religious component simply be dropped, out of respect for diversity of belief and to preserve and enhance the general dignity of humankind. Those who wish to privately call upon their assorted gods to bless such events can still do so in the inner recesses of their minds (which is where all such gods exist) so there can be no *reasonable* objection to the proposal to abandon *public* expressions of petitionary prayers at such events. The word reasonable is deliberately emphasized in the foregoing sentence, because most objections are not based on reasonable grounds; they are emotional, irrational, and essentially intolerant in nature.

12. Politics

There is no specific humanist political agenda. Although there are many Humanist Associations all over the world, and indeed an International Union of such associations, there is no such thing as the official Humanist Party, at any national or international level. There is no Humanist Election Platform, proposing the overthrow of existing government regimes and the consequent establishment of a new Humanist World Order. There are no Humanist Armies, ready to impose Humanist Ideology by force. However, reference to any of the Humanist Manifestos identified later (see Chapter 1.5 *Manifestos*) will disclose several articles dealing with ideologies, economics, ecology, world government, conflict resolution, and similar related issues about which the humanist movement has deep concerns regarding appropriate policies for the conduct of world affairs.

Humanists are generally looking beyond politics for methods to solve social problems. The method proposed for implementation of these policies is generally through the development of *literacy* and the *education* of the people of the world to abandon old, unfair, and unworkable systems of state and church government and economics, and to consider the adoption of new systems, many of which have yet to be invented. As was said in the play "*Richelieu*" by Edward Lytton, the pen is mightier than the sword. We may not see the implementation of these new systems in our lifetime, but the basis for them can begin to be laid now by the spread of humanist ideals on a one-to-one personal basis.

13. Education

For humanists, education poses some problems. These occur largely because of the fact that at present, education of the great mass of the population of the world is still primarily in the hands of those who belong to one or other of the major world religions or ideologies. Such people are neither free nor willing to introduce the rational and secular principles of humanism into programs over which they have control. The deliberate, overt, and widespread teaching of specifically secular humanist values in public and private schools is virtually non-existent; indeed, it is deliberately suppressed in many areas. In those places where it does occur, its beneficial voice tends to be overwhelmed by opposing ideologies.

Nevertheless, in subject areas as communications, literature, sociology, and the earth sciences, the scientific methods in for example biology, chemistry, mathematics and physics developed by pioneers of every religious persuasion (and some of none) and endorsed by humanism is continuing to gain ground, and will result in a growing number of maturing students who will be increasingly skeptical of the claims of their educators. The techniques of lateral and critical thinking, now being introduced into many curricula, will have a beneficial effect on young adults of the future.

14. Gender

In humanism, males and females at every age and stage of their respective developments are considered to be worthy of equal treatment. While it is undeniably true that men and women are different in many respects (such as in biology and physiology) as a result of evolution, each should be accorded dignity, respect, and expectations relative to their gender and condition. Humanists do not believe that men should be able to do everything that women can do, or vice versa, nor that every person is equally capable of doing what many others may be able to do. Those things which both genders can do with equal facility are worthy of equal rewards (or occasionally, punishment); those things which one can do and the other cannot should be valued by both on their own merits, relative to benefits to individual development, relationships, and to society as a whole. Unlike many religious groups in which women are required to play roles subservient to men, under rules created by men, in humanism women, like men, may undertake any political, familial, managerial or service role to which they are genuinely and freely inclined and for which they are suitably qualified.

15. Fun and Games

To conclude, it can also be stated that the majority of humanists are not overly preoccupied with or fanatic about all the weighty issues mentioned or alluded to in the foregoing paragraphs. They also like to have a bit of fun. They enjoy the ordinary pleasures of eating and drinking (usually in moderation), of getting together with family, friends and relations, of going to movies and plays, attending sporting and cultural events, arranging picnics and social gatherings, watching TV programs and video tapes. Many have special interests and skills in baseball, chess, choral work, dance, fitness, golf, hockey, music, opera, photography, skiing, swimming, and travel, to name some of the more obvious pastimes. A disproportionately large number of humanists (compared to the general population) have academic or professional qualifications in many fields, including (but not limited to) accounting, the arts, aviation, communications, construction, education, engineering, finance, industry, law, media, medicine, nursing, psychiatry, and social work, as well as organizations and sciences of all sorts.

ENDNOTES

1. *New Arrivals—A Guide to Naming Ceremonies* by the British Humanist Association.
2. *It's Your Wedding: a Workbook for Creating your own Ceremony* by the American Humanist Association.
3. *A Humanist Wedding Ceremony* in "Humanist in Canada" Volume 75, Winter 1985, pp 27, 28
4. *Guidelines for Officiants at Non-Religious Funerals* by the British Humanist Association.
5. *A Humanist Funeral Service* in "Humanist in Canada" Volume 7, Winter 1969, pp 6,7

1.2.3 HUMANIST AUTHORITIES

It often happens that people who find themselves holding views that can best be described as humanist think that they are alone or unusual, and that the thoughts that they are harboring are new or dangerous or unpopular. They look around and see that most of their friends profess to be believers of one sort or another, and they therefore sometimes think that perhaps they themselves are on the wrong track or tack. It may be of some comfort for them to realize that humanism is as old as humanity, and that for thousands of years, millions of people have held identical or similar views about the worth of humankind and its destiny.

It is only in recent years that it has become less risky to speak out on the subject, as fear of reprisals from religious sources has diminished. In France in 1757, a decree established the death penalty for anyone found guilty of questioning the established religion. Most religions have a sorry history of repression, torture, and murder of those who would disagree with their views. Even today it is not altogether safe in every part of the world to publicly voice opinions which call the basis of religious beliefs into question; the forces of darkness are still regrettably very much in evidence. Nonetheless, the rational humanist voice has an increasing need to be heard amidst the babble of incantation. There is also a general dearth of clearly humanist material in many local libraries, and a lack of organized humanist activity in many local regions, so it is common to find few popular and readable works or little current information readily available on the subject.

As mentioned in the *rationale* for this book, at a local chapter meeting of a humanist association, the author once asked the participants to write down the name of at least one humanist author of whom they had heard. They did not even have to be familiar with his or her work, but only to mention the name. It was interesting to learn that about 15% of the group could not name one name. A question immediately arises: how can such people call themselves truly humanist if they have not read or at least heard of one book or author. Most Christians could name all the (alleged) New Testament authors; most Jews could name two dozen of the Old Testament writers; most Catholics could name at least a dozen Popes; most Hindus could identify half a dozen gods by name. Why then can humanists not list their own heroes? There are probably two main reasons for the gap: most humanist writers are not specifically identified as being such, and most children are not exposed to the work of these writers *as humanists* at home, in school, in church, or elsewhere, unless they happen to have literate and educated humanist parents or sympathetic free-thinking friends or teachers.

Although there have been hundreds, even thousands, of humanists in every country and in every age, the very nature of humanism restricts the emergence of humanist "deities" or "saints." That is not to say, though, that humanists do not turn to the works of notable and respected authors, both past and present, for guidance, to more fully grasp the elements of the humanist frame. Some names immediately come to mind: *John Dewey* for education, *Bertrand Russell* for logical argument, *Corliss Lamont* for humanist philosophy, *Edwin Wilson* for humanist organization, *Paul Kurtz* for analysis of humanist values, *Mordechai Richler* and *Kurt Vonnegut* for light-hearted and novel humanist observations on life and its many foibles; these are seven among hundreds. One does not have to be a scholar to be a humanist, but it helps to read at least some of the works of such people.

The purpose of this Section of the book is to correct a gap in the educational opportunities, first for those who are already dedicated humanists and want more information, secondly for those who are perhaps "closet" humanists and want to come out onto the broad sunlight uplands of rationalism, as well as thirdly for those who would be humanists but have no idea where to start to get information. No one book could possibly contain all the works that have been produced by humanist authors over the centuries, nor contain the names of every person of humanist outlook who has ever lived on earth. But it is possible to identify some of the more major figures of early and more recent history to whom recognition and attention might be given by those wishing to improve their knowledge of humanist theory and practice. Because of their pragmatic approach, their logical arguments, and the simplicity of the ideas presented, most humanist authors are relatively easy to read and understand. The names of many humanist authorities are listed below and the titles of some of their works are to be found in more detail in Appendix A.2 *Bibliography*.

As stated, the list is nowhere near complete; it only contains about 200 of well over 1000 names known to this author. It is at best an introduction to a few people about whom humanists in general could do well to know more. Furthermore, it should be said that not all of the people included in the list might have viewed themselves as true-blue humanists; some clearly were or are, while others, who might be more correctly classified as freethinkers, have either directly or indirectly contributed to the humanist cause by their lives and works. Many famous, not so famous, and indeed infamous people, such as Joseph Stalin, Mao Tse Tung, or Fidel Castro, to name only three, may be acknowledged as atheists or agnostics, but they clearly do not belong in a list of humanists. Similarly, there are many other names, such as Martin Luther King, Andrew Carnegie, and Mahatma Gandhi, to name only three, who have advanced human affairs in a way generally consistent with humanist ideals, but who could not realistically be included in the list because of their overtly stated religious affiliations.

It might also be observed that so far as is known, no wars have been fought, no repression imposed, no torture inflicted, no pillage committed in the name of anyone on the list; there is nothing but good to be said on behalf of all names included. The exclusion of other equally well-known names or well-intentioned people is occasioned solely by the constraints of space and the decision (or ignorance) of the author. The list is arranged alphabetically.

1. European:

Matthew Arnold, A.J. Ayer, Irving Babbitt, Francis Bacon, Charles Beard, Arnold Bentham, Simone de Beauvoir, Jeremy Bennett, Cyrano de Bergerac, Ingmar Bergman, H.J. Blackham, Sir Herman Bondi, Charles Bradlaugh, Bertold Brecht, Josef Bronowski, Ludwig Buchner, Albert Camus, Geoffrey Chaucer, Paul & Patricia Churchland, Auguste Compte, Joseph Conrad, Jaques Cousteau, Marie Curie, Charles Darwin, Richard Dawkins, Denis Diderot, Albert Einstein, George Elliot (M. Evans), Frederick Engels, Fransisco Ferrer, Ludwig Feuerbach, Elliot Fitzgerald, Gustave Flaubert, Anthony Flew, G.W. Foote, Anatole France, Sigmund Freud, John Galsworthy, Andre Gide, Johann W. Goethe, Maxim Gorky, Baron Holbach, J.B.S. Haldane, Thomas Hardy, Hector Hawton, Georg F. Hegel, Thomas Hobbes, Baron

Holbach, Frederick Hoyle, David Hume, Aldous Huxley, Julian Huxley, Thomas Huxley, Henrik Ibsen, C.E.M. Joad, Margaret Knight, Kathleen Knott, Richard Leakey, John Locke, Horace Mann, Thomas Mann, Christopher Marlowe, Kingsley Martin, Somerset Maugham, Guy de Maupassant, John Stuart Mill, Jacques Monod, Kit Mouat, Gilbert Murray, A.A. Neill, A.S. Neill, Reuben Osborn, George Orwell, Louis Pasteur, Ivan Pavlov, Robinson Ritchie, Jean J. Rousseau, Salman Rushdie, Bertrand Russell, Marquis de Sade, Jean Paul Sartre, Ferdinand Schiller, George Bernard Shaw, Percy B. Shelley, Adam Smith, Barbara Smoker, Herbert Spencer, Benedict Spinoza, Leslie Stephen, Marie Stopes, Algernon Swinburne, Peter Ustinov, Francois M. Arouet (Voltaire), H.G. Wells, Rebecca West, Barbara Wooton, Emile Zola, and some say William Shakespeare.

2. North American:

Theodore Abel, Steve Allen, Woody Allen, Dana Andrews, Susan B. Anthony, Isaac Asimov, Margaret Atwood, J.A.C. Auer, Edwin Backus, Dan Barker, Edward Bellamy, Pierre Berton, Norman Bethune, Annie Besant, Leon Birkhead, Joseph Blau, Raymond Bragg, R.W. Brockway, Edward Brower, George Carlin, Dick Cavett, Brock Chisholm, Noam Chomsky, Robert Buckman, Arthur C. Clarke, Samuel Clemens (Mark Twain), Lowell Coate, Daniel Dennett, John Dewey, John Dietrich, Frederick Edwords, Albert Ellis, Ralph Waldo Emerson, Edward Ericson, Stella Falk, Bernard Fantus, Jules Feiffer, Tom Flynn, Larry Flynt, William Floyd, John Fremont, Betty Friedan, Erich Fromm, John Kenneth Galbraith, Bill Gates, Ann Nicol Gaylor, Stephen J. Gould, Matt Groening, Ernest Hemingway, Pat Hutcheon, Robert Ingersoll, E. Haldeman-Julius, Wendy Kaminer, W.P. Kinsella, Paul Kurtz, Corliss Lamont, Tom Lehrer, Sinclair Lewis, Abraham Lincoln, Joseph McCabe, James Madison, Barry Manilow, H.L. Mencken, Henry Morgentaler, Farley Mowat, Lloyd and Mary Morain, Kai Neilsen, Jack Nicholson, Robert Nozick, Thomas Paine, Kenneth L. Patton, Linus Pauling, Sean Penn, Paul Pfalzner, James Randi,

Mordechai Richler, Gordon Rodgers, Andy Rooney, Jane Rule, Carl Sagan, Jonas Salk, Carl Sandberg, Margaret Sanger, George Santayana, H. Sellers, B.F. Skinner, Rod Steiger, Donald Sutherland, David Suzuki, John Steinbeck, Charles Templeton, Henry Thoreau, Ted Turner, Gore Vidal, Kurt Vonnegut, Wendell Watters, Andrew D. White, Walt Whitman, Frederick Woodbridge.

3. Others

There are of course many more ancient literary figures who might be considered to fall into the humanist category, such as Aristotle, Confucius, Epicurus, Helvetius, Heraclite, Omar Khayyam, Mencius, Protagoras, Lao Tzu, and Lucretius, in addition to those who lived more recently or who still live elsewhere in the world. Humanists are to be found in virtually all sectors of society, such as music, art and sculpture. Readers can set themselves some challenging and rewarding research tasks to discover the names and read about the lives and works of these and many more interesting people at home and abroad. An excellent way to start such a study would be to purchase a copy of *"The Bibliography of Humanism,"* published by the International Humanist and Ethical Union, whose address is listed in Appendix A.4; that *Bibliography* lists approximately 1800 titles, of which about half are written in or have been translated into the English language. Another useful source of information, containing the names and synoptic thoughts of about 800 major non-religious literary and historical authorities, is *"The Biographical Dictionary of Ancient, Medieval, and Modern Freethinkers,"* written early in the last century by a former priest called Joseph McCabe, and published by Julius Haldeman in North America as part of a series entitled *"The Blue Books."* The series dealt generally with aspects of atheism and free thought. Another excellent general reference work is *"The Encyclopedia of Unbelief,"* edited by Gordon Stein, Ph.D., and published by Prometheus Books of Buffalo, New York. Many books written on specific humanist topics also contain useful bibliographies, of which a good example is *"The Genesis of a Humanist Manifesto"* by Edwin Wilson.

One can also find more references for humanist authorities on the InterNet. Usually, one can access the necessary information by just typing in the full name of the association into an InterNet search engine, and then clicking on a specific topic within that web-site. Two examples of extensive personal reference sources on the InterNet are (1) the list of *"Humanists of the Year"* recognized by the American Humanist Association (every year from 1953 to the present) and (2) the continually up-dated list of noted *"Atheists and Materialists"* recognized by the Humanist Association of Canada.

CHAPTER 1.3

MORALITY

1.3.1 INTRODUCTION

It was the American humorist and humanist, Mark Twain, who dryly stated that there is nothing so much in need of reform as *other* people's morals. And the Scottish poet, Robert Burns, in his address to the "Unco Guid" (uncommonly good people), observed:

> *"O ye wha are sae guid yoursel'.*
> *Sae pious and sae holy.*
> *Ye've nought to do but mark and tell.*
> *Your neibours' fauts and folly."*

There is unquestionably a righteous streak or a superior element related to almost all everyday examples of moral thought and behavior, and the reasons for this are not difficult to discern. Traditionally, moral behavior in western society has been closely linked with religious belief. There are, of course, some religions such as Taoism where to be a superior human is regarded as the ultimate or ideal objective, as suggested in the following excerpt from the *"I Ching"* or *"Book of Changes"*:

> *"Thunder over the lake.*
> *Thus the superior man*
> *understands the transitory*
> *in the light of the eternity."*

In general though, most ordinary moral issues or aspects are regarded by the majority of people as being inextricably bound up with religious ideals. However, it should be realized that one can be the most confirmed atheist and still lead a profoundly moral life; any person who understands and practices the principles of humanism will lead a life of acceptable moral quality. There is no need for threats of religious retribution to keep willing and informed people on paths of righteousness. One may also encounter a firm believer who also leads an exemplary moral life; his or her religious beliefs are simply laid on top of the fundamental morality. In this section of the book, some general aspects of moral behavior are presented first, leading to the identification of the elements of morality.

The argument that, without punitive sanctions from gods there are no constraints on moral behavior, does not pass even superficial scrutiny. Historically, few religions have shown much respect for the rights of others, or in many cases, even for the rights of their own adherents. Those few religious practitioners in particular who have shown consideration have largely done so, not on temporal, secular, or moral grounds, but out of respect (or more accurately fear) for their own spiritual safety or salvation.

Moral behavior can have a rationale completely independent of religion. To illustrate this point, consider the so-called Decalogue or Ten Commandments, allegedly handed down to Moses by God on stone tablets, as described in several places in the Bible [e.g., see *Holy Bible*, Exodus 20]. Needless to say, like so many other biblical and religious miracles, these tablets, though absolutely priceless, were soon broken and lost, and were therefore no longer available for review or checking by independent observers. It appears that a duplicate set of commandments was prepared and then also lost. The events surrounding this literally incredible action are described in some inconclusive detail in the Old Testament; these need not concern us in this discussion. The content of the second set is at variance from the first set, and includes such trivia as an injunction not to cook goats in their mother's milk [Exodus 23:19]. This hardly seems the stuff on which to base a world-class moral code.

First, the ten exhortations in the Decalogue consist of two positive statements and eight negative ones, in itself an inauspicious balance of forces. Secondly, five of the ten deal exclusively with restrictions in purely religious matters, such as worship of God, the making of idols, and observing the sabbath day. Thirdly, the remaining five commandments embody advice on human relationships which have a universal application not restricted to Jews, Christians, or any other sect (including humanists) and indeed predating Moses himself: not to murder, steal, lie, covet possessions of neighbors, nor to commit adultery. These are simply fundamental behavioral standards for any civilized society, regardless of religious belief, although the last one bears some examination. In some countries, a man is allowed only one wife, whereas in other countries, a man can have as many wives as he can support; in yet other countries, a woman can have as many husbands as she likes. In some countries, divorce is almost unattainable, whereas in others, it is a simple matter easily obtained. But adultery has got more to do with dishonesty and inappropriate behavior between individuals than societal procedures or national niceties.

There are a few interesting points that might be extracted from the foregoing paragraph. First, as mentioned, the replacement tablets of the decalogue made by Moses for placement in the famous Ark of the Covenant are missing, notwithstanding their priceless historical value, as is the Ark itself. People appear to have been very careless with the preservation of heritage properties in earlier times. Secondly, a curious comment to be found in one of the commandments concerns an admission by God that he is a jealous God, raising two points worthy of note: it suggests that God is not perfectly good, to the extent that jealousy is not good, and furthermore, the use of the indefinite article "a" implies that there may be other Gods who are not so jealous. Third, God says that he intends to punish children for the sins and transgressions of their fathers, which seems, at the very least, to be unfair on the children who have no control over their father's actions. To conclude this short section on the commandments, it might be noted that there are many additional ordinances or rules following on from the basic ten, which readers might find of interest to review for themselves in the biblical chapters cited (such as Exodus 21) and elsewhere. For example, one of these clearly states that if money is lent to a poor person, interest shall not be charged. One wonders how often that ordinance is strictly observed today by Judeo-Christian people carrying on *any* commercial business involving financial credit in the current century. And the admonition in Exodus 20:13 that "Thou shalt not kill" is clearly in conflict with the assertion in Ecclesiastes 3:3 that there is "a time to kill."

The subject matter of this chapter is set against a humanist outlook, articulated as follows: "There is no supreme exemplar of humanist ethics, because, on humanist assumptions, there is no *summum bonum*, no chief end of all action, no far-off crowning event to which all things move and for which all things exist, no teleology, no definitive human nature even." [Blackham, 1965]

1.3.2 MORALS IN GENERAL

First, one should keep in mind that the distinction between self interest and societal interest is at the heart of moral behavior. Secondly, one must separate moral issues from factual issues; we cannot deduce that people ought to do something just because they do in fact do it or don't do it. It may be an historical fact that modern western society got some of its moral values from religious origins, but it is an accepted principle of logic that the validity of a belief is independent of its origin. Third, the religious moralist's argument is based on one principle: because God is good, we ought to do what God wills. The humanist's moral argument is based on two principles: that every human should be treated as an end and not as a means; and that happiness for every human is good. If one can commit to one principle, why not to two (or as many as necessary, for that matter)? In any event, why commit to any principle which is based on an apparent absurdity in preference to principles which are based on fairness and reason?

In theory, if all humans were of equal strength, ability, and reason, it is likely that they would band together in communities where each person was deserving of equal respect; to give it would be to receive it. It is reasonable to believe that social life, organized according to this principle, is likely to be better for all than life not so organized. In practice, all humans are not so equal. What restraints are there on egoists who hold power, not to hurt others who do not hold such power? One minor restraint is that in society, circumstances often change, and the egoist may lose the position of power, but ultimately a moral decision as to how to act must be made by the power-holder.

Before examining secular morality in general, it is appropriate to consider two specific aspects of morals in particular, namely the elements of morality, and the basis of moral judgements.

1. Elements of Morality

For a person to hold a truly moral opinion about any issue, the opinion must be impartial as between people, it must be prescriptive, and it must be rational. With respect to *impartiality*, the recommended thought or behavior must apply to all appropriate people, including oneself. With respect to *prescription*, the thoughts or behaviors must not just be observed and commented upon in retrospect, but predicted and prescribed in advance. With respect to *rationality*, the opinion must be based on *good* reasons, and not simply taken on faith or order.

To be a truly moral person, one must develop attitudes about the civil and social rights of oneself and others, the ability to understand what others think and feel, the skill to acquire necessary and pertinent facts or knowledge, and the capacity and will for action. One can see from the foregoing explanation that there is no requirement whatsoever to hold religious beliefs or to adopt anything on faith in order to develop sound standards for moral conduct in any society. It is the answer to those who say that humankind needs to acknowledge the existence and intervention of a god to establish moral standards.

It might be said that the sum of one's moral experiences coupled to one's ability to make moral judgements give rise to one's conscience. Although the intellectual ability to have a conscience is a characteristic of humankind, conscience itself is not inherent; it is learned from the study and teaching of community standards. Because of this, there is a fair degree of interpretation involved in matters of conscience. Where a society has a strong religious influence, that regrettably will be adopted into the conscience of individuals brought up in that society. The word "regrettably" is used in the foregoing sentence because the great bulk of people exposed to such moral codes as promoted by the traditional religions simply adopt them by default. It is easier, safer, and therefore more acceptable to do so than to think carefully, deeply, correctly, and possibly controversially about what it all means. Like religion in general, much of what passes for good moral conduct based on religious values in contemporary western society does not withstand careful scrutiny; it may make one feel comfortable and virtuous, but it may not be very good for one's self-respect.

It might be fitting to end this short excursion into some basic issues concerning morals and morality, by making reference to the views of Stephen Jay Gould, Professor of Paleontology at Harvard University, expressed in an article in a humanist journal. He reminds us, by quoting several examples selected from natural history and biology to show that, as nature is neither kind nor cruel, there are no inherent moral messages to be found in nature.

We know that humans are also part of nature, albeit endowed through evolutionary processes with the ability to attribute values of good or bad, right or wrong, to certain sets of conditions found in natural circumstances. But the scientific study of nature will not provide answers to moral questions, as science can only provide information about the way our universe is constructed. Only humans can ascribe moral values to what is observed and experienced. And they should do so without reference to any sort of alleged divine intervention, despite certain religious authorities that make spurious claims to the contrary.

2. Moral Judgements

Moral actions involve judgements about outcomes. When we are about to do or say something, we have to make a judgement about the weight of each and all of the various factors surrounding the activity or statement and the possible effects or ends to which they may lead. The result may be to do or say nothing, but the judgements still have been made.

There are two main elements involved: self interest and societal interest. The great majority of morally correct actions and thoughts naturally involve issues in which these two sets of interests coincide. In other words, most things which you have to do (or are expected to do) are things which you probably want to do anyway. The conflicts, where they exist, are usually relatively minor. However, the greater the conflict or disparity between society's interest or expectations and the individual's self interest, the greater the moral stress experienced by the person concerned. It is a question of degree of moral obligation, of things which one knows ought to be done or said. The process involves cognitive dissonance, or the amount of disparity between what one feels should be done and what is actually done in any given set of circumstances. As someone once said, this can lead to hardening of the "oughteries."

There are several classes of moral judgements. First, there is the *personal* judgement, where a person makes a decision about a situation, followed by personal action. For example, I could decide that I am going to help old people (if they need the help) to cross busy streets safely (if that is what they wish to do); then I do that, whenever the opportunity arises. Secondly, there is the so-called *spectator* judgement, made about past personal actions or the current or past actions of others. For example, I might think that I or others ought to have helped some old people to cross a busy street when the opportunity arose.

Thirdly, there are *conditional* judgements, affecting a person's short or long term self interests; these usually involve an "if-then" situation. For example, *if* I help old people to cross the street, *then* they (and perhaps others) might think well of me, and this may be to my advantage. Religious people might add that their God will also think well of me. Conversely, if I steal some money, then I may be caught and punished, not only by law, but also by public censure or ridicule. Fourthly, there are *unconditional* judgements about perceived moral obligations, about things one literally ought to do or say; these of course vary from time to time and place to place. For example, most mature people in western society would consider it a moral obligation not to lie, steal, or cheat (in most circumstances; there are exceptions). Some people do lie, steal, and cheat, but not without experiencing a degree of mental dissonance and moral stress if they are not caught and usually more severe social penalties if they are caught. More often than not, moral judgements over-ride personal inclinations, having regard to outcomes. Some authorities, such as Immanual Kant, considered moral duty to be of the highest human order, a duty not open to choice and regardless of possible outcomes [Kant 1965]. A case often quoted in this regard concerns a passerby who is asked by a potential murderer if he saw which doorway the intended victim ran into. Is it the duty and therefore the moral obligation of the passerby give a truthful and correct answer thereby contributing to the victim's demise, or should he lie and thereby mislead the murderer with incorrect directions? (It might be noted, however, that Kant did expressly state that he believed in the existence of a God and the likelihood of an afterlife in his particular God's company [Kant p.650])

Some moral obligations have been codified into law, which gives an added weight to their universal application by the members of any society. Broadly speaking, it might be said that correct moral actions and statements should exhibit a universal societal application—that is, they should be capable of being applied by all people at all times in any specific society without reservation. In a society which values property rights, it is wrong to steal someone else's property, because if everybody did it, there would be no security of the rights. In any society which does not value private or personal property, stealing is not a matter for moral consideration or standards. To consider the example of abortion for a moment, it seems clear that, while early abortion may not be desirable or appropriate for every pregnant woman, there are many cases where it is the correct course of action. The correct moral position in this instance should therefore be: abortion if necessary, but not necessarily abortion.

For further reading, the following titles are suggested:

1. *Moral Thinking* [Wilson 1973]
2. *This View of Life* [Gould 1986]
3. *Moral Philosophy* [Duncan 1965]

1.3.3 SECULAR MORALITY

So far, morals have been described in a general sense. However it is necessary to be more specific to fully comprehend the main issues relating morality to humanism and to show how morality, while separate from religion, is at the core of humanism. It is of course quite difficult to be absolutely objective about a broad topic which embraces a very complex and essentially subjective mode of human experience, but the attempt should be made to establish a sound philosophical base for morality by those who aspire to humanism. As will be seen, it is possible to lead a life of good moral quality, free of religious crutches. People who simply act on so-called conscience, or who parrot what their friends say about right and wrong behavior, or who think what their church instructs them to think about moral questions, can hardly be said to be living truly moral lives. To be moral, one has to think and act by and for oneself, having regard to the benefits to oneself and to society as a whole. There are no "simple answers" or "quick fixes" to moral questions; we have to think out logically defendable solutions. There are no absolute, objective moral values, although an admonition like "to do no unnecessary harm" does come close.

No leap of faith will satisfy the rational mind in moral matters. Take a simple example, based on a complex issue: the Roman Catholic Church says divorce is wrong in principle. It has arrived at this position because its leaders believe that divorce is against its God's will, and it therefore requires its members to hold this view. The members don't have to think about it; they just have to accept it. This Church would also like to enforce its views on this topic (and many others) on those who are not Catholics. Some of these people who are not Catholics may also feel, think, and say that divorce is wrong, but they have to come to this opinion by a much more difficult route, involving the nature of mature sexual and familial relationships as well as property rights in a modern society.

A really careful examination of the subject by an open and rational mind could just as easily come to the conclusion that divorce is right in principle as well as being right in many specific situations. Those who hold this view after such examination have made a perfectly correct decision from a moral point of view. It may also be noted in passing that such people seldom wish to impose their view on the Catholic Church; they simply demand the freedom to decide for themselves what is right or wrong. No one group should have the right to impose or enforce its particular moral stance and choice, held only by some members of society, on others holding an opposing stance; to do so is immoral as well as being unconstitutional. In the field of law, a contract entered into under such conditions of duress or enforcement would probably be void or voidable. To be moral in a democratic society, every person must act freely, rationally, and with adequate knowledge of all significant facts, and then take responsibility for all outcomes of the chosen course of action.

For those readers wishing to further their knowledge of this interesting aspect of human relationships, the works of William Lecky on morality are recommended for review. One excerpt, not exactly chosen at random, gives a flavor of what might be in store for the curious mind, where it is asserted:

> "The writers of the middle ages are full of accounts of nunneries (*church convents*) that were like brothels, of the vast multitudes of infanticides (*murder of unwanted babies*) within their walls, and of that inveterate prevalence of incest (*sexual intercourse between blood relations*) among the clergy, which rendered it necessary *again* and *again* to issue the most stringent enactments that priests should not be allowed to live with their mothers or sisters" (*parentheses by this author*).

It would seem that the church authorities had extensive experience of the very things that they were keen to suppress among the laity or common folk.

If a human could possibly live an entire life in solitude, it might not be necessary for that person to develop moral standards, as all actions could be presumed to be in the direction of self interest. Robinson Crusoe on his desert island had no real need for morals until he met Friday. All humans belonging to groups, however small, do have a necessity for holding moral beliefs, and these are usually developed or attained as the result of education to the standards of that group. It might be observed that the standards in each group may not necessarily be the same as any other group, as standards will change from time to time. Some groups see no harm in lying, nakedness, homosexuality, or adultery, whereas as others frown on such behavior and impose sanctions against it. The moral issue is not whether such behavior is intrinsically right or wrong, when measured against some imaginary absolute standard, but rather what a given society at a given time and place freely thinks, says, and does about it. The standards reflect each group's understanding of its physical, social, and economic situation in the natural world. Of course, understanding involves thinking about the issues. To think properly, one must have a good grasp of language, clear logic, and some knowledge. In discussions of morality, authorities use obscure language, convoluted logic, and endeavor to suppress knowledge.

A number of psychologists have articulated concepts of moral development, particularly in the young child, where moral training is of the greatest importance. At the earliest stage, moral judgments made by the child are primarily based on response to parental commands, with obedience classified as good and disobedience as bad. Coupled to and following this stage is the view that conduct that satisfies a personal need is good, and vice versa. By the early teen years, moral development permits actions approved of by others as being good, as well as actions involving one's perceived duties, with their respective corollaries. At maturity, if and when it occurs, this schema is broadened by each individual to include the rights and well-being of others, often further refined as each individual clarifies his or her sense of common justice, based on life experiences. Many under-educated people do not reach this third level of development. If the foregoing concepts are correct, one can easily see how moral standards are shaped in the minds of young people, and then maintained well into adult life at the second uncritical level. It is therefore important that moral ideas in young minds should be very carefully shaped to suit the purposes of society at large, and that opportunities are presented to ensure the proper maturation of each individual.

Secular morality has to do with human conduct and the concepts of right and wrong. It involves intention and knowledge, as well as freedom of choice. Humans speak, and their words indicate their moral beliefs. Humans act, and their actions indicate their moral values. Humans think, and have ideas about their own and other's actions. These actions and ideas are controlled by certain constraints, relating to what society thinks ought or ought not to be done. Right actions ought to be done; wrong actions ought not to be done. Right actions are socially beneficial; wrong actions are socially harmful. The word "ought" is of critical importance in discussions about moral behavior, suggesting as it does a duty, an obligation, or a bond of some sort.

In moral issues, one is not dealing with absolute values. For example, in modern western society, it is generally assumed that it is right to tell the truth (however truth is defined); to tell the truth is considered morally correct. To lie intentionally is considered to be morally improper, and it is on this basis that we go about our daily lives and businesses, relying on or assuming that most of the information being presented to us is essentially truthful and therefore reliable. It may be of some comfort to realize that one cannot lie unintentionally.

But what about a situation where to tell a lie might be the more morally correct action, as say in the case of a doctor who diagnoses that a patient has a serious medical problem, but decides not to tell the patient about the problem immediately, for sound psychological reasons. This raises the interesting issue of medical ethics and its relationship to moral duties, a topic regrettably beyond the limited scope of this book.

In our western society, most people perform specific functions in various roles which they play as parents, teachers, workers, students, entrepreneurs, and so on. They have a duty to perform these functions according to the standards (moral, legal, ethical, and otherwise) which society sets for the various roles. The duty is expected to be done, notwithstanding the preferences or indeed the interests of the individual charged with the duty, or the fact that standards in some roles may sometimes conflict with standards for other roles at different times or places. For example, it is the duty of a student not to cheat on examinations, even though it may appear to the student to be in his or her best interest to do so on occasion. It is considered morally wrong to cheat in this fashion in our society. Another example involves the case of a policeman who was delegated to stand guard outside an medical clinic where abortions were being performed. He refused to do so on religious grounds, and was relieved, not only of this duty, but also of his job, for refusing to obey a legal command to execute a legitimate task which he had a sworn obligation to perform. The conflict for the officer in this case was between his legal duty, based on his oath of office, and his moral duty, based on his religious beliefs. The issue of tolerance and compassion towards clients of the clinic does not seem to have been much of a factor in his thinking.

For further reading, the following titles are suggested:

1. *Ethics: Inventing Right and Wrong* [Mackie 1990]
2. *A History of European Morals* [Lecky 1911]
3. *Morals without Religion* [Knight 1983]

1.3.4 NOTIONS OF SIN

To the humanist, there is no such thing as sin, although this is not to say that there are no such concepts as right or wrong in humanist philosophy. Right and wrong in any society at any given time can be determined by applying the basic principles of morality, as described in Section 1.3.2 *Morals in General*. When examining these principles, it might be useful to further consider the topics of sin and repentance, to better understand how proper moral conduct can be achieved, independent of all religious influence. If it were not for religion, there would be no such mental concept as sin, and the misery that such a concept initiates and maintains would be abated, if not entirely eliminated.

Ever since the rise of the concept of social organization in human affairs, religious practitioners have always interfered with the possibility of humankind to develop sound moral values in life independent of religion. As the concept of sin is so widespread in the Western World, any well-informed humanist should have some grasp of the main issues involved in sin, in order to develop arguments against belief in the concept.

1. Establishment of Sin

Sin has been loosely defined as deliberate opposition to the alleged will of any God. To be sinful, an action or thought must break some alleged law of a particular God. So-called original sin involves mythology about a woman called Eve eating forbidden fruit in the Garden of Eden, in contravention of a command from her God not to do so. According to those who believe it, we are all therefore sinners, as we are all supposed to be descended from Adam and Eve, the original (and unmarried) sinners, if we ignore biblical references to Lilith. The basic Christian message is that we should believe that we are indeed born as *sinners*, which means that we are in need of salvation, and that Christianity with save us. Humanism contends that we are all born as *agnostics* (that is, with no knowledge of gods) with the potential to learn with proper guidance how to distinguish between right and wrong, but not many religious people would agree with that notion.

As there is no God, there can be no sin. For those who believe that there is a God, sin involves both imagination and free-will. To sin, one must be able to imagine and recognize good and evil, and be able to make a choice for evil. On this basis, animals do not sin, because they allegedly have no imagination and only limited power to choose; they act mostly on instincts. To be evil, one must be free to choose to be or do evil. Like the rest of the animals, if one could not so choose, then one could hardly be considered to be sinning.

The concepts of sin and repentance were early invented by religious Christian protagonists to suit their own ends, specifically to secure control over other people's lives. All religions have some stated policies and views on good and evil (addressed elsewhere in this book), on blessings and curses, on sin and repentance, because they are in that business. Most ayatollahs, bishops, cardinals, gurus, ministers, priests, rabbis, shamans and other religious experts can spot sin at any distance, and then arrange for appropriate absolution; after all, it is their job to do so. Having manufactured sin as a concept, and thus being expert at recognizing it, they then set themselves up as arbiters or judges regarding sin in others. This does not necessarily preclude them from engaging in some sins themselves, whenever it is to their advantage or inclination to do so. Much of what humans value is tainted by religious injunctions and sanctions regarding sin.

2. Elimination of Sin

There are only two requirements for the elimination of sin: first, the abolition of religions which perpetuate the concept, and secondly, the education of people in secular techniques to distinguish between right and wrong in thought and action, and how to choose to do right. As it is doubtful when the first requirement will be met by society, attention might be profitably focused on the second one.

Every new-born baby has the potential to learn and thus to do or think right or wrong things—it is up to society to train the child as it develops to distinguish between good and evil and to choose to do good. Learning has been defined as a change in human disposition or capability, which can be retained, and which is not simply ascribable to the process of growth.[Gagné 1970]

Learning includes not only the acquisition of subject-matter, but also of habits, attitudes, perceptions, preferences, and ideals. Learning also usually involves the measurable modification of perception and behavior. Learning, being knowledge acquired by systematic study and life experience, cannot be observed directly by others, but can only be inferred from changes in behavior or capability in a person.

The purpose of this short explanation of learning is point out two necessities. First, society in the current century must start to teach children the techniques of rational and critical thinking and to give them scientific knowledge of the world in which we all live from the earliest of ages. Secondly, it is necessary to understand the learning process, so as to be able to interrupt the teaching of religious dogma handed down from parent to child. To quote a simple example of the kinds of problems that faulty teaching can produce, it appears that recently in Israel, Hasidic Jews are taught that it is sinful for any woman to expose any part of her body not officially approved by their religion. As a result of this preposterous, undemocratic, and repressive concept, gangs of Hasidic Jews took it upon themselves to destroy bus shelters in down-town Jerusalem, because advertizing panels in these shelters displayed department-store promotions of young girls in scanty swim suits. In retaliation, gangs of Orthodox Jews took to burning down synagogues frequented by the Hasidic Jews. It should be obvious to all but the most rigid believer that such action and reaction will never solve the basic problem, which is essentially one of a mixture of faulty training, fanaticism, and religious intolerance. It is clear that society has got to learn how to overcome such ignorance and bigotry, and also to teach and practice tolerance, understanding, and acceptance of differing viewpoints on a massive scale.

This will be an extraordinarily difficult task. In effect, we will have to ask every parent in the world to resist passing on their own religious beliefs (and prejudices) to their children, and to assist the children to mature to the point where they can decide for themselves what is right and what is wrong in the world, based on reliable and impartial knowledge of that world. They should also be trained to become personally and increasingly responsible for their own thoughts and actions, to be fully developed upon reaching the age of their majority (usually around 20 years of age) and not to develop moral values based on mythical threats of sin and repentance. If then, at age 20, an individual chooses to add religion on top of an otherwise sound, social, and secular moral base, then in the democratic society that should be his or her choice. It is, however, an option which few would probably choose to exercise.

There will always be some actions (such as murder, rape, or theft) perpetrated by some disturbed individuals that society as a whole considers to be wrong at any given moment or period in time, but these actions would not be *sins* in a secular society; they would be classified as *crimes* and dealt with accordingly, through secure incarceration and proper treatment.

For further reading, the following titles are suggested:

1. *Summerhill* [Neill 1960]
2. *The Construction of Reality in the Child* [Piaget 1971]
3. *The Conditions of Learning* [Gagné 1970]

CHAPTER 1.4

APOSTASY

1.4.1 DEFINITION

Many humanists were born into and raised in homes or families where humanist principles and practices were the norm. Consequently, these people had no religious affiliations. However, many others who now consider themselves to be humanists came to that life stance by abandoning adherence to former religious denominations. Such abandonment may have occurred suddenly, but more usually it occurs over a period of time, as interest in and acceptance of religious beliefs simply fades away. However it happens to occur, the process is called apostasy and such people are called apostates.

1. Origin

The origin of the words *apostate* and *apostasy* are from parts of two Greek words: *stas* which means "to stand"; and *apo* which means "away from." Later, in medieval English, these words came to have a meaning more like "desertion." By definition, then, apostates are people who have deliberately (but as often as not unconsciously) abandoned religious beliefs at some point in their lives. There comes a point in their lives at which they realize that they no longer have any emotional involvement or investment in their former or any other religion, although they often retain an intellectual or social interest in it. The abandonment may occur within a short space of time, but it is more commonly developed over a few years, as other influences, such as family or business or social contacts, increasingly intrude upon one's life and times. In most cases, interest in religion just fades away.

2. Religion

Before discussing apostasy, which is the conscious rejection of previously-held religious beliefs of any kind, it may be helpful to briefly reiterate some of the definitions of religion given later in Section 2.2.2. According to one dictionary, religion means: "a set of beliefs concerning the cause, nature, and purpose of the universe, when considered as the creation of a supernatural agency or agencies, usually involving devotional and ritual observances and often containing a moral code for the conduct of human affairs." A secondary definition follows: "a specific fundamental set of beliefs and practices generally agreed upon by a number of persons or sects, e.g. the *Christian* religion."

3. Apostasy

As stated, apostasy is the conscious rejection of previously-held religious beliefs of any kind. In most Western countries, freedom of conscience is guaranteed by their Constitutions. Technically, in a multi-cultural environment, people are free to hold religious beliefs or not as they choose. Although there is still great societal pressure put on most citizens to belong to one or other of the many religious denominations, there is a growing trend on the part of many people to opt out from religious beliefs. The world-wide rise in religious non-affiliation has grown from about 2% in the year 1900 to about 21 % in the year 2000 (Momen, p.504).

However, just because a person claims no affiliation with any religion, it does not mean that he or she is therefore an apostate (or an atheist, or an agnostic). Many of these people may have never held religious views; religion is a subject which is of no interest to them. However, it is not unreasonable to assume that a proportion of them is apostate, and as the total number of non-affiliates is growing, then so must be the number of apostates. Formal public testimony purposefully given by an increasing number of apostate individuals at meetings of various groups of Canadian agnostics, atheists, humanists, skeptics, and the like also, constitute evidence of the change in thinking of many such people. Religiosity involves 3 components: behavioral (participation), affective (commitment), and cognitive (beliefs). To simply drop out need only involve the first two; apostasy requires a change in all three components.

4. Probable cause

The reasons for this diminution leading to abandonment of belief are not clearly understood. Recent investigation into a new *and as yet controversial* medical field called neuro-biology suggests that specific neural activity in selected portions of the brain give rise to religious feelings and impressions of being in the presence of supernatural beings. Such brain states can vary on a continuum all the way from those approaching epileptic seizures at one end to an extremely benign state of disengagement at the other. Near the active end, we encounter a fundamentalist or rigorously evangelistic type of thinking, whereas at the inactive end, we encounter people for whom any sort of religious experience is literally a closed book. As one might expect, the majority of people tend to congregate towards the average or middle of the scale; such people naturally view their religious experiences as being normal to their place in their societies. They generally feel little need to question their beliefs, but neither do they go out of their way to proselytize.

For further reading, the following title is suggested:

1. *The "God" Part of the Brain* [Alper 2000]

1.4.2 CHARACTERISTICS

Apostates who abandon religion differ from many agnostics or atheists who have never held religious beliefs as defined above. It may be comforting for apostates to know that, according to many studies, apostates display certain uniformities and thus cannot be considered as aberrations. For example, according to one researcher (Beckwith 1985), apostates are generally well-educated, have higher than average levels of intelligence, and enjoy better than average economic circumstances. In North America, people tend to become apostates at younger rather than older ages, are more predominant in the West, and are most likely to be male. Beckwith attributes these characteristics to the growth of knowledge, education, freedom of expression, social reform, health care, and the rise of logical positivism and scientific method, among other factors.

Another researcher (Bromley 1988) made a study of what he termed religious disaffiliation occurring in American mainstream and alternative religious groups. He also examined the rapid growth of those who claimed no religious affiliation in the first place, as well as apostates from any one group who adopted another (usually more liberal) set of beliefs. Bromley found that research into the topic was incredibly complex, with problems stemming from inconsistent questionnaires, non-uniform terminology, conflicting methodology, and the variety of studies of the many social and psychological consequences of apostasy, both for groups and individuals concerned.

Another author (Hendricks 1993), in a book compiled from interviews with people who have left various Christian churches for various reasons, makes the statement (on p.17) that: "While countless "unchurched" people are flocking in the front door of the church, a steady stream of the "churched" is flowing quietly out the back door." He also points out that many of the claims by churches to increasing memberships can be attributed to individuals from one congregation switching to another. Such movement cannot be considered as an overall gain. One premise of his book is that an increasing number of Christians are becoming *disillusioned* (his word) with the church. Of course, not all who leave a church necessarily abandon their faith; some are seeking a different form of spirituality. However, a considerable proportion of these apostates do give up on religion as a significant force in their lives. In passing, one notes that Hendricks' book contains two interesting pieces of data, among many others. One (on p.246), taken from the *World Christian Encyclopedia* (Oxford 1982), states that there were, at the time of that publication, in excess of 20,000 religious denominations worldwide. It is little wonder that there is so much friction and tension as a result of so many religion divisions throughout the world today. The other (on p.251) asserts that: "Since 1980, there has been *no growth* in the proportion of "born-again" Christians. The number remains fixed at 32%." Hendricks attributes that situation to lateral movements and the actual lack of conversions which are often claimed.

There are of course, many books which have been written on the topic of apostasy, some of which might be of interest to those people who have left an organized religious group, but do not feel inclined or able to abandon their religious or theological beliefs. One such book is titled *Leaving the Fold* [Winell 1994]. As a self-described apostate from Christianity, Dr. Linell, a psychologist, asserts that many people who suffer from harmful religious indoctrination have a difficult time breaking free from the trappings of their former denomination. She offers such people a step-by-step process to assist them to come to terms with their newly adopted stance, and to work through some of their natural concerns regarding family relations and social or business contacts. The style of the book is a mixture of therapy, anecdote, and personal interview.

One final study (Caplovitz 1977) deals with religious drop-outs among college students, in which factors such as parental relationships, peer pressure, radical political orientation, and individual commitment to intellectualism and rationality are cited as significant. For readers who may find this topic of interest, there is a wealth of useful material to be absorbed in any well-stocked city or college library.

As a corollary to the foregoing outline, Cormac Murphy-O'Connor (Archbishop of Westminster and a leader of the Roman

Catholic Church in Britain) was quoted* as saying at a religious conference that "Christianity as a background to people's lives . . . has almost been vanquished." And one year previously, George Carey (Archbishop of Canterbury and a leader of the Protestant Christian Church) publicly declared* that Britain is "a country where tacit atheism prevails" with "thoughts of eternity rendered irrelevant." (*Source: Vancouver *SUN*, 2001-09-06).

For further reading, the following titles are suggested:

1. *The Decline of U.S. Religious Faith* [Beckwith 1985]
2. *Falling from the Faith* [Bromley 1988]
3. *Exit Interviews* [Hendricks 1993]
4. *The Religious Dropouts* [Caplovitz 1977]

2.4.3 SOME FAMOUS APOSTATES

History is replete with the names of famous and not-so-famous apostates, of whom the following men and women are but a minuscule selection:

Isaac Asimov (1921-1992), a science educator who wrote over 400 science fiction books. He came from a Jewish background and was a president of the American Humanist Association. One of his major works of non-fiction is a secular history titled "A Guide to the Bible."

Dan Barker (1950-), a former Pentecostal preacher for nearly 20 years in California before it became evident to him that he no longer believed the evangelical message of salvation. His apostasy cost him his job as a preacher and ended his first marriage, but he later remarried and is now involved with the Freedom from Religion Foundation in Madison, Wisconsin.

Charles Bradlaugh (1833-1891), a British parliamentarian and lawyer. He is remembered today chiefly for two things: his role in permitting people to take public office by *affirmation* rather than by *swearing* an oath, and his outspoken support of women's issues in an era long before that was a popular cause. Bradlaugh was involved with the Anglican Church, but while preparing for his confirmation, developed doubts and permanently dropped out.

Julius Haldeman (1889-1931), one of a family of Russian Jewish immigrants to America, left that faith in early manhood, to turn his attention to philosophy, skepticism, and socialism. He is best known for the publication of a series called *"The Little Blue Books"* which dealt with a variety of topics such as literature, socialism, religion, and philosophy.

Robert Ingersoll (1833-1899), one of the best known orators on atheism of the 19th century in America, was the son of a Congregational minister. He abandoned religion when he married a woman who was already an atheist. In his day, Ingersoll gave speeches on atheism to audiences numbering in the thousands.

Taslima Nasrin, (1962-), born in Bengal, this physician, author, and atheist had a price put on her head for writing a novel about repression of Hindus by Muslims, and was later charged in Bangladesh for defaming religion.

Thomas Paine (1737-1809), author of *"The Age of Reason"* was raised as a Protestant Christian in England, but abandoned that involvement at an early age. Apart from his many political struggles in America, France, and elsewhere, one major part of his life's work was to discredit the Bible as a repository of revealed truth.

Mordecai Richler (1931-2001), a Canadian author of 10 world-acclaimed novels and hundreds of articles, book reviews, and screen plays. Richler was raised in the orthodox faith in a Jewish enclave in Montreal, but abandoned it to become an atheist. He said he "could not obey all those little sabbath laws." He described himself as a humanist.

Carl Sagan (1929-1996), of "Cosmos" fame, came from a Jewish background, but his scientific studies into the cosmos led to his abandonment of his former religion and his adoption of a skeptical and agnostic outlook.

Elizabeth Cady Stanton (1815-1902) suffered mental anguish at the hands of a fundamental evangelist, causing her to abandon all her former religious beliefs, and later to take up the cause of women's rights, both politically and socially, as well as the abolition of slavery, and written and oral criticism of organized religion.

George Bernard Shaw (1856-1950), the Irish playwright, was born into an Irish Catholic family and was accordingly baptized in that faith. As a young man, he dropped all religious pretense when he became involved first with a socialist group called the Fabian Society, and later with the National Secular Society in Britain.

Charles Templeton (1916-2001), a TV evangelist, was a colleague of Billy Graham for about 20 years. Templeton realized that he had grave doubts about the veracity of much of the Bible and therefore no longer believed what he was being asked to preach. He published his experiences in becoming an agnostic in a book titled *"Farewell to God."*

Ted Turner (1935-), media magnate, became an apostate from Christianity upon the death of his sister, despite his prayers to God to spare her. In a speech to the American Humanist Association, he stated: "The more I strayed from (religious) belief, the better I felt."

Mark Twain (1835-1910), the pen name of Samuel Clemens, was raised in a thoroughly God-fearing family and community, but despite it all, became one of America's foremost skeptics, as evidenced by his little known essay *"Letters from the Earth"* and other papers published after his death.

Most readers familiar with the history of humanism and freethought could (and probably will) add many more names (and places) to this admittedly short introductory list.

For further reading, the following titles are suggested:

1. *Women without Superstition* [Gaylor 1997]
2. *The Encyclopedia of Unbelief* [Stein 1985]
3. *Celebrities in Hell* [Smith 2002]

CHAPTER 1.5

THE ESSENTIALS OF HUMANISM

1.5.1 THE HUMANIST MANIFESTOS

It can be argued that in an introductory primer of this type, it is not necessary to include extensive background material on the main topics and themes of the book. However, there are some documents of significant historical value of which all humanists should be at least aware and which are worthy of study by the more serious student of humanism. These documents are generally referred to as the Humanist Manifestos. Although each in itself is not very lengthy, to save space, time, and cost, none of these original documents are reproduced here. Instead, extracts are discussed and references to a current source of each are given, and all readers are urged to have a look at the originals and related material. It often helps to know where we have come from, to know where we might be going. These Manifestos can also be distinguished from many other useful documents, variously titled as *Statements of Principles, Objectives of Humanism, Declarations of Humanist Values* and the like, which various individuals or associations have produced from time to time, for reasons of legal incorporation, internal organization, or public promotion.

1. 1933 CE

The first modern Humanist Manifesto was developed in the United States in 1933 by a group of about 30 people who managed to achieve an acceptable and, given the times, extraordinary consensus of opinion on what they described as matters of final concern. That document contained a Preamble, **15** Articles of Affirmation, and a brief Conclusion. It was first published in the "New Humanist," Vol. 5, No. 3.

Briefly stated, Article **1** asserts that our world was not divinely created and **2** says that humans have evolved as part of a process. Article **3** rejects dualism of mind and body, while **4** acknowledges the roles that religions have played in civilizations. Article **5** deals with the role of science while **6** considers religions to be passé. Article **7** notes the necessary human contributions to all religions while **8** outlines the primary ends of humankind. Articles **9** and **10** both deal with social well-being, emotions and attitudes. Article **11** deals with the application of knowledge and reason in human life and **12** deals with humans creative instincts. Article **13** emphasizes the role of various institutions to aid in human fulfillment, while **14** promotes a socialist rather than capitalist form of economic order. The final Article **15** is a general statement about core humanist values.

2. 1973 CE

The second Humanist Manifesto, which was based on the first one, was developed 40 years after it and was first published in the September/October issue of "The Humanist" magazine in 1973. It also contained a Preamble, **17** Articles, and a Conclusion.

Briefly stated, Article **1** deals with the rejection of dogmatic religion but the retention of some of its ethical teachings while **2** deals with the rejection of notions of salvation and damnation. Article **3** deals with the sources of moral values and **4** asserts that reason and intelligence are the most powerful of human instruments. Article **5** recognizes the intrinsic worth of each human being and **6** addresses issues of sexuality. Article **7** discusses civil liberties and **8** discusses democracy. Article **9** advocates the separation of church and state. Article **10** suggests humane approaches to general social well-being while **11** deals with diversity and equality of opportunities in education and culture. Article **12** comments on negative aspects of nationalism while **13** deals with the renunciation of violence as a means to solving disputes. Article **14** deals with world-wide ecological issues and **15** deals with economic issues. Article **16** examines technology and **17** discusses international communication and transportation.

3. 1999 CE

A more recent Humanist Manifesto was published in 1999. Primarily developed by Paul Kurtz, a noted American humanist philosopher and editor who was also involved in the 1973 Manifesto. It is divided into **10** major Sections, starting with an introductory Preamble, followed by eight subdivisions, each of which contain a number of topics which more fully deal with the subject matter of some of the corresponding Articles of the earlier Manifestos, and concluding with an optimistic statement about humanist prospects.

Briefly stated, Section **1** gives some historical background to the present Manifesto and present a plea and the case for what is called planetary humanism. Section **2** points out that humans, for the first time in history, now have the material means to generally improve life for all, although we are reminded that there are still many obstacles to overcome. Section **3** deals with the basic tenet of humanism, namely scientific naturalism. Section **4** outlines the many benefits of technology. Section **5** addresses issues of ethics and reason, while **6** attempts the difficult task of fitting humanist principles into existing societal practices. Section **7** outlines humanist elements for inclusion in a *Planetary Bill of Rights and Responsibilities*. Section **8** proposes a new *Global*

Agenda, involving improvements to human development, justice, international law, multi-national corporations, and the environment. Section **9** makes the case for the development of new world-wide institutions to deal with democratic representation, security, disputes resolution, environmental monitoring, taxation, legitimate dissent and the free exchange of ideas and opinion. Finally, Section **10**, while recognizing that there will always be some challenges for humans to face, outlines the basis of and the need for optimism in the development of Planetary Humanism and the possibility to eradicate most human gloom and doom.

The original document was signed by more than 120 individuals significant to the humanist movement, from about 30 different countries. Some of these individuals include Richard Leakey, Richard Dawkins, Taslima Nasrin, Levi Fragell, Robert Buckman, and Daniel Dennet, among many others.

4. 2003 CE

A revised Humanism Manifesto, published by the American Humanist Association and based on the first two mentioned above, appeared in 2003. It consists of a one-page summary, starting with a short outline of humanist principles, followed by 6 Articles addressing specific core values and features of humanism, and concluding with what might be described as humanist aspirations.

Briefly stated, Article **1** addresses our knowledge of the world, Article **2** deals with evolutionary influences, Article **3** sources humanist values in experience, Article **4** discusses human potential and development, Article **5** talks about societal relationships, and Article **6** points to ways to maximize human happiness.

The document concludes with an assertion that the quality of our lives and the kind of society we wish to live in are the responsibility of human beings alone. The document also notes that the words "Humanist Manifesto" constitute a registered trademark of the American Humanist Association.

For further reading, the following titles are suggested:

1. *The Genesis of a Humanist Manifesto* [Wilson 1995].
2. *The Philosophy of Humanism* [Lamont 1982].
3. *Manifesto 2000, "Free Inquiry"* 1999 Fall Ed.[Council for Secular Humanism]

1.5.2 THE ESSENCE OF HUMANISM

Having now outlined some of the broad definitions and elements of humanism and reviewed the main features of some humanist manifestos, we can now examine what might be called the essence of humanism with some minimal repetition or overlap over what has already been discussed. In many attempts to define what it means to be a humanist, a large number of general issues relative to leading a so-called "good" life seem to be inextricably bound in with what might otherwise be referred to as core humanist values. By general issues, we mean notions which are applicable to any reasonably sound life, religious or otherwise, such as love of family, the formation of friendships, truth-telling, promise keeping, useful employment, enjoyment of music and art, and the pursuit of happiness (however defined), among many other things. It is possible, for our purposes here, to separate these issues from the core values

It is acknowledged that many people who subscribe to any of the hundreds of current religious creeds aspire to lead such "good" lives. They love their families and cherish their friends, tell the truth as they understand it, discharge obligations, enjoy art, and so on. So the primary difference between humanists and religious people would seem to be found in aspects of worldviews separate from these general issues. The main difference lies in the fact that all religious people, by definition, hold religious beliefs of one sort or another, where religious belief is (somewhat superficially) defined to mean acceptance of the existence of one or more supernatural entities or effects and their alleged impact on our universe. Humanists do not hold such beliefs, and that certainly is a primary feature which distinguishes them from the others. However, it is not considered appropriate to define positive values in negative terms. One should not focus on what humanists do not believe; one should review the elements, distinct from the general issues, which make up the positive basis of the humanist world view. Some of the more significant of these elements follow, in no particular order of priority; most are further elaborated elsewhere in the book.

One is the application of the **scientific method** to solve many of the problems which confront us in life. This process is distinct from petitionary prayer to alleged gods. As someone once said, "Life is what happens while we are making plans." The scientific method has four parts: *hypotheses* or making suggestions about possible solutions to identifiable problems, *testing* or trying various ways to see if the proposals will work, *reporting* or sharing the results of one's experiments with others, and *replication* or checking to see if others can reproduce the same results or effects. If a proposal survives the scrutiny of the scientific method, then it probably has some merit. If it fails, now or later, then it should probably be abandoned. If life presents a solvable problem, then application of the scientific method should lead to one or possible solutions. It is also acknowledged that some problems are not capable of solution, given our present knowledge and resources.

A second element is the cultivation of **skepticism** towards unproven claims of every sort. This is distinct from the unquestioning acceptance of so-called revealed truths by persons who have assumed positions of responsibility. The origin of the word (also spelled *scepticism*) means to *examine, consider,* or *inquire*. It does not mean to dismiss possibly worthy suggestions or proposals arbitrarily; it means to question the validity of claims until they have been proven or demonstrated to be correct. A distinction should also be made between healthy *skepticism* and corrosive *cynicism*, which is the development of selfishness and disbelief of any claim, no matter what the evidence.

A mind open to possible changes in all matters is an attribute of the truly skeptical humanist (setting aside for the moment

Cartesian arguments about the improbable duality of mind and body and the resultant doubts about any entity called *mind* existing separately from the body). Although humanists are usually monists who believe that mind is a function of the brain which is an inseparable part of the body, a true skeptic should be able to accept dualism or the even existence of supernatural beings, *if such could be conclusively demonstrated or proven.* So far, no such unequivocal irrefutable proof has been forthcoming. So humanists can relax on this point.

Thirdly, humanists accept the general principles of **evolution**. This is distinct from a belief in creationism. Humanists mostly have open minds about the origins of the universe. They say the jury is still out on a number of theories on this topic. Whatever its origin, organic life could and obviously did arise on planet Earth (and probably on a multitude of other planets in other galaxies). The fossil records, though incomplete, show evidence of evolutionary development along a number of lines. Many species have come and gone, while others are still in the process of development. While some humanists favor Darwinian notions of "survival of the fittest," others prefer "punctuated equilibrium" as suggested by the late biologist Stephen J. Gould of Harvard. Authors such as Richard Dawkins of Oxford have demonstrated that even the most complex of organisms has evolved to its present states through a mixture of chance and natural selection, as a result of tiny but beneficial incremental improvements accumulated over truly enormous amounts of time. The present state of many such organs may as yet be only rudimentary; we do not know what changes may occur in the limitless future. We can be fairly certain, though, that evolution is not progressing in some supernaturally pre-ordained direction, because there is no evidence to support such a view.

Humanists assert that there is no observable **purpose** in the universe (beyond purposes ascribed by human beings to their aspirations and activities) not because of absence of evidence but, as the astro-physicist Victor Stenger succinctly put it, because of *evidence of absence.* This is distinct from religious assertions about intelligent design in nature. While there certainly are a multitude of observable patterns in nature, such as in atoms, molecules, crystals, snowflakes, flowers, insects, animal behaviors, and so on, science has not yet discovered any necessary connection between these natural phenomena and alleged supernatural forces or entities. These patterns all appear to be the result of natural forces. Deer do not have white tails so as to make them easier for humans to hunt, as was once believed. Studies in quantum mechanics are now showing that there are random occurrences in nature which conform to no particular pattern.

Humanists understand that **moral behavior** primarily springs from human experience, relative to circumstances. This is distinct from claims that moral authority is absolute and flows from nonexistent divine sources or the alleged words or works of deities in holy books. Morality has a secular basis, involving three elements: *impartiality* as between people, *prescription* or predictability, and *rationality* based on good reasons; there is no need to add extraneous religious sanctions. Limitations on public behavior are necessary in organized and civilized communities. Such controls arise from self-interest, a learned sense of duty, and by way of the imposition of legal codes, i.e., behavioral standards accepted by and imposed upon the members of specific communities. Moral actions should be judged on their outcomes, and all normal human beings should be held to be accountable for their actions.

With respect to **politics**, there is no specific humanist political agenda to which all humanists must subscribe. Most humanists tend toward a (small-l) liberalism, however articulated. They believe in the democratic process and generally support political parties having a demonstrated social conscience. They advocate choice in matters of reproduction and euthanasia and generally oppose the death penalty. However, many humanists are involved with some so-called "right-wing" or conservative parties. The point to note is that, in most communities, the humanist message of tolerance and kindliness is usually spread through advertisements, by education and word-of-mouth, and by trying to lead groups by example and not through the imposition of political power.

One often hears the question posed by religious people: "But what do humanists do?" Well, humanists do many of the things that non-humanists do. Some get married and some have children, some separate and some get divorced. They seek gainful and satisfactory employment in virtually all of the professions, trades, businesses, and avocations. They go shopping and pay their taxes. They tend their gardens and go to shows and concerts. They contribute to charities and do volunteer work. They go on vacations and participate in political campaigns. A small proportion, comparable to the general population, is homosexual. In general, humanists conduct themselves as useful citizens in the localities in which they reside and work. They also try to face the inevitable fact of death with composure and compassion, accept its sad significance, and offer condolences and assistance to the bereaved.

In Europe, many humanist organizations operate hospices for the sick and rest-homes for seniors. In some places, they provide part-time voluntary schools which inculcate secular moral values in their children. In North America, many humanist organizations run summer camps for children, arrange for members to visit patients in hospitals, provide officiants for various secular ceremonies, such as births or baby-naming, legal marriages between people whether of opposite or same sex, and funerals. They present lectures and discussions of interest to their members and the general public, and they provide fellowship and support for each other. They also engage in advocacy with government agencies to bring about social improvements in line with humanist values.

One thing which humanists as a group do *not* do is to engage in crimes which result in significant prison sentences. Statistics show that humanists form an infinitesimally small proportion of incarcerated populations, particularly when compared to the vast majority of jailed inmates who claim religious affiliations of one sort or another.

In conclusion, humanists try for the most part to understand nature and the society in which they live, to tell the truth, to keep their promises, and to act based on reasonable knowledge and with genuine compassion. They are prepared to live with some uncertainty about the great questions of life and death. They are accepting of diverse opinions provided these are not forced on the humanist community, and in general they try to stay happy, healthy, wealthy and wise. As can be seen, the essence of humanism is indeed a sweet perfume.

For further reading, the following titles are suggested:

1. *The Philosophy of Humanism* [Lamont 1982]
2. *Humanism* [Smoker 1984]
3. *The Humanist Alternative* [Kurtz 1973]

PART TWO

Religion and Mysticism

CHAPTER 2.1

THE HUMAN CONDITION

2.1.1 INTRODUCTION

There are a number of things that all humans need and value, regardless of their political, religious, sexual, social, or other persuasions. The purpose of this preamble to the various religious beliefs that people hold, is to identify and classify some of the more important of these things, first under the category of *needs* and secondly under the category of *values*. Discussion of these two is followed by a brief description of some of the salient features of human communication in the graphical, numerical, and verbal modes. In this context, the term "humans" means those normal, mature, reasonably stable beings which comprise the great bulk of humanity. It does not refer to chronic substance-abusers, eccentrics, fanatics, masochists, neurotics, or members of social fringe groups which comprise a regrettably large, usually noisy, and sometimes irritating minority of modern society. Such people have needs of a different kind, in addition to the needs of otherwise normal human beings.

2.1.2 HUMAN NEEDS

Human beings have a number of needs. Some of these are reasonably objective, such as the basic needs of food, sleep, shelter, and clothing. Most religions place restrictions or interference on all of these basic needs at one time or another, to get and keep people's attention. Others needs are more subjective or abstract, such as feelings of belonging, happiness, satisfaction, and trust. Again, most religions have not ignored laying claims to these types of needs as well.

Because of these needs and the motivations which they trigger, a number of theories regarding human motivation have been developed and articulated by psychologists from time to time. Some of these theories deal generally with topics such as existence, relatedness, and growth, or more particularly with motivations to work, working conditions and responsibilities, as well as achievement and recognition.

Of all of these models, probably the best known one was developed by a psychologist Abraham Maslow in 1943, when he articulated a five-part motivational hierarchy which placed the basic human physiological needs of hunger, thirst, and sex first, followed by safety and security needs. These in turn were followed by belonging needs for friendship, affection, and acceptance, and by self-esteem needs, such as recognition and status. At the end, or top, of the hierarchy, Maslow placed what he called needs for self-actualization in the areas of opportunities and growth. At least minimal awareness of these theories of human needs is required if one is to make sense of the issues raised for study in this section of the book.

Humans also need to experience a reasonable degree of meaning and satisfaction in their occupations. Although it appears not to be absolutely essential to survival, most humans need to experience some love and friendly companionship with their fellow humans. They need to feel a reasonable degree of security and emotional peace, relative to their general situation, their occupations, and their relationships. They need outlets for creative expression through art, music, dance, drama, writing, or other media. They desire self-consciousness and self-identity for their own sakes. All such normal and relative needs and desires can be satisfied without religious influence or interference.

One common human desire is what is generally referred to as the pursuit of happiness, a condition described by Aristotle as being the "highest good.". A large amount of the energy expended by the ordinary human is directed towards that oftimes elusive goal. There are a number of difficulties in this subject area, but it might be said that happiness is not to be found in the future (or indeed in the past). It is not so much a goal or a memory as it is a standard or stance to be achieved in the present. It is therefore best to arrange one's affairs to bring as much happiness as possible into being right now.

Happiness can be defined in a number of ways, but in general it might be held to represent a life consisting for the most part of satisfactions and the fulfillment of needs and desires. It does not necessarily mean complete freedom from wants, pains, or fears at all times. In general, life experiences can be said to be relative, and not absolute. One can hope for the best, but one takes what comes and makes the best of it.

For further reading, the following titles are suggested:

1. *A Theory of Human Motivation.* [Maslow 1943]
2. *Nicomachean Ethics* [Aristotle 1985]

2.1.3 HUMAN VALUES

It will soon become clear that the twin subjects of human values and value systems are extraordinarily complex. The purpose of introducing a simplified version of these topics at this point is to give the reader a feeling for some of the issues involved in this interesting branch of human activity, and to show its relationship to human needs and to the general subject matter of the remainder of the book. For further detail, attention is directed to the original sources from which the paraphrased excerpts were extracted.

First, the word "value" has several discrete meanings. One implies *specific significance,* such as the value assigned to a numerical quantity. A second meaning implies *worth in exchange,* wherein a valuable object might be exchanged for its monetary equivalent. A third meaning implies *qualities ascribed* to specific tones in music or colors in art respectively. Yet another meaning relates to the things in social life towards which there is an *affective regard*, of either high esteem (such as freedom) or low esteem (such as crime). Although there are other meanings for the word "value," it is with some of these latter things that this section will deal. Secondly, the term "human values" has been defined to mean enduring beliefs that specific modes of conduct or end-states of existence are preferable to their opposites. The term "value system" has been defined to mean an enduring organization of such beliefs.

It is evident from the foregoing definitions that a value is held to be a belief. These beliefs can apply either to on-going activities (means) or final outcomes (ends). Such beliefs are of two somewhat related types: *prescriptive* beliefs involving the opposites "good or bad" or *descriptive* beliefs involving "true or false." Prescription applies to subjective judgements about whether an activity or end-event is desirable or not (e.g.: "I believe that humanism is beneficial for society"); description applies to statements that are subject to objective empirical testing (e.g.: "I believe that humanism is a growing phenomenon"). Values are not absolute or unchanging, but only relative and reasonably stable. Many societies, and the individuals in these societies, change their values over time. Some examples include the abolition of slavery and the development of gay rights.

Furthermore, values are either *instrumental* (involving means) or *terminal* (involving ends). Examples of some instrumental values would include words like *ambition, courage, honesty, logic, obedience,* and *responsibility*. Terminal values include words like *beauty, equality, freedom, happiness, peace,* and *wisdom*. Each of these can be further subdivided, wherein instrumental values can have either a personal or social focus, and terminal values can have either a moral or competence focus. Each value has three component parts, applying to both means and ends: *cognitive* (involving knowledge), *affective* (involving feelings), and *behavioral* (involving action). According to some authorities, the total number of terminal values does not exceed about 20 and such terminal values are more centrally located in the system of values adopted by each person than are the instrumental values, which may number as many as 60 by some estimates.

Value systems enable individuals to function in a manner generally consistent with their own values and those of the society in which they live, although any specific situation which arises may cause some conflicts between specific values in the system. The entire value system is not brought into play to resolve every action or thought; rather parts of the system are selected in a manner more or less consistent with the whole system, with some parts being temporarily suppressed as dictated by circumstances and judgement. It may be instructive for the reader to try to relate human values as discussed in this section with human needs as described in the preceding section.

For further reading, the following titles are suggested:

1. *The Nature of Human Values* [Rokeach 1973]
2. *Values in Education and Society* [Feather 1975]

2.1.4 COMMUNICATIONS

The purpose of this short discussion of human communication is to make the reader aware of the power of language and of the many difficulties involved with the meaning ascribed to words, particularly in philosophical and religious contexts, and to be wary or critical of dogmatic statements or unfounded assertions made by theists and atheists alike.

Also, the manner or circumstances in which an idea is presented can often influence the way in which it will be accepted or rejected, regardless of the intrinsic worth of the idea itself. If a person attends a "Crusade for Christ" rally in a large auditorium filled with thousands of enthusiastic people, encouraged by speakers using carefully chosen audio-visual aids, urged on an affective emotional basis to make an immediate commitment, and all accompanied by beautiful music, bright lights, clean clothes, nice smells, and promises of salvation, one might make a decision to "Go with God." In contrast, if one was to sit quietly at home and read 10 books on the topic (five advocating belief and five not) and then discuss one's findings with an impartial but knowledgeable and concerned observer (assuming that such a paragon can be located), it is unlikely that one would as readily choose to "believe."

Our modern language is full of blatant inaccuracies and contradictions used in every day speech. We say, for example, that we are watching the sun setting, when we know very well that the sun does not set, or we talk about using a paper clip, which is made of steel, not paper, but is used not to clip but to attach separate sheets of paper to one another. People still talk about the souls of the dead being "up" in heaven, when Buckminster Fuller has made it clear that there is really no "up" or "down" in the universe but only a "here" or a "there." How then can souls be up in heaven if there is no "up?" And are there really such things as souls? There is not one shred of evidence to prove it. Before one can talk or even think about concepts such as being, or existence, or god, or heaven, or morality, or sin, or souls, one must try to understand what these words might mean. One must also be on the look-out for loopholes in semantic arguments so as not to be misled by skillful and smooth talkers with vested interests.

To function as a human being, some means of communication is absolutely essential. Even those few humans who live in total seclusion communicate with or within themselves. We all use communications of one sort or another to express ideas and to describe and categorize objects or events, either to ourselves or to others. The techniques of communication include use of marking devices on traditional hard copy, such as cloth, glass, paper, stone, or wood, and nowadays a myriad of electronic media, such as radio, television, telephone, telegraph, recording devices, and computers and InterNet servers and search engines, in all their debatable glory. There are essentially three modes of practical communication: graphical, numerical, and verbal, leaving aside other methods such as music or touch, and telepathy or other alleged forms of extra-sensory perception.

1. The Graphical Mode

The graphical mode is probably the most ancient and efficient method of communicating information. People have been drawing pictures to convey ideas since the earliest periods of human evolution. The inclination and ability to draw is very widespread; almost every normal person has some talent in this field. One reason for this is perhaps the ease with which an idea can be presented graphically; this is also a reason why it is so difficult to be really outstanding in the field of art. As the saying goes: one picture is worth a thousand words; one can look at a picture and absorb its meaning literally at a glance. For this reason, a number of sign languages have been developed having a graphical base. A common example is the directional system used on the highways, in which most instructions to drivers are given by symbols, such as shapes or arrows, rather than by words. Another more complex example is the use of stained glass windows in church buildings, in which a message is conveyed to the senses in a number of ways, directly through graphical symbolism and indirectly through the skillful use of colored glass and subtle lighting effects to create an atmosphere of mysticism.

A digression dealing with graphics may be appropriately introduced at this point, to relate an incident which occurred in Western Canada while this book was being written. It was reported that a facial image, alleged to be in the likeness of Jesus Christ, had miraculously appeared in the plaster-work of the living room wall in a small and insignificant house on Vancouver Island. Hundreds of Christian believers showed up to view and participate in this "miracle;" dozens of cures and other marvelous phenomena were reported among the enthusiastic witnesses. TV newscasts showed film of the events and of the image; the owner of the house enjoyed some short-lived fame or notoriety. The image did indeed appear similar to the standard Western likenesses of Christ (namely, a caucasian man with long hair and a beard) to be found in pictures on the walls of any church or Sunday school hall.

Interest in the case collapsed for one minor scientific reason and more interestingly, for one major religious reason. The scientific reason involved an explanation of the precise reasons for the phenomenon by the painter who had applied the paint to the plastered wall some time previously. He said he had had similar difficulties in the past, which he was able to correct, having knowledge of local plaster, paint, and weather conditions. He predicted the image would soon disappear, and it did. The religious reason was that the local Roman Catholic bishop tersely observed that as there were no pictures of Christ in existence, it was impossible to say whether this was a likeness or not. He did not state outright that it was or was not a sign from God; he simply said he did not know. Here we have a bishop saying he is agnostic about a possible sign of the actual workings of the God which he says he serves. One can understand the reluctance of the bishop to commit himself on such flimsy evidence (after all, he is an alleged expert on God's miraculous works), and one can understand the news media in hot pursuit of a good though silly news story. One can also understand the scientific explanation of the painter. But one cannot help but wonder at the mental condition of the other people who traveled some distance to stand in line to enter that house to view some accidentally discolored paint and plaster.

2. The Numerical Mode

The numerical mode is probably the most precise and reliable method devised and used by humans to communicate ideas, although there are some drawbacks. For one thing, people have to learn and accept the assumptions on which mathematics are based, and they have to understand the special processes by which ideas in mathematics are developed and conveyed. Not everyone has the inclination or the capacity or the training to fully grasp these intricacies (such as occur in calculus, algebra, or trigonometry) in the first place, nor to properly utilize them in the second place. As a result, many people have difficulty using this mode to express ideas. One commonplace example of this effect is the trouble that many people experience keeping their check-book and domestic financial accounts in order.

Some attempts have even been made to mathematically prove the existence of God. For example, a Muslim sect in the United States recently used a modern electronic computer to review mathematical relationships between the number 19 and parts of the Koran, as well as to develop a formula based on the frequency and sequence of letters which precede 30 of the chapters of that holy book. They then asserted that the complexities of these mathematical curiosities proved the existence of God, as they considered that no human mind could have invented or derived equations of such refined beauty. The fact that they used a computer and a program invented and manufactured by humans to generate the refined proof of aspects of a holy book which has also been produced by humans was not addressed in their conclusions.

3. The Verbal Mode

The verbal mode is probably the most widespread method of communication. After all, almost everybody has the inherent capacity to speak and to listen to some extent, although everyone's ability in this regard is different. There is a natural propensity and ability in the brain to develop language skills. Leaving aside physiological defects in speech or hearing resulting in impairment, virtually everyone learns to speak at least one language, however basic their understanding of grammar and vocabulary may be. Most people in North America also are taught and learn to read and write the language which they speak, whether that may be English, French, Spanish, or Chinese, although their ability may be only minimally developed, just sufficient for them to exist at an acceptable level in our society. In addition, it should be remembered that there are literally hundreds of different languages and that most of them have developed through custom and usage and are thus full of irregularities and confusion, although some (such as *Esperanto* and the newer *Inuit* languages) have been deliberately composed (or engineered) to be essentially rational and regular.

Furthermore, one may be highly educated in one language, but if ideas have to be communicated to others in another language, then problems arise. One current example of widespread illiteracy among otherwise educated people is their lack of facility with the languages used to program computers, resulting in difficulties to convey ideas using these programs. To introduce a personal comment, this author holds two degrees and speaks two languages, but is virtually illiterate with respect to any of the special languages used to program computers. Another aspect of this general topic concerns the difficulties of adequately translating scriptures from their original languages to our more modern languages, because of the varieties of the interpretations which can be placed on so many critical or key words. The Bible, for example, has been translated from Hebrew and Aramaic and other languages to ancient Greek or Latin to old English, medieval English, and then to modern English, with modifications appearing as historical research necessitates. There can be little doubt that this process alone has introduced ambiguity into the precise meaning of some of the original passages, many of which were not too carefully researched or composed in the first place.

To use just one biblical example, in Luke 18, verse 24, Jesus is reported to say: "For it is easier for a camel to go through the eye of a needle than for a rich man to enter the kingdom of God." The semantic problem in this saying revolves around the translation of two parts of this sentence. The first is that the Greek word *kamilos* (or Latin *camelus*) apparently at one time could mean either "camel" or "rope"; the second is the use of the phrase "eye of a needle." The sentence may mean what it at first appears to mean, that it is relatively easy to thread a sewing needle with some very fine "rope." It would, of course, be impossible for a camel literally to go through the eye of an ordinary sewing needle. However, there is a second more obscure meaning, and that is that the entrance to many ancient walled cities was through a main gate, large enough to permit animals and carriages to pass. Beside the main gate there was usually a smaller gate, intended for people to enter, under the scrutiny of guards. The smaller gate was apparently referred to as "the eye" and it would be difficult, though not necessarily impossible, for a camel to pass through such a small opening. While the meaning of the phrase is still more or less clear, regardless of which set of words or phrases is used, it does show up some of the potential problems that can arise through in-expert translation of dubious or obsolete words or expressions.

Human language consists of linear patterns of sounds and shapes. The sounds are the spoken words, and the shapes are the written words. The process of interpretation of these patterns between their sources and their terminals is affected by all sorts of filters and barriers, such as distractions, interruptions, mistakes, ambiguities, and the like. It follows that the better the quality of language training given to people, the better will be their understanding of the meaning of what is being said and written. It is therefore somewhat ironic that the beginnings of adult education in the early part of the 19th century involved a movement to teach the ordinary or common people to become literate at least to the point that they could read the Bible, so that they could better understand its message. As a result of the training, however, the general populace began to discover that it could not only read the Bible to try to understand it, but that there were many parts of the Bible that contained conflicts and other parts that defied understanding. Furthermore, with their new-found literacy skills, the people discovered that they could also read other printed material, and they proceeded to do just that, to the consternation of the religious sponsors of the literacy programs. Regrettably, the general societal problem of illiteracy (affecting about 1 in 5 people world-wide) is still one of global proportions.

Estimates of the number of words in the English language alone run up to half a million, with new words (such as "high-tech" and "telemetry") being formed all the time, and old words (such as "zounds" and "forsooth") being abandoned. Also, some existing words take on new meanings (such as "cool") while others lose formerly popular meanings (such as "gay"). Almost every one of these half million words is subject to interpretation, and explanations of their meanings often differ in different dictionaries. Many of them have more than one distinct meaning (such as "pitch" which has more than ten), and many can be used in several different parts of speech, as nouns, verbs, adjectives or adverbs. The word "paint" is such a word, when used as a subject (a can of paint), describing an activity (paint the can) or qualifying an object (a paint can). The point of these comments about the use of words is that when one starts to try to comprehend and explain complex issues, such as are found in human affairs, the language becomes of critical importance to understanding. Words that are not fully understood should either not be used, or should be defined as to their meaning in the context in which they are being used. The difficult word "God" comes to mind in this context.

For further reading, the following titles are suggested:

1. *I Seem to be a Verb* [Fuller 1970]
2. *Contemporary Epistemology* [Dancy 1989]

2.1.5 THE COSMOS

From time immemorial, human beings have naturally considered their condition relative to their position in the universe. As a result, there are many theories about the origin and ultimate disposition of the universe. Five of the more common of these theories are briefly summarized below for review, before a more detailed examination is made of specific aspects of belief and religion.

1. The Big Bang

The "Big Bang" theory suggests that the universe suddenly came into being several billion years ago in one gigantic explosion. Just what it was that exploded, or where it came from, or why it did explode, has not yet been made very clear by supporters of this theory. Several scientists have asserted that, as the universe appears to be expanding, its origin can therefore be deduced by looking backwards in time to the so-called "big bang." They allege that everything came into being in one cataclysmic split-second, and that humans cannot discover whether the universe existed prior to that moment. This proposition ignores the seemingly obvious fact that for something to explode, that something must have existed in the milliseconds before the bang, so the bang was not in itself the moment of creation, even if there was such a moment. Some scientists say that time and space started at that moment, thereby avoiding these other questions.

If matter (or force) could have pre-existed for any period of time, it does not really matter whether one believes it to have been milliseconds, seconds, minutes, months, centuries, or eternity. Other scientists have said that, in any event, any such pre-existing matter would have been annihilated in the big bang, so there is no point in looking for it, which is a curious argument to make for those who call themselves scientists. Surely one might look, until it is clear that it is not to be found. Also, for what reason would the pre-existing matter be annihilated? No answer is given.

It is more plausible to believe that although one present view of the universe may give rise to the possibility of a big bang explosion at some remote point in the past, and that explosion obscures our view of what preceded it, it does not necessarily follow that the big bang theory is either correct or explains the beginning of the universe. If the bang occurred, we may not yet or indeed ever know what caused it, but we do not need to invent weak arguments to support a weak claim. We can just leave the question unanswered for a while longer. After all, it is not of any great importance to our practical daily lives.

2. Steady State

Another theory is known as the "Steady State" theory, which suggests that the universe as a whole is stable, although parts of it expand and contract, but always maintaining an overall balance. Some scientists assert that the universe is not expanding, that it is generally stable. They feel that it is just in our part of the universe that we and our immediate neighboring galaxies are rushing towards a gigantic black hole of some unknown type and magnitude, and that the involvement of our small solar system in this movement gives rise to the appearance of expansion in our immediate galactic neighborhood.

In other words, matter closer to the hole will appear to be accelerating away from us as it is increasingly affected by the gravitational pull of the hole. Matter further out from the whole, behind us in effect, will appear to be receding from us because it is not yet accelerating as fast as we are; we are in effect pulling away from it.

3. Oscillation

A third theory is the "Oscillation" theory, which suggests that although the entire universe appears to be in a state of expansion at present, it will reach a limit of that expansion at some future date, and then start to contract again towards its earlier compressed primordial state, and then explode again to start a new expansion, and so on indefinitely. It has also been argued that although the various star systems and galaxies may be receding from each other and therefore taking up more space in the universe, the universe itself may not be expanding, for two reasons: it may already be infinitely large, in which case it need not (or can not) expand, or it may be of finite dimensions but large enough to contain all the galaxies and their expansions.

One difficulty with all of the preceding arguments is that people often confuse astronomical knowledge with philosophical beliefs, instead of making a clear separation between the two. Recent work on wave theory by the world-renowned British physicist and cosmologist Stephen Hawking of Cambridge University and others seems to confirm the view that the universe simply exists, that it has always existed, though not necessarily in unchanged form, that there was no start and there will be no end, so proponents of the other theories are not without formidable opponents.

4. Thermodynamics

A further physical argument is occasionally presented regarding the second law of thermodynamics which concerns the loss of energy in the form of heat, leading to the theory that the universe is sort of running down, like a clock that cannot be rewound. Where did the energy come from? Where does the lost energy go? It surely must be somewhere in the universe, although in a different form. If energy can just disappear for no reason, then it can just as easily appear (and have appeared in the first place) for no reason. Arguments involving selection of one such law should also introduce elements of all other related laws, such as those regarding the conservation of energy, to rationalize the relationships between them. It should also be remembered that all such so-called laws of nature are man-made, and they are based on observations of probabilities, not absolutes. Occasionally, such laws have to be revised in the light of new knowledge.

5. Creationist

This theory suggests that a God exists and created the universe in approximately seven days, starting at about 9:45 one Friday morning about 6000 years ago. The theory also suggests that the end of the universe is near, although the specific date is constantly postponed as the event obviously has not yet occurred despite repeated though incorrect predictions astrologers and clergy. Although believed by most Christian fundamentalists, the theory is generally weak, having no scientific base, and plenty of scientific opposition. Other religions have similar theories of equally un-compelling strength. In general, people should place a higher value on the scientific attempts to explain the facts of the universe, than on the recitation of ill-formed opinion quoted from ancient scriptures written by men largely ignorant of significant and appropriate facts about the cosmos.

6. Additional Issues

In this section of the book, a few theories of the origin of the universe have been introduced for review. Some thoughts on these theories are presented below. First, if the universe has always existed, then it is also plausible to believe that life in the universe has always existed. There long has been and still is a great deal of pernicious nonsense being spread about by religious apologists regarding the start of life. Stories which debunk the so-called primordial soup (from which life on earth allegedly sprang) abound in the theological literature, and yet, if an infinite life force is universally pervasive (as it appears to be) and if the correct chemical, physical, and electrical conditions prevailed at some point in time on earth, then life as we know it would (and did) start on earth and probably has done so in other forms that we do not know elsewhere in the universe.

Secondly, regardless of big-bang or steady-state theories, if the universe is expanding, as it may well be doing, then everything in it is also expanding. That would suggest that we, who are part of this universe and who are observing this expansion, are also expanding. But is this true? If we are expanding, would we be able to observe the expansion, because the devices which we might use to measure the effects would themselves be expanding at the same rate. Is it not just the spaces between the stars and galaxies which appears to be expanding? And what is the direction of this expansion? Are there one or more directions? To consider another issue, increasing attention has been paid to the existence of what is referred to as universal "dark matter" in recent years. It is so-named mostly because it cannot be observed, but it appears to pervade the entire universe. Calculations regarding the overall mass of matter and energy and the general stability of the observable universe suggest that the dark matter could comprise as much as two-thirds of the whole. There are no clear answers understandable to the layman regarding many such questions. But even if there were clear answers, it is really doubtful whether our ordinary lives would be affected in any significant manner. For the foreseeable future, it is just a topic for interesting speculation among scientists who specialize in such studies.

Certainly, there are still many other unanswered questions about natural organic and inorganic processes which are not now understood, but people should be prepared to live with such uncertainty for the time being, to go about their daily lives with some equanimity, but ready to rise to the continual challenge of seeking more and better answers to life's many marvelous mysteries, including explanations about the origin and characteristics of the universe.

For further reading, the following titles are suggested:

1. *A Brief History of Time* [Hawkin 1988]
2. *Not by Design* [Stenger 1988]
3. *Fallacies of Creationism* [Young 1985]

CHAPTER 2.2

BELIEF SYSTEMS

2.2.1 INTRODUCTION

For many humans (indeed for the majority), religious beliefs hold a major place in their thoughts and actions, rightly or wrongly with regard to acceptable evidence. There seems to be a need in many humans to grapple with a number of questions concerning destiny and reality and the like, as well as a need for fulfilment of a so-called spiritual nature. One may question whether this should be the case or not, but one cannot deny the fact.

It is therefore considered appropriate to briefly examine the nature of these needs and beliefs, to more fully understand their causes. Added to this, recent research into this topic is beginning to suggest that there may be some aspects of evolutionary predisposition or "hard-wiring" in the brain which causes people to have what seem to be (and are called) religious experiences and therefore to hold religious beliefs. To accomplish an adequate level of knowledge about this complicated aspect of humanity, it is proposed to discuss some definitions of religion, some bases of faith, some justifications for beliefs of various sorts, some recent research, and to consider some aspects of and arguments about beliefs held in general and in particular.

2.2.2 RELIGION DEFINED

Webster's *College Dictionary* (Random House) defines the word "religion" in the following terms: 1) the quest for the values of the ideal life, involving three phases: the *ideal*, the *practices* for attaining the values of the ideal, and the *theology* or world view relating the quest to the environing universe; 2) a particular system in which the quest for the ideal life has been embodied; 3) recognition on the part of man of a controlling superhuman power entitled to obedience, reverence, and worship; 4) the feeling or the spiritual attitude of those recognizing such a controlling power; 5) the manifestation of such feeling in conduct or life; 6) a point or matter of conscience—to make a religion of doing something; 7) other now obsolete meanings.

None of these meanings indicate the origin of the word "religion" itself. It appears to stem from a latin root "ligare" which means to tie or to bind, and the prefix "re" which means back or again, thus giving the word its true meaning: re-ligion—to tie or to bind back to a set of ideals. The use of the word "religious" was originally and correctly restricted to those priests and nuns who had taken vows to become bound to a particular set of beliefs; it did not have the wider and less correct meaning now ascribed to people who lead apparently "good" or "moral" lives as a result of their beliefs in the existence of supernatural entities.

However, there are always difficulties associated with attempts to define a word about which there is such a wide diversity of approaches to determine meaning. Some of these approaches lead towards the vacuously infinite; others tend towards a kind of pseudo-scientific finiteness; yet others attempt to satisfy a sort of academic subjectivity. Naturally, all of them will involve and reflect the point of view and beliefs of the person attempting the definition. In this case, some of these definitional difficulties stem from the extraordinarily complex origins of this particular word, from Latin, Greek, and Old English roots (such as *legere*—to gather; *relegere*—to recollect; *legare*—to appoint; and *religare*—to constrain, to give some examples).

In any event, such simplistic definitions do not fully convey what the word "religion" means. One reason is that there simply are so many different religions shared by so many different people around the world. Some religions, such as Christianity, primarily comprise a set of shared theological and perhaps moral *beliefs*, apart from which one tends to lead an otherwise mostly secular life. Because of this, it is relatively easy to adopt some other set of beliefs or to abandon beliefs altogether; the change to one's daily life would be minimal. But other religions are much more of a *way* of life, with religious ritual deeply pervading almost all aspects of daily routines. To ask Muslims or Hindus what they believe about their religion would not elicit a very succinct reply, as they would be hard pressed to separate such beliefs from the rest of their being.

Whereas Christianity is based on a creed or set of beliefs, taken from a holy book, a religion like Islam is based on a set of laws, embodied in a holy book. Many oriental religions, such as Buddhism and Taoism, have virtually no theological content at all; instead, they feature daily practices of meditation and ritual. To ask Buddhists what they believe about gods may cause them some difficulties with an answer; it is just not a issue for them. So, while a Buddhist or a Muslim might relatively easily become a Christian by adopting the set of Christian beliefs, it would be more difficult for a Christian to become a Jew or a Hindu, because there are far more hereditary family and ritualistic elements to those religions than just a set of beliefs. And for much of the world's population, religion is often not a matter of choice; it is an inescapable fact of the geographical, historical and political structure of their societies.

The purpose of trying to clarify this word in this work at this point is to give the ordinary person a practical meaning for the word to use in ordinary conversation and thought. Consequently, some further definitions are given in more common parlance, from which it is hoped that the reader will be able to get a grip on this elusive and confounding topic.

The first is a definition composed by Bertrand Russell, the well-known British philosopher, thus: "Religion is a set of beliefs held as dogmas, dominating the conduct of life, going beyond or contrary to evidence, and inculcated by methods which are emotional or authoritarian, not intellectual." The second is a definition proposed by Trevor Cobeldick, as reported by the Humanist Information Service of New Zealand, thus: "Religion consists of beliefs about mystical or supernatural forces (or powers or beings) that are interactive with the world; and the behaviors and practices which the believer feels mightily encumbered upon (or obliged or bound) to have and to follow." A third definition has been quoted recently by Paul Pfalzner, a former president of the Humanist Association of Canada, thus: "Religion is a system of beliefs, centering around belief in a supernatural being (or beings, powers, or forces), which affect human life and are objects of ritualistic worship."

A definition in the *Dictionary of Philosophy* (Pan Books) takes a different tack. It acknowledges the difficulty of distinguishing between philosophizing about and explicating religious belief. In doing so, it lists a couple of assertions by notable philosophers, such as: "The essence of religion consists in the feeling of an absolute dependence" (Schleiermacher) and "Religion is what the individual does with his own solitariness" (Whitehead). This dictionary also asserts that a satisfactory answer to the question "What is religion?" would be more like an encyclopedia than a sentence. The following three chapters of this book present an abridged form of a primer on the topic.

2.2.3 BASIS OF FAITH

The essence of faith is to be determined to believe in an idea or notion, no matter what the evidence might prove to the contrary. One simply keeps telling oneself (or is told) to believe long enough until one believes or no longer doubts. Reason, evidence, exploratory discussion have little to do with it. It is often said by believers of religious ideas that it is morally wrong and mentally foolish to reason about the existence of God or gods, and that people should just have faith. It is therefore appropriate to give some thought to the meaning of the word "faith" to clarify our understanding of what is expected of those who have faith, and to decide whether or not to have faith is always a reasonable proposition. Several of the ideas in this synoptic section were extracted from parts of a book by Michael Scriven [1966].

The word "faith" in the context of normal conversation means no more than to have confidence in something, usually based on experience. When we say that we have faith in a person, we mean that we know that person to be reliable, based on evidence of previous behavior and actions. In this case, our faith is based on experience and to some extent, reason. Now, just as there are degrees of reason, there are also degrees of faith. But in the religious context, the word faith is used to mean an alternative to reason, not as something based on reason. In the first and normal context, the use of faith is a possible route to truth, but not so in the second case. We can be reasonably (but not absolutely) assured and therefore have faith that a person will be reliable in the future if he or she has proven to be reliable in the past, but how can we have faith that God exists or is good, when we are simply told to believe it, without any proof of existence and some evidence of lack of goodness, on the basis of a fundamental leap of faith? Are we expected to have faith in faith, solely because of faith? It is a curious expectation. We could be asked to believe that there are wild tigers in orbit around the planet Jupiter, but should we accept it without proof? Few would.

One cannot show that God exists or is good or has any other attributes, just by having faith in the possibility that such a belief is true. Whatever faith of this kind may be, it is certainly not based on knowledge or experience; it is more likely to be based on fear and conditioning. Of course it is possible to have faith in a large number of things, in the hope that some of them might turn out to be worthwhile, whereupon, on a selective basis, one might argue that faith in the things that worked out was therefore justified all along. This amounts to little more than gambling, which is a poor basis for (and a sore trial of) faith. It also does not explain those residual things that did not work out in which one had faith that was apparently misplaced.

It is of course sometimes argued by believers of religious notions that there is such a great feeling of comfort and confidence to be derived from having faith that that in itself is an indication of its worth. One cannot deny that feelings of comfort and security are good and desirable and therefore worthwhile. However, such a line of argument does not prove anything, as it does not present any reliable facts on which the faith is based. Indeed, if such facts could be demonstrated, there would be no need for faith, as the evidence itself would justify the belief. It is argued by nonbelievers that the validation of such beliefs involves reference to ordinary logic and scientific knowledge; but is it not possible that religious faith may give humankind access to some new domain or level of truth? Well, it is certainly possible, but possibilities are neither veracities nor probabilities. It is also unlikely. It produces a circular argument: we might believe it to be possible, but as we cannot prove it, we would have to have faith.

One so-called proof occasionally offered is that so many people claim to have had religious revelations or experiences, many of which are astonishingly similar to each other, that there therefore must be "something to it." The difficulty with this proof is that though many may be in general agreement, the agreement may be about a communal or shared mistake or at least a misinterpretation. It is more likely that these people are just sharing normal phenomena of a physiological or psychological nature. Recent research into brain states, being done by Dr. Michael Persinger at Laurentian University among others, has given rise to the notion that there may actually be parts of the brain that trigger so-called religious experiences and beliefs.

Two common human medical disabilities are migraine headaches (caused by neural disturbances) and glaucoma (caused by pressure on fluid in the eyeball). Many people who suffer painless migraines mentally experience bright flashes of light in the center of grey tunnel-like areas; this author has had this disturbing experience on three occasions. One could confuse this phenomenon with having a vision of supernatural beings. Those who suffer even mild glaucoma (which painlessly impairs vision) tend to see auras around lights and people; this could give rise to the notion that some people see others with halos over their heads.

We can easily interfere with our bodily constitutions. It has been observed that if you give a person too much or too little to eat or drink, that person will have unusual experiences; but should such experiences then be classified as religious experiences? If many people experience the same effects from the same causes, does this lend any more credence to the theory? If people (individually or collectively) starve or gorge themselves or otherwise alter their perceptions with drugs like alcohol or mescaline, and then have visions of bliss, are they really to be taken seriously by normal people who eat and drink in moderation relative to their needs? It is doubtful that such distortions should be considered of much value to society, even though they may offer some insights into the human conditions that causes people to engage in such behaviors.

In Ireland a few years ago, a number of deeply religious people claimed to have seen a plaster statue of the Virgin Mary move slightly. They naturally believe this to be a manifestation of the work of their God, although why any god would choose such an odd and insignificant way to show his, her, or its universal power is not clearly explained in the reports of this event. One would think that an intergalactic collision or a supernova explosion or at the very least a major earthquake would be a more fitting signal of omnipotent presence. No actual measurable proof has been offered that the statue did in fact move, beyond the claims of these devout and indoctrinated believers, and no independent non-religious observer has been privileged to witness this extraordinary phenomenon. One or two scientists who informally reviewed the situation later observed that, at certain times and in certain lights, the color, size, and appearance of the statue, seen against its own special background in relation to flickering candlelight (and coupled to the possibility of hallucinations in such strong believers) could give rise to an optical illusion of movement. It can be said that the Vatican reserved judgement in this case. It is also curious, and sad, that otherwise normal people would choose to believe such religious claims in preference to the much more likely explanations of the scientists.

However, it should not be forgotten that believers of religious notions want to (indeed may feel that they have to) believe; they are therefore susceptible to beliefs that favor their causes and ideals, and they are not much interested in contrary or missing pieces of evidence. Such believers are also susceptible to contrived influences in their childhood and early adulthood. In particular, many Christians still believe in things like holy ghosts and virgin births, however improbable these notions may seem to the rational and scientific community. If one believes such things are possible, then one might also believe that an almighty god would choose to make a small plaster statue move, for some indiscernable reason or perhaps for no reason at all, but just for the fun of it. God, being allegedly perfect, must have a sense of humor, although it is not much in evidence in these difficult times of poverty, disease, religious wars, terrorist attacks, natural disasters such as earthquakes and hurricanes, and unnatural disasters such as oil spills and other industrial catastrophes.

Another difficulty that faithful believers face is that those who lead them are themselves caught up in the superstitions which characterize so much of religion. To give only two examples, one Roman Catholic bishop has been quoted as stating in public that the death of soldiers in battle was part of his God's plan for populating the kingdom of heaven which was probably small comfort to the families of the now dead soldiers [Lamont]. On what reasonable basis could anyone worship such a cruel and selfish God? Could God not just perform another miracle and populate his kingdom in some other less painful and disturbing way?

Another Roman Catholic priest observed how prudent Almighty God was to provide rattles in the tails of rattlesnakes to warn men (sic) so that they would not be killed by these animals and then in the very next sentence described how he killed such a dangerous snake [Meyer]. No mention is made of the inconsistency that man is thus more dangerous to the snake than the snake is to man; yet neither God nor the priest appears concerned to warn snakes against men. On what reasonable basis can one worship such a partial and uncaring God? Could God not have devised some way of warning the snakes about the potential dangers of man?

Many other examples of such superstitious beliefs abound. One involves the religious nonsense which prevailed around the repeated sightings of Halley's Comet right up until the visit of 1985, when the most ordinary citizens of all beliefs finally had ready access to reliable scientific information about the orbit and other properties of this natural (though astounding) celestial object. In contrast to previous epochs, right up to and including the previous sighting of the Comet in 1910, the churches of the world were notably silent about the now-debunked religious significance of this now well-understood scientific phenomenon. One does not need faith when one has knowledge; it is not an act of faith to photograph and measure a comet from a space ship. It is instead an example of human achievement and advancement on two grounds: the development of useful science and technology with the corresponding retreat of useless and often harmful religious belief.

Many believers in occult (i.e: hidden) powers also make attempts to introduce aspects of technology into their procedures to lend an air of reliability and respectability to their nonsensical claims. Apart from the use of simple artifacts such as the crystal balls, tarot cards, and tea-cups used by fortune-tellers, there are charts and other gizmos used by astrologers, and many larger but equally fraudulent deceptions involving various types of concealed apparatus used by spiritual mediums in seances. Another example is to be found in the practices of a small but dedicated group who believe that the lines of magnetic force that impinge on the body of a baby at the *moment* of birth (whatever that means, as birthing is a *process*) determine the future health and wealth of that child as it develops to adulthood. They employ a number of gadgets, such as magnets, or divining or dowsing rods of various types, in their attempts to realign these alleged forces around some sort of imaginary central life axis. There is of course no scientific basis to support any of these useless practices, although there may be a minor quantum of psychological benefit that may accrue to the practitioners and believers. However, the extent to which the psychological credit is offset by the credibility debit is a moot point.

Another gambit of religious believers is to argue that many scientific beliefs have been shown to be false, and that faith in such beliefs is therefore pointless. This is of course true in those instances where the belief is shown to be false; part of the scientific method involves the potential or ability to falsify data. However, it is largely beside the point, and moreover, the same argument can be applied to religious beliefs. The difference is that scientific beliefs are subject to constant and usually independent testing, and if found to be deficient, they are modified or abandonded by knowledgeable people. For example, we could all believe that we could fly through the air without mechanical assistance, but as soon as we put such a belief to the obvious test, it would fail. Yet many people believe that angels exist and can fly through the air without mechanical assistance, without demanding any verification of this incredible claim. Most people are just not prepared, nor willing, nor brave enough to take the time and risk to consider such a study, much less actually do it. This is interesting, because the criteria for religious truths are not connected with the criteria for every-day truths, and thus they should have little bearing on our every-day lives. They constitute no explanation of what we see around us nor do they provide us with any useful guidance for our course through time that cannot be found in purely secular bases. Yet such beliefs persist.

In many cases, religious beliefs are harmless, but there are other cases where unrestrained faith becomes fanaticism, and people adopt truly harmful notions which can result in truly harmful actions. The tragedy of the air attacks on the World Trade Center in New York and the Pentagon in Washington, D.C. on September 11, 2001 is an extreme case in point. The attackers were alleged to be members of an ultra-fanatical Middle Eastern religious sect, who apparently believed (apart from their extreme political beliefs) that this present human life is of no value, other than as preparation for a so-called afterlife in some sort of heavenly paradise. If such people place no value on their own lives, it is little wonder that they care nothing at all for those who are killed, wounded, or aggrieved by their selfish actions. To compound their beliefs, members of many of such cults are taught that all political and religious regimes, other than their own, are evil and not worthy of consideration in actions to bring about their eradication. Some other similar examples are described later in Section 2.5.6 *Mythology*.

There is also an argument that humans ought to act on faith, because there is simply not enough time to wait for proof of everything before acting. Some assumptions should just be made (so goes the argument) and one of these assumptions is to have faith. But by definition, faith is belief, regardless of evidence or probability, which are two valuable commodities to consider before acting. It is also unlikely that a perfectly good God, if such exists, would expect or require humans to act regardless of evidence or probability. To do so would be illogical: "God", being perfect, cannot be illogical, and "Man", allegedly being made in "God's" image, should not be illogical either. The logical basis for living a valuable life is one involving sound values chosen as the result of critical and rational thought, and not one based on "ready-to-wear" values adopted through hearsay or duress, or simply taken on faith.

For further reading, the following titles are suggested:

1. *Primary Philosophy* [Scriven 1966]
2. *The Philosophy of Humanism* (Lamont1982]
3. *Honore-Timothee Lemfrit, OMI* [Meyer 1985]

2.2.4 ASPECTS OF BELIEF

In this section, some aspects of religious beliefs are addressed, such as the general range of beliefs, the fundamental categories of belief, and the numbers of adherents to various religious denominations, as well as a related issue: literacy.

1. Range of Beliefs

The range of religious beliefs held by humans and the number of religious denominations is simply staggering to contemplate. There are thousands of separate denominations (some reports say more than 20,000) and their beliefs range literally all the way from worship of gods to worship of devils, and touch upon every possible or conceivable intermediate object or notion along the way. While the majority of people understandably belong to one or other of the so-called traditional religious groups, there is no dogma too far out, abstract, weird, abstruse, or nonsensical not to have a few believers and proselytizers. Some people still believe that the earth is flat; others think that the moon landings were filmed in Hollywood.

2. Categories of Belief

All religious experiences fall into one of two categories: *first* hand and *second* hand. Experiences of the *first-hand* category include the kinds of "visions" that mystics and so-called holy men occasionally report after lengthy meditation or experimentation, as well as spontaneous "enlightenments" which sometimes occur to unsuspecting believers, bringing them to some form or state of apparent grace or bliss. Many of these experiences are no doubt perceived as being real enough by the participant, although they are often hard-pressed to describe such experience in terms which are meaningful to others not so privileged. In philosophical terms, this is called "the problem of other minds." Although they may be difficult to explain, they are not hard to understand, as it is often not easy to express even many overtly conscious feelings in simple language. For example, imagine trying to describe the taste of cheese to a person who has never tasted anything like it; more precisely, try to describe the taste of a specific type of cheese to such a person. Or try to explain the experience of color to a blind person who has never seen such phenomena.

It is fair (and safe) to say that many such *first-hand* religious experiences do occur, and that they can be very real and powerful for the person involved; what is not so clear (or safe) to say is what they really signify, in any meaningful and rational way. The fact that a person has such an experience and perceives it to be a sign from God does not in itself prove the existence of God or confirm that it is such a sign. All that can be definitely said is that a mental or even physical experience of some kind has occurred, and even for that, we have to take the word of the "experiencee." There is no ordinary every day test to actually prove to others that he or she had the alleged experience, despite statements or affidavits to that effect, or subsequent and even measurable changes in physiology or overt behavior. In recent years, though, some laboratory experiments have been developed to monitor brain scans taken during such events; the results of these tests do show some altered brain states during the reported experiences, as might be expected. Finally, the rate of incidence in such genuine experiences in the general population is apparently quite low, although fraudulent quackery abounds in this specific philosophical arena.

The second category of religious experiences are the *second-hand* ones. The great majority of believers of all faiths fall into this category. They feel some religious quality in and around their lives, for no more complicated reason than the fact that they have been taught to think that way since birth and that their brains are so constituted. They hear a constant and repetitive message about religion from all authority figures in their lives: parents, teachers, preachers, and from friends, relations, and numerous forms of media. A very large segment of western society is still not yet ready to favor open dissent or even much discussion about religious matters that might conflict with their own deep and long held views, and thus cause some discomfort and uncertainty. On the contrary, a colossal amount of time, energy, and money is expended annually by millions of people seeking to further their knowledge of specific religious concepts, not with an attitude of rational inquiry, but simply to further their attempt to more securely save their own souls from the wrath of their own Gods. It is not made clear to onlookers why one should worship vengeful Gods, but it may have something to do with the vengeful streak which one finds in many who hold firm beliefs about specific and exclusionary religious ideas.

In addition to the two fundamental categories identified above, the range of beliefs held sacred by humans can be further subdivided into two broad classifications: *theistic* and *non-theistic* religions. Under each classification, a number of subtitles can be subsumed. Naturally, no one chapter, indeed no one book, could possibly cover this enormous subject in any depth. However, a brief synopsis of the main religions in both of these classifications has been included in Sections 2.3.0 and 2.4.0 of this book, to make the book more useful for the uninformed reader. A review of the primary features of the major religions of the world will give the open-minded reader some idea of the nature of the many beliefs still held sacred by so much of humankind.

Non-believers like atheists, agnostics, pragmatists, humanists, and other free-thinkers, are located on the sidelines of all of this activity, looking on in amazement and with some amusement at the extraordinary lengths to which much of the rest of humankind will go to save its spiritual hide. It should be noted, however, that while there is a need for understanding, there is little room for condescension. Although non-believers of religious notions may not believe in spiritual divinities, they still sincerely believe whatever they do believe to be true. So it is with believers—they mostly believe whatever they do believe, to be true. One cannot really denigrate the act of belief in itself.

For religionists, their beliefs are real enough to them; it is the premises on which these beliefs are based that is false, in the opinion of the non-theistic believer. And so that is one task for the non-believer: to show that the basis of religious beliefs are false. A second task, which logically precedes the first one, is for non-believers to understand the nature of what it is that believers believe, so that the weaknesses may become apparent and therefore capable of explanation to believers. A third task for non-believers is to recognize the elements of belief and to become familiar with existing arguments or to develop new arguments against irrational belief. They should also try to realistically grasp the approximate magnitude of the preceding tasks.

3. Numbers of Adherents

To get some idea of the magnitude of religious influence, it is appropriate to give some perspective to the numbers of people who hold religious beliefs, and to do this, it is necessary to introduce some statistical data. There is a tendency on the part of non-believers in North America to hold among their beliefs that they are an indistinct minority of society. The facts tend to show otherwise, although the figures given cannnot be considered as very accurate, considering that many religious denominations have no clear idea of just how many members they themselves have, and that many such data conflict with official sources, such as government census figures. Because of the vast size and complexity of this statistical topic, religious beliefs throughout the world in general shall not be addressed here; this review is limited to North America.

The current combined population of Canada and the United States is approximately 300 million people. Approximately 60% or 180 million of these people profess to have some type and degree of religious affiliation. About another 20% claim to believe in a god, though they do not appear to belong to any specific denomination. The largest single identifiable group is the Roman Catholic Church, with about 50 million adherents; no other group comes close. There are about 25 million Methodists and another 25 million Baptists. The remaining 80 million encompass well over 350 separate denominations, bodies, sects, or cults, ranging over the entire alphabet from Adventists and Anglicans, through Hindus and Hutterites, Mennonites and Muslims, to Zen Buddhists and Zionists. It should of course be noted that in other parts of the world, such as China, India, and Japan, the distribution of beliefs are notably different from the North American pattern, with Islam being a major influence.

About 130 million of these 180 million North American believers could be classified as Christians of one sort or another; the remaining 50 million subscribe to other theistic religions such as Judaism, or to non-theistic religions such as Taoism. This still leaves about 60 million people (the other 20%) who apparently profess no religious belief. This proportion coincidentally echoes that of many western European countries. It is interesting to consider that if these 60 million Americans and Canadians could simply acknowledge their inherent humanism, they could form the single largest denomination on the Continent, with a membership as large as any other, and bigger than most of the remainder taken together. To achieve this position, it would not be necessary to make a convert of a single believer. For further treatment of this topic, see Chapter 1.4.0 Apostasy.

4. Literacy

According to United Nations statistics, the United States was recently ranked 49th out of 158 countries with respect to literacy levels. It has been estimated that 1 in 8 (or about 37 million of the 300 million) of the population of North America are functionally illiterate. This means that a very large number of people are not able to fully participate in all that their constitutional rights guarantee. In addition, there are another 1 in 5 (or 60 million) North Americans whose literacy skills are so poorly developed that they could not read this book well enough to comprehend its meaning or significance. Taken together, these data indicate that about 1 person in 3 does not have the skill necessary to read or research written information accurately or usefully on their own; they have to get whatever limited amount of information they do get second-hand, most often from radio, TV, and other aural sources. These sources are frequently biased, dogmatic, incorrect, melodramatic, political, superficial, transient, and uncritical.

It does not take much imagination or investigation to see an enormous problem inherent in such a widespread societal deficiency. Quite apart from making a secondary decision as to which form of religion to accept or reject, how do such people make primary decisions regarding their fundamental democratic rights, if they cannot even read the constitution and legislation that guarantee such rights? It is a serious question, and one which the people as a whole must address in a form understandable by the bulk of the population.

For further reading, the following titles are suggested:

1. *The Religious Heritage of America* [Shulman 1981]
2. *The State of Religion Atlas* [O'Brien 1993]

2.2.5 NATURE OF BELIEF

First, an explanation of the word "belief." It means that which is believed; an accepted opinion; and (significantly) conviction of the truth or reality of a thing, based on grounds *insufficient* to afford positive knowledge. Early humans quickly noticed that they had within themselves some limited power to change local circumstances according to their wishes. They noticed that there were larger powers in nature capable of making much larger changes. They also noticed that their dreams and wishes occasionally came true. After all, there are several billion dreams dreamed every night; some of them will coincidentally appear to come true. People were thus drawn to several conclusions leading to beliefs of various sorts: first, that there were powers outside of their own beings; second, that these powers had considerable influence over their environment; and third, that appeals of various sorts might be made to these larger powers in attempts to bring about beneficial treatment. In some cases, these appeals appeared to be granted. And so the concept of supernatural powers developed, as the brain evolved to permit more sophisticated thoughts, leading through refinement to concepts of gods. These concepts led to the development of more specific religious practices and procedures, such as worship, prayer, and sacrifice. These beliefs and practices later became codified into so-called Holy Books, such as the Bible, the Koran, the Torah, and the Vedas, giving rise to the priestly hierarchies which are a feature of most religions of the present day world.

People who belong to specific religious denominations seldom question their own fundamental personal beliefs, any more than people who speak a particular language or dialect question that fact. Religious belief, like language, is a coincidence of birth and family as much as anything. As one gets older, it becomes more difficult to learn a new language or adopt a new belief. Believers seldom openly speculate about their god or gods; they concentrate on the alleged actions and pronouncements of the god or gods. They simply state that their God *Is* or that *God Exists*, and then, believing it, act on the directions of those priests, gurus, or leaders who are self-appointed or appointed by other believers to interpret the alleged words of their particular god. Needless to say, these interpretations usually favor the adherents of the specific denomination to the detriment of all outsiders. Of course this is not to say that all religious believers do not have any doubts whatsoever; they do, but they tend to dismiss them (or more probably, not to publicly admit them) as signs of weakness or uncertainty.

Many religious humans feel and therefore believe that their particular God is the supreme God, and they therefore think that worship of and obedience to that God is the supreme good. These thoughts or actions which embody their creeds produce immense feelings of satisfaction and comfort, giving rise to the feeling that the universe is important, and that their own part in it, however humble, is therefore also important as part of some grand plan or scheme of things. Comforting as these thoughts about life obviously are, there is yet greater comfort to be found in connection with death. Religion lets people believe that physical this-worldly death is not the end of metaphysical other-worldly forms of life and therefore offers the hope (however false), indeed the likelihood (however remote), that people and their loved ones will live forever in perfect peace, justice, harmony, and happiness in valhalla or heaven. The precise nature of that eternal life is usually not specified with scientifically acceptable clarity or precision, but the very vagueness of it appears to be an additional comfort to believers.

Non-believers question the amount of pleasure to be derived from such alleged infinite, uneventful, and boring bliss. Are there news-casts in heaven? How is the weather there? What do souls talk or think about in heaven, when they are not praising their Lord? How do souls become reunited with those of friends or relatives from among the uncountable trillions of souls in heaven? It is difficult to get clear answers to these questions from religious believers.

It is important to understand these beliefs, because they do in large measure support the curious dogma that religion is intrinsically good, and that anyone who challenges religion is therefore intrinsically bad. Theistic believers do not engage in polemic or argument to discover whether or not they are mistaken in their beliefs; they simply believe, regardless of the evidence against such belief or lack of evidence to support it. Most true believers feel surprised and even pained that such evidence should be considered necessary, and they frequently attempt to intimidate non-believers by attacking their characters (and sometimes their bodies) instead of their arguments.

A classic (though non-religious) example of this type of activity occurred when the management of General Motors sought to discredit Ralph Nader as a worthwhile person after he published his first book exposing some of the devious practices of the automobile industry. They later apologized when it transpired that what he had said was true. Believers argue that the atheist is by definition impious and therefore wicked, and on that basis is therefore not worthy of a fair hearing because his or her views are false. The atheist's argument is, of course, that humans should value truth and reason above comfort and happiness, but that is an argument which regrettably falls on many deaf ears.

Many believers simply think that it is wrong not to believe in God, or to consider that God may not exist, or to try to convince others that there is no God, although they seldom make it clear just on what basis such thoughts or actions are intrinsically wrong, other than the fact that they do not like them. In short, they have been taught that they should believe, and they therefore believe that all others should also believe. The main irrationality, intellectual dishonesty, and pragmatic fallacy of religion is the cynical, immoral, and harmful propaganda that spiritual comfort and security are to be preferred over experiential truth and reason. The suggestion that members of any society should adopt and adhere to any specific religion, whether it is true or not, on the erroneous supposition that people will be somehow less cruel, or less criminal, or less mischievous, is not only unproven, but there is much historic and current evidence to the contrary. Moreover, it is degrading to more rational human aspirations.

Other fallacies adopted by religious believers include a curious one: rather than rejecting religion because it is possibly false, they accept it because it is not certainly false. Believers are also biased in their selections of instances that they maintain proves their contentions, such as the occurrence of so-called miracle cures or the answers to self-serving petitionary prayers; they simply ignore all contrary cases. Many believers say that their beliefs keep them free of fear, yet according to the British philosopher Bertrand Russell, the primary reason for all religious belief can be summed up in that one word: fear. Specifically, fear of death; generally, fear of the unknown and of disapproval.

A couple of digressions concerning aspects of belief can be introduced at this point, to illustrate the difficulties that contemplation of the topic of belief entail. For example, questions of observations and perceptions of reality have puzzled people for centuries. In earlier times, it was thought that the Earth was at the center of the universe and that human beings were God's greatest creation. After all, in the light of knowledge available at that time, people could only believe what they thought they saw and experienced. Later scientific thought and discovery altered these views, placing Earth, and therefore humankind, in a considerably less prestigious position on the edge of a minor galaxy. More recently, a theory has emerged from the field of quantum physics to suggest that perhaps human beings are at the center of a reality and a universe of a type and form not heretofore understood. In short form, the theory suggests that at the subatomic level, the universe exists only insofar as human beings exist to observe it. It is a theory that will no doubt generate considerable debate among and between believers and non-believers alike.

Another example concerns the effect of religious belief on day-to-day experiences. In Maryland some years ago, a man named Roy Toscaro applied to the State for a license to practice as a notary public. To get the license, a State law required that applicants swear an oath that they believed in God. When he refused that portion of the oath (on constitutional grounds) his application was denied. He took the case all the way to the US Supreme Court (at considerable personal cost) and won. Such legislation contravenes several elements of the Constitutions of both the United States and Canada, such as freedom of conscience and belief, and freedom from discrimination in employment.

A third example concerns an apparent conflict in the vows of celibacy required to be undertaken by priests and nuns in certain sectors of the many divisions of the Christian faith. According to their bible, it is the law of God that all should go forth and multiply, that is, engage in sexual intercourse for the purpose of conception of offspring. Leaving aside discussion of the enormous amount of misery that such an uncontrolled concept has caused, how can people who really believe in such a law deliberately swear an oath of celibacy and not go forth and officially multiply themselves as their own law requires? There appear to be some problems with belief in religious contexts.

The Essence of Humanism | 153

For further reading, the following titles are suggested:

1: *Why I am Not a Christian* [Russell 1957]
2: *Science Digest* [Summer 1986]
3. *Modern Man in Search of a Soul* [Jung 1933]

2.2.6 ARGUMENTS ABOUT BELIEF

A number of arguments have been used to support the idea of the existence of God or gods. There are a corresponding number of arguments against such beliefs. Before examining these arguments in more detail, the following simplified chart may assist the reader to place degrees of belief relative to evidence on an informal and approximate scale:

100%	Disprovable	Rejectionism	Atheist
75%	Improbable	Skepticism	Skeptic
50%	Possibility	Agnosticism	Agnostic
75%	Probability	Pragmatism	Pragmatist
100%	Provable	Theism	Theist

Table 1—Scale of Beliefs [see endnote 1]

The data in the foregoing table mean that if the existence of a supernatural being is absolutely not provable, then some form of atheism is the logical stance for the rational mind; conversely, if it can be proved conclusively that a god exists, then theism is the rational point of view. Others, who hold less dogmatic views, might classify themselves under one or other of the remaining three categories. The majority of humanists probably consider themselves to be skeptics or agnostics, taking the stance that the proofs for the existence of God have more weight against them than for them, and that in any event, such considerations are of little consequence, when compared to the real problems which the world is currently facing.

What follows are simplified outlines of several arguments that purport to prove the existence of God. Most of the originals of these proofs were originally propounded and subsequently developed by professional theologians, who can hardly be considered to be impartial bystanders in this debate. However, only believers have any reason or motivation to provide such so-called proofs, and so examples must be necessarily chosen from their ranks. Furthermore, both they and their proofs should be taken at their face value, and non-believers wishing to discredit such proofs should also avoid attacking the people who present the proofs; in fairness, criticism should be directed at the proofs themselves. To do otherwise is to treat believers with the same disdain and belittlement with which many believers treat non-believers, when these believers find it difficult to attack arguments against belief on semantic grounds and impossible to defeat skeptic or agnostic conclusions on rational grounds.

It may also be of interest to incidentally contemplate that the Torah, the Koran, and the Bible do not contain any proofs for the existence of God; such existence is simply an unquestioned assumption made in advance. The first five of the following arguments are accompanied by a rebuttal.

1. First Cause Argument

This Argument suggests that everything in the universe must have had a cause, and that if one goes back far enough, one will come to the first cause, and that cause is (or can be called) God. Before examining rebuttal to the assertion, which is also called the cosmological argument, the meaning of the word "universe" requires some clarification. According to the dictionary, it means the totality of existing things; therefore if God or gods exist, the universe must include them. If gods can exist outside the universe, then there is a defect in the accepted meaning of that word. Further, there are those who say that the universe, while being the totality of things, is not a thing in itself, and so likewise, God may not be a thing like other things.

The general thrust of rebuttal to this argument is that if

everything must have a cause, then logically God must have had a cause. Conversely, if God could exist without cause, then so could the universe or any part of it. To put it slightly differently, if anything can exist without cause, then God might exist without cause. However, if things could exist independently of God, then God cannot have been their cause. Another weakness of this argument is the assumption that everything must have had a cause. This may be so, but this argument does not prove it. This concept is tied to our concept of time. Most humans believe that time passes in a linear fashion, leading from one thing to another, but in fact it may not do so. Scientists now know that time passes at different rates under different conditions of speed and direction. To a large extent, our concept of time is tied to our way of measuring distance, specifically the distance traveled daily by any and all points on the surface of the earth as it rotates in its orbit around the sun. The universe as a whole may not be at all concerned with or even have any concept of the passage of time which occupies so much of our thoughts.

The concept of an infinite number of causes of actual events is difficult for most people to grasp, but there appears to be no mathematical constraint or barrier to the concept. Indeed, the fact that so many events in the natural world can be described in mathematical terms is itself often used to suggest that there therefore must have been some master mathematiciam, namely God, who originally worked it all out. It will be evident to any rational mind that systems of mathematics are simply ways developed by humans to describe natural events that are occuring above, below, at, or beside the levels of human sensibilities; there is no divine influence at work here. And one might note that if it is indeed possible to have an infinite number of causes, then one will never get back to a first cause.

Furthermore, there is no evident reason why the universe should have had a cause or indeed any beginning; it may simply always have existed in one form or another. In spite of the so-called Big Bang Theory (discussed in Section 2.1.5), the forces or matter of which the universe is composed must have been available in some form prior to that event, if it did in fact occur.

2. Natural Laws Argument

This Argument suggests that the operation of the entire universe is governed by natural laws, and that these laws must have been established by God. By natural laws, reference is made to the principles governing such phenomena as gravitational attraction, planetary orbits, electrical characteristics, chemical combinations, genetic arrangements, and so on. This argument stems from the confusion that these natural laws are somehow the same as human laws, which are behests by some people telling other people how to behave in specific situations. These so-called natural laws are literally not of the same nature as human laws; instead, they are general descriptions, devised by humans, of how things appear to work in the natural world. As such, it cannot be successfully argued that there must have been something that originally told or continues to tell things to act as they do in fact act.

Let us suppose for a moment that God does exist and did in fact actually issue these particular natural laws. A question immediately arises: why just these laws and not others? If God had reasons for these specific laws, then he/she/it was or is subject to reason, and therefore cannot be the ultimate law-maker. If God had no reasons, then the whole concept of natural law is thwarted, because there could and would be things in nature not subject to natural law, which is absurd.

The correct answer to this argument is that the Natural Laws have been formulated through observation by humans to assist themselves to understand how things work in the present and to make reasonable predictions about how things might work in the future.

3. Design Argument

This Argument suggests that the entire universe exhibits patterns and order which point to the work of a supreme designer called God. This argument, also called the *teleological* argument, presents the idea that everything in the universe is so precisely and beautifully arranged (by an master designer) so that we and everything else manage to live in the world and the cosmos just as it is. The word "teleology" means the study of evidence of purpose in nature, and the argument proposes the existence of God on the assumption that order in the universe implies an orderer, and cannot be a feature of chance occurrence. The argument ignores the weakness of its own basic assumption, namely that nature has a purpose, as well as the obvious fact of adaptation to environment, which suggests that things are not well designed at all; in fact, quite the opposite. If they were so well designed, then why would they have to make adaptations? There is a great deal of imperfection in nature, partly stemming from a tendency of most things towards a state of entropy or disorder. The weather is a case in point; social organizations are another, as is decaying organic matter, such as dead plants and animals. The reader will be well aware of others.

Apart from the fact that we do not yet know everything about the universe (so we should not perhaps make such a sweeping claim for universal perfection at this point in time), proponents of this argument have to believe some astonishing things. For example, they have to believe that God, with all the power, wisdom, and time in the universe at his disposal and command, has produced a world with so many patent imperfections, such as earthquakes and disease, to name only two. Surely a competent (indeed perfect) designer would have produced a better (indeed perfect) design? Why would any god create life on a planet which is itself doomed to extinction? Why would any god create a planet so hostile to human life, allegedly the greatest creation of all? Not many humans, who have less wisdom than God (or so we are told), would go to so much trouble for so little return, although one might argue just how much or how little trouble it was for God to engage in such slip-shod creation in any event. Perhaps it is some grand cosmic joke. In any event, evolutionary naturalism, as proposed by humanists, provides a more satisfactory alternative explanation for apparent design.

4. The Moral Argument

This Argument asserts that if there were no God, there could be no right or wrong; but there is right and wrong, so there must be a God. One variation of this argument states that if there was no God, there could be no difference between right and wrong; there could only be actions not so classified. Assuming (for the moment) that there is a difference, the question is: Is the difference due to God or not? If it is due to God, then for God there is no difference, as he permits both to occur. If it is not due to God, then right and wrong have some meaning independent of God.

Another variation of this argument states that, if there were no God, there would be no justice prevailing in this world. It seems abundantly clear that there is extremely little justice prevailing, so this particular application of God's all-powerful work is somewhat spotty, to say the least. The religious believer's response is to say that to have justice, you have to have a balance. If there is injustice here on earth, then there will be justice in heaven, with hell on the other side to balance injustices in this life which were not unjust enough in the opinion of the great and final Judge, curiously called a loving God.

An analogy presented by Bertrand Russell points out that if one opened a crate of fruit and found all the top layer to be rotten, one would be unlikely to think that the lower layers must therefore be good, to bring about a balance; experience shows us that natural laws do not work that way. Similarly, one might say that the amount of injustice which we observe in the world today is in fact the way things are, and there is no evidence or reason to suggest that they are going to be rectified at some later point in time or in some hypothetical after-life. It is also pointless to argue that if human beings were only better than they are, then things of course would be different. We have to take life as we find it, not as we might wish it to be, although any opportunity for moral education without religious overtones should be seized by society.

Another aspect of this argument has been presented as follows: God is all-powerful and all-good. But evil exists. Therefore, either God can not or will not abolish evil. If he *can* not, then he is not all-powerful; if he *will* not, then he is not all-good. There are two standard rebuttals to this line by believers: (1) God has just not yet gotten around to abolishing evil, and (2) God gave men free-will to do as they please. They sometimes choose to do evil; if men could only do good, then they would not have free-will. This of course does not explain why innocent (and particularly) pious victims should fall prey to people who freely choose to do evil. Nor does it explain the occurrence of evils in which humans exercise no choice, such as diseases and natural disasters, evils which an all-powerful and all-good God could abolish or avert, if he/she/it so chose. Some believers deflect that approach by saying that such problems serve to bring out the best in people. Human beings do make efforts to alleviate the miseries brought about by diseases and natural disasters, and to censure those who transgress human laws of conduct, regardless of their involvement with religion or otherwise. Furthermore, many disasters do not appear to be particularly selective; they strike down religious believers and non-believers alike. There are many examples of church buildings collapsing on worshipers inside, which would appear to make their God seem somewhat ungrateful for the praise these worshipers were attempting to heap on him. It is hard for non-believers to understand how such an ungrateful being can be worthy of praise.

Few believers will acknowledge that God, if such exists, must be the source of evil. However, the Bible itself records (at Isaiah 45:7): "I form light and create darkness, I make weal and create woe. I am the Lord, who do all these things." As "weal" means good and "woe" means evil, it would appear that, for those who accept the truth of the Bible, God is admitting to being responsible for the evil in the world. Again, it is hard to understand why anyone would want to worship such a god, except out of feelings of fear as Russell said.

5. The Ontological Argument

This Argument suggests that as God is a perfect being, he/she/it must possess every attribute, including the attribute of existence, and must therefore necessarily exist. The word "ontology" refers to the science or metaphysics of "being" and the ontological argument is based on the assumption that being or existence is a property that every thing possesses. The basis of the argument appears to be that a perfect being, such as God, would of necessity possess all properties, otherwise he/she/it could not be perfect. Proponents of this argument say that as existence is a property, God must therefore exist. In other words, God being perfect, cannot lack the attribute of existence. There are two defects in this line of thought.

First, there is the philosophical and infinitely debatable question of whether an immanent concept such as God can be considered as a "thing" of the same order as other things. As this question is really not capable of categoric answer, the development of possible rebuttals shall be left to the reader. Secondly, there is a technical semantic question with respect to the use of the word *exist* in this context. You may recall from grammar instruction that the predicate is the active verb in a sentence along with the word which it governs. If one were to say that a circle is round, one is describing an attribute of the circle, specifically its roundness. The word "round" is an adjective. If one were to say that a circle exists, one is merely saying that something has the nature of a circle, but unless specific attributes are listed, we have no way of knowing what it really is that is being called a circle. We can say that it exists, but we do not and can not prove it just by saying so. If we can describe and then observe the attributes, or conversely observe and then describe attributes, then we can say that a thing exists.

In the sentence "God exists," the word *exists* is a predicate verb, not an attribute of God. In the sentence "God does exist," the word *exist* is a predicate adjective, but not an attribute of the noun. It is not much of an argument to say that God does exist just because someone says he/she/it exists; non-believers require to be presented with a better proof than that by religious believers. One cannot break the rules of grammar in just this one instance, to make a point in just this one argument. As the British philosopher G. E. Moore put it: "One can say that some tigers *growl* and some do not, but one cannot say that some tigers *exist* and some do not."

In general, St. Anselm, a 13th century Scholastic philosopher is credited with first articulating the ontological argument in the following form: "God is that than which nothing greater can be conceived. But that which exists in reality must be greater than that which exists only in the mind. Therefore God must exist outside the mind." So many objections have been raised to this line of argument by so many philosophers (from David Hume to Immanuel Kant) that the concept is now discredited. For example, Kant suggested that one real dollar is clearly more valuable than one imaginary dollar, and everyone know what one real dollar is worth (ignoring exchange rates for the moment!). However, the relevant concept of "God" is not in itself shown to be legitimate or proper, prior to its appearance in the argument. Moreover, there is no provable link between the first and second premise. Also, if God is everywhere, then he/she/it could exist in the mind and outside of it at one and the same time. And so on . . .

6. Other Arguments

A sixth argument involves *experience*. It suggests that the existence of God can simply be experienced, in much the same manner as one might experience a tree or a house or any other object. One might close one's eyes, and think about an object, and then open the eyes and see the object, or vice versa; an impression is made on the brain by the light reflected from the object and in that manner the object is experienced and perhaps comprehended. So it is with God, say the religious believers. If one opens one's mind to the concept, then God will signify his presence. The impression of God will be made on the brain, and the person will have no doubt as to God's existence. There may be some difficulty in proving it, but there will be no difficulty in believing it, and the impression can be understood by anyone else having received a similar impression. This argument is hardly proof of God's existence; at best it merely indicates some specific activity in the brain, and the acceptance of a belief or opinion about what it might mean. Recent research on brain states is beginning to show that the experience of the presence of supernatural bodies is essentially an internal function of the brain, and not the other way around.

A seventh argument again involves semantics; it goes as follows. If the real is totally intelligible, total intelligibility exists. If total intelligibility exists, then being exists. If being exists, then its components exist. One component is understanding. Man can understand some things; an entity which could understand everything would be supreme. This entity is named God by Man. Therefore, God exists. This argument makes a number of assumptions. Notice that the the word "if" is used in three separate places. One assumption is that the real is totally intelligible; the argument does not say what to think or do if the real is not totally intelligible (as new discoveries in quantum physics are indicating). It also does not prove, as it should, that total intelligibility is beyond the scope of man's imagination or power; it may be, but the argument does not show it. It also ascribes contrived meanings to ordinary words and derives doubtful conclusions from phrases with which few literate people would agree. There are of course other even lesser arguments that have been presented to sustain belief in supernatural gods; space does not permit their inclusion here. The first five of the foregoing are refuted as stated, while the last two appear to refute themselves.

For further reading, the following titles are suggested:

1. *An Atheist's Values* [Robinson 1964]
2. *Why I am Not a Christian* [Russell 1957]
3. *`Atheism—a Philosophical Justification* [Martin 1990]

2.2.7 PROVERBS AND CHARMS

Society has a rich heritage of useful proverbs which attempt to direct people as to how they should live. Much of this knowledge falls under the category of "old wive's tales," many of which have kernels of truth in them. For example, the saying that "there is many a slip twixt the cup and the lip" is undeniably true. "Once bitten, twice shy" has the strength of simplicity as well as the air of common sense. Similarly, a red sky at night may be a sailor's delight if it predicts fair weather for the morrow, whereas a red sky at dawning may also be a sailor's warning, for the same reason. There are literally hundreds of such sayings, most of which are as harmless as are they amusing.

But why should a person who breaks a mirror be inflicted with the thought that he or she may be in for seven years of bad luck? What is the possible benefit of this saying? How many of us go around deliberately smashing mirrors, to bring bad luck on ourselves? How many of us have accidentally broken good mirrors and found our lives no worse than before, and sometimes even better? Or deliberately smashed an old or cracked mirror to dispose of it? What about the expression "to touch wood" for good luck? The wood referred to is, of course, the wood of the Christian Cross, pieces of which were peddled as good luck charms in the Middle Ages by all sorts of wandering mendicants. This allegedly sacred wood was intended as a talisman to ward off life's ills. Incidentally, enough of this wood was sold over many years that the quantity would not only reconstitute the original cross, but also build a few of Noah's Arks as well. Yet there are still people today who feel the need "to touch wood" if an event involving some risk should occur. The fact that much of the wood is now made of plastic doesn't seem to matter. And there are difficulties with the number 13, because there were reputedly thirteen men at Christ's last supper, one of whom was considered to be a traitor. Even today, there are a few high rise buildings in which the elevator signals do not indicate a 13th floor. There IS a 13th floor, but the superstitious beliefs of some people prefer to imagine that it does not exist. Such beliefs are harmful, because they raise false hopes or perpetuate false fears in people's minds, thus detracting from the inherent dignity of humankind.

For example, the possible social or mental value that a dead rabbit's foot, or perhaps a lucky coin, can have is known only to those who buy and sell such over-priced rubbish, but there are many people who actually believe in the alleged attributes of such good-luck charms. The fact that bad luck often overtakes them does not seem to shake their faith in these useless artifacts. Many a corpse has been removed from a wrecked automobile having a Saint Cristopher statue glued to the dash. Saint Cristopher is, of course, the patron saint of travelers; he is supposed to guard them from harm, but he seems to fail on the job occasionally. Generally, gods seem to have a problem with quality control; specifically, there has been some talk lately of demoting Saint Cristopher to a position of lesser prominence in the public view. Perhaps he is giving superstition a bad name.

As a result of such sayings, society has been burdened with an incredible mish-mash of nonsense of the foregoing types. Much of it introduces an element of fear and irrationality into people's minds. Non-believers are, however, encouraged to study this material, not only for the fun of it, but also to learn how to avoid stepping on cracks to avoid breaking their mother's backs, staving off bad luck by not whistling or raising umbrellas indoors, or having their paths crossed by black cats, especially on Friday the 13th if about to put to sea in a ship. Triskaidecaphobia (fear of Friday the 13th) is still a problem for some people.

In former times, people believed that the earth was at the center of the universe, that it was flat, that it had four corners, and that the sun moved across our sky. Not very many people believe those things today, because science has given us more reliable data. In many parts of the world, people believed in spirits in the rocks, seas, and trees; most educated people do not now believe in such things. Yet in other parts of the world, some people still believe in spirits floating around in heaven, although many of them no longer believe that the Devil or the biblical version of Hell exists. It is to be hoped that these questionable and debatable beliefs will give way to a wider acceptance of a more rational understanding of nature in the future. What is more serious is that many people who do NOT really believe in spirits floating around, ACT as if they did, for entirely selfish reasons. And so the nonsense is perpetuated.

To paraphrase a comment attributed to Anatole France, a French novelist and humanitarian of the early 20th Century, even though a million people say a foolish thing, it is still a foolish thing. This piece of common sense applies to sayings of all sorts. Many popular proverbs and other so-called aphorisms do not stand up to even superficial examination or testing. Even though a billion people say that gods exist, it is not necessarily so; so far, there has been no proof, evidence, or even the vaguest indication of the existence of any god, and "goodness" knows, there have been enough of them created (and abandoned) by human beings over the centuries, with no observable benefit to the human condition. Most benefits have come about by the application of the scientific method and basic humanistic values to society.

For further reading the following titles are suggested:

1. *Proverbs from Around the World* [Secaucus 1992]
2. *The Good Luck Book* [Harris 1996]

CHAPTER 2.3

THEISTIC SYSTEMS

2.3.1 INTRODUCTION

The range of religious ideologies and beliefs held sacred by humans can be subdivided into two broad classifications: *theistic* and *non-theistic*. Under each, a number of subtitles can be subsumed. This review of the primary features of the major religions of the world will give the open-minded reader some idea of the nature of many of the many beliefs held sacred by so much of humankind.

This chapter of the book deals with *theistic* religions. The next chapter deals with *non-theistic* religions. More detailed study of all of these religions will reveal a number of similarities among and divergences between the various theologies and ideologies. Books or tapes for further study of any or all these philosophies and ideologies are to be found in any well-stocked public or college library, and readers are urged to make whatever further review of this subject matter their time and inclination permit.

For further reading, the following titles are suggested:

1. *Man's Religions* [Noss 1974]
2. *The Religious Heritage of America* [Shulman 1981]

2.3.2 ABORIGINAL BELIEFS

There is reliable archaeological proof that the indigenous people of North America lived on this continent for tens of thousands of years before the coming of Europeans to America. There is anthropological data to suggest that the native population may have been as high as ten million people, just prior to contacts with white explorers and settlers. These people were, of course, scattered all over the continent, and gathered together in many small groups, with an extraordinary diversity of languages, customs, and culture. They were incorrectly called *Indians* by the early European explorers, who thought they had arrived in India.

In general, there was some commonality of belief among all of these groups of aboriginal people. First, they all appear to have had some sort of religious concepts or explanations for apparently supernatural events, by which they attempted to understand natural phenomena to their own satisfaction. Second, virtually all groups viewed the land on which they lived as being sacred. Third, they generally felt that the spirits of their ancestors were still extant in the sounds of the winds, rains, rivers, and storms, and that specific parts of inanimate nature (such as rocks, caves, or mountains) and of animate nature (such as trees, animals, or birds) were imbued with supernatural powers by unseen gods, all contained somewhere between Heaven and Earth. Finally, the majority of these people appeared to have believed in some form of Great Spirit, guiding and overseeing all others.

There was (and still is) widespread belief in a former time of paradise, when all men, animals, birds, fishes, and insects lived and communicated together in harmony and under utopian conditions. There was (and still is) widespread faith in the abilities of magic men or shamans to heal or kill or otherwise intercede with the mystical forces of nature. These select men (seldom women) usually received their own alleged powers through miraculous visions involving sacred animals or birds. There was (and still is) widespread ability to adapt to or adopt new forms of religious practices, such as the concept of monotheism in contrast to polytheism, with old concepts being merged with new to produce hybrid styles.

These aboriginals did not feel that anything of their old religion was being lost by such adoption; the problem was that their Christian converters viewed them as heathens until all vestiges of the old religious thinking had been eradicated. The oppression and other excesses practiced by the Christian newcomers increased in both magnitude and ferocity, to the point that a proportion of the indigenous population in the American Southwest actually rebelled against the Catholic Spaniards in 1680, destroying virtually all Christian priests, churches, symbols, and rituals throughout the region. By a somewhat ironic coincidence, the leader of the rebellion against these Catholic incursions was a shaman named Pope.

One thing that puzzled the aboriginals about the new European religion was the fact that, although it admitted of only one God, there seemed to be constant argument and many views as to how that one was to be worshipped. In their own religions, the aboriginals had many gods, but they never argued about how to worship them. Another thing that they found difficult to accept was that the word of this one God was contained in the Bible, and that this book was only available to the Europeans. The aboriginals argued that if this God was really as good, and loving, and powerful as was claimed by the Europeans, why had the Indians not also been favored with a Bible of their own, or a least a copy of the European one. One prominent aboriginal leader, Chief Dan George, is quoted as saying: "Before the white man came, they had the Bibles and we had the land. Now, we have the Bibles and they have the land."

A third and perhaps more profound puzzle to the aboriginals was the white man's view of land as a commodity to be bought, sold, or traded. To the American Indian, land was part of their creation and their heritage; the land was there to be used to advantage by and for all people and animals alike, but they did not consider that it belonged to them in the sense that it was capable of private possession. This view was eloquently expressed in a letter allegedly written by Chief Seattle of Washington to President Franklin Pierce in 1855, in which he apparently drew a clear distinction between the social, spiritual, and economic values that the Eastern Whites and Western Indians attached to the land. In Seattle's opinion, the Whites regarded the land as a commodity to be conquered, plundered, used, and then abandoned. In contrast, the aboriginals revered the land of their ancestors and their birth, and their religions were closely tied to specific tracts of land. If the white man could not understand the relationship of so-called Indians to their land, how could he understand the relationships of the aboriginals to their religions, even if he made the effort? Although the exact wording of the Seattle letter has been severely edited and modified over the years (some now say that perhaps he did not say what he was supposed to have said), the ideas contained in the original still have some currency.

Notwithstanding that there appears to be a genuine human need to hold beliefs about things not yet understood, and acknowledging the fact that such beliefs appear to be very widespread as evidenced in the native populations of North America before the coming of the Europeans, the nature and magnitude of such beliefs do not in themselves prove or indicate that gods, spirits, or any other supernatural authorities exist, no matter how sincere the belief. Furthermore, as many missionaries have found to their dismay, native populations often hold notions which make the teaching of divergent religious values impossible, and in some cases downright dangerous to all concerned. Trobriand Island is a case in point, where the indigenous people had no concept of fatherhood as they did not understand the biological significance of sexual intercourse. They therefore could not comprehend the significance of having a god alleged to be The Father, when they placed greater value in brothers and uncles. There is also evidence that some aboriginals are abandoning

Christian teachings and returning to indigenous beliefs which are equally compelling in their view.

For further reading, the following title is suggested:
1. *Native American Testimony* [Nabokov 1978]

2.3.3 BAHA'I

The Baha'i religion is of relatively recent origin, having been founded towards the end of the 19th century CE by a man called Mirza Hoseyn Ali Nuri in what was then called Persia. Nuri sought to bring about the fulfilment of an earlier prophecy regarding a so-called "gateway to God, called "The Bab." In 1850, Nuri became leader of one of several Babi factions, adopting the name Baha'u'llah. Shortly thereafter, the government of the day did not look with favor on this new religion, persecuting (indeed killing) its followers and imprisoning its leaders. Nuri remained a prisoner in various locations until his death in 1892.

The Babi faith, established in 1844, predicted the arrival of a messiah-like figure, not unlike other religions. In 1863, Baha'u'llah took it upon himself to be that figure, the latest in a long line of historical and legendry characters to deliver what they considered to be divine revelations. His followers were called thereafter Baha'is, and considered themselves to be part of this new religion. In later years, Bahaullah's son, Abd ol-Baha, after his own release from prison in 1908 as a result of the collapse of the Ottoman Empire, traveled to Europe and America to spread the faith.

Some of the principles of Baha'i teachings, in addition to showing reverence towards the Bab, include the desire to abolish racial and social prejudice, the achievement of gender equality, universal education, adoption of a universal secondary language (like Esperanto) and universal government (like the U.N.). One distinct difference between Baha'i and other religions is that there is neither a priest class nor a prescribed ritual for services. Headquarters for the faith is located in Haifa, in Israel. The administrative center for adherents in North America is now located in Illinois, with about 800 local assemblies scattered throughout all 50 states as well as Canada.

For further reading, the following titles are suggested:

1. *Resurrection and Renwal - The Babi* [Amanat 1989]
2. *The Reality of Man* [Baha'u'llah 1969]

2.3.4 CHRISTIANITY

Christianity is essentially a monotheistic religion centered about the personage of a man called Jesus Christ who, according to some biblical records, believed he was the Son of God. Problems immediately arise. First, the word *Jesus* is a Greek derivation of the Hebrew word *Joshua* which means *savior*. Secondly, the word *Christ* means *anointed* (from the Greek word *chrism*); its Hebrew form is the origin of the modern word *messiah*. Anointing allegedly imbues the person so recognized with magical or mystical qualities. So what at first glance appears to be a *name* (like John Doe) is in reality more like a *title* (like appointed preacher). There is debate about the true given or family names of the person now called Jesus Christ. And to further confuse the issue, the Aramaic equivalent of the name Jesus was very popular in the Middle East a couple of thousand years ago. Thirdly, some argue that no such individual as Christ ever actually lived, and that the person really a composite of several characteristics of actual people having similar background and ideas. Leaving that controversy aside for the moment, at the time Christ allegedly lived, the countryside in that part of the world was full of wandering mystics and mendicants, proselytizing all sorts of salvation. For the present purpose, the assumption will be made that there was in fact such an individual, and that the circumstances attributed to his being did in fact occur at some time.

The general Christian belief is that this present earthly life is merely temporary, a probationary or test period in which one gets the chance to prove oneself as being worthy of entry into God's Kingdom in Heaven. If you pass, then you are in; if you fail, then your soul is relegated to Hell. By this logic, one might think that the ideal life would therefore be infinitesimally short (or at least somewhere between conception and birth), so that one could enter heaven with the least accumulation of earthly debits. However, Christians, in common with all other forms of life, seem to wish to cling to life for the very longest period. Self-preservation seems to be an intrinsic part of natural life, regardless of belief. With respect to the concept of God's Kingdom, it is also difficult for non-believers to grasp why political leaders of democratic or republican states would wish to embrace any religion having the stated objective of establishing a kingdom of any type on earth, but such are the enigmas of religion.

A distinguishing feature between Christianity and other monotheistic religions is the concept of the Trinity. This concept requires a view of God as existing in three forms: Father, Son, and Holy Spirit, collectively though peculiarly called the Godhead. Each form is equal to the others and is interchangable with them, although commonly God is considered to be the Father, Christ is the Son, and the Holy Spirit is the Church. Another fundamental concept is the Eucharist, a simple meal of unleavened bread and red wine, which is symbolic of Christ's last supper during which he was betrayed by one of his followers, a man named Judas Iscariot. The bread represents the body of Christ and the wine his blood. Although presumed to be merely symbolic by most adherents to Christianty, some scholars see overtones of cannibalism in these rites of (even symbolically) eating and drinking products representative of a human body.

A powerful concept in Christianity is the possibility believed by adherents that Christ did in fact rise from the dead, thereby overcoming the most fearful of all of humankind's panoply of fears, that death is the end of life. The argument is that if Christ could escape death by belief in God, then so could anyone else who held that opinion. Oddly, this concept appears to conflict with a passage in the Old Testament, where (at Ecclesiastes 9:5) it says:"For the living know they will die, but the dead know nothing, and they have no more reward." Another feature of Christianity is adherence to the Church; it is essentially a communal kind of religion, with acceptance of the offical church dogma by adherents being of prime importance. The two main events of the Christian year are the celebration of the birth of Christ, nominally placed in December to coincide with one pagan holiday, and of his alleged death at Easter, for which the precise timing varies according to the phases of the moon, because Easter is named after another pagan holiday, honoring a goddess having a similar name.

For further reading, the following titles are suggested:

1. *The Historical Evidence for Jesus* [Wells 1982]
2. *The Jesus Puzzle* [Doherty 1999]
3. *Christianity—the Debit Account* [Knight 1975]

It is understandably impossible to satisfactorily condense the two thousand years of turbulent, inaccurate, biased, and often violent history of Christianity into a few paragraphs. However, the following synopsis, admittedly rudimentary, may give the uninformed reader some feeling or flavor of some of the distinguishing features of this wide-spread religion, in addition to the foregoing details. Christianity is essentially divided into two doxies or schools: Eastern and Western. Eastern Orthodox Christianity still hews very closely to the original ideals contained in both the old and new Testaments, as its name suggests. As the Eastern subdivision of Catholicism has little influence in North America, it will not be further discussed here. The Western Branch is probably more familiar to most readers. It is can be examined under the following two sub-titles.

1. Catholicism

Catholicism consists of two main rites or subdivisions based on traditional practices: Roman and Byzantine. The Roman Rite has its origins in Rome in Italy; the Byzantine Rite has its origins in Istanbul (formerly Byzantium), Turkey. Within these major rites, there are many minor rites, such as the Alexandrian, the Armenian, and the Antiochan Rites, each named for a city or region. Each minor Rite has a number of subdivisions or churches, such as the Coptic and Ethiopian Churches within the Alexandrian Rite, or the Greek Orthodox Church within the Antiochan Rite. As can be extrapolated from this brief introduction, it is a very complex structure, further complicated by the fact that some sectors, such as the Ukrainian Orthodox Church, still bases its religious celebrations on the old Gregorian calendar, while other use the more modern Julian calendar. This results in many identical occasions such as Easter and Christmas being celebrated by different Catholic groups at different times of the year in any one region. From time to time, Councils of high Church officials have been convened to address specific issues. One such was the Council of Nicaea, called in 325 CE to settle controversy regarding the Trinity. Much later, the Council of Trent, called in 1564 CE, initiated a general organizational reform and re-defined essential dogmas which were in effect for the next 400 years, to mention two significant examples.

Roman Catholicism is not unlike the traditional Eastern Orthodoxies. This division of Christianity claims its superiority over the others by reason of its alleged direct descendency from one of Christ's original followers, St. Peter, reputed to be buried in Rome, Italy. The Pope, who is the leader of the Roman Catholic Church, claims his authority directly, though not genetically, through this descendency. The main church of the Vatican in Rome is called St. Peters and is located over what Catholics believe to be the actual tomb of St. Peter. This church is based on a world-wide organization of dioceses, each of which is governed by a bishop. The bishops rule over the clergy, consisting of both religious and lay personnel; the bishops in turn report to arch-bishops, who report to cardinals, who report to the Pope through a system of councils.

The Roman Catholic Church takes a fairly literal view of the bible and lays claim to catholicism (or universalism) of its practices. It claims the right to teach morality based on its own interpretation of its own Christian dogma, and it sees its own church as being imbued with the so-called Holy Spirit (exactly like but in opposition to the Shintoists in Japan). The religion involves worship of Mary, the Mother of Jesus, veneration of saints, observance of masses (or ceremonies) of different sorts, participation in a number of ritual sacraments such as communion, taking of holy orders, baptism of adherents, and giving last rites to the dying, among other mystical, liturgical, and financially profitable practices. A strict and conservative line is offically drawn by the Church in most aspects of family life, such as marriage, births and deaths, and all matters concerning sex including abortion. Such limitations are not always fully observed by many who claim to be members of the Church, and many others cannot be supported by biblical reference. Propaganda, censorship, and political interference on a world-wide scale are features of modern Roman Catholicism.

2. Protestantism

As with Catholicism, it is impossible to fully explain the Protestant Movement in a few paragraphs. Broadly speaking, it was a revolt or protest against the self-ordained authority of the established Roman Catholic Church and the excesses and corruption of its officials. It started at the beginning of the 16th century CE with reformation within the Church, a process which lasted for about a century, but it ended as a separate movement.

In Europe, the theologians Martin Luther (1483-1546) and later, John Calvin (1509-1564) primarily focused the criticism, the object of which was to give the individual person more freedom and flexible responsibility for his or her own interpretation of the Bible scriptures and subsequent salvation. Within a short period, these relatively liberal religious views became enormously popular with all levels of society. Largely for personal and political ends, Henry VIII of England, who was by no means a liberal, passed the Act of Supremacy before the middle of the same century, rejecting papal control of religion in that country.

Other forces, such as Puritanism (advocating simpler religious rituals) and Evangelicalism (advocating personal conversions), were also becoming influencial around that period, and more so subsequently. In North America at the time of this writing (2003), Protestants outnumber Catholics 3 to 2. However, unlike Roman Catholicism which is relatively rigid and monolithic, Protestantism is characterized by diversity, communality, innovation, and a sort of quasi-liberalism. Some of the major branches of Protestantism include (in alphabetical order) Anglicans, Baptists, Episcopalians, Methodists, Presbyterians, a small number of large United Churches, and a much larger number of smaller separate orders, literally too numerous to mention by name here. Some of these branches, such as the United Methodists, have memberships approaching 10 million people, while others, being little better than esoteric cults, claim membership not exceeding two hundred people.

One particular branch of Protestantism which also grew out of the Reformation, but in reaction against Calvinism, is Unitarianism, whose adherents deny the concept of the Holy Trinity common to most Christian sects. Unitarians believe that a single God can be implied (though not demonstrated) by logic and reason, and they view the biblical Christ simply as a teacher of moral values, based on God's so-called laws. They also doubt the possibility of the miracles described in scriptures. Some Unitarians believe in an afterlife, contingent on this present life, while others with equal standing and sincerity do not hold such beliefs. Unitarians stress fellowship and commonality of ideas, freely discussed and mutually accepted. Many members of Unitarian Churches have become humanists or free-thinkers, while still finding some acceptance by members of that branch of religion. Others have left that church because of its insistence on promoting a metaphysical spiritual dimension to human life, for which there is no discernable scientific foundation.

For further reading, the following titles are suggested:

1: *Catholicism* [Brantl 1962]
2. *Protestantism* [Dunstan 1962]

2.3.5 HINDUISM

This word has its origin in the Indus River Region of India around the 5th century BCE. The religion which it designates predates the use of the word by about 1000 years. Because of its enormous longevity, and its capacity to absorb new influences, modern Hinduism is an extremely complex religion, deeply interwoven into the daily life of about 600 million people.

Hindus believe in a single source of divine power, but that source has multiple theistic forms. Because it is a polytheistic religion, Hindus theoretically have some choice as to the specific god they select for worship, although the choice is restricted to some extent by family and caste origins. Consequently they generally worship either the god Shiva, who has warlike (and phallic) attributes; the god Vishnu, the creator who created the creator Brahma; or the goddess Devi, considered by some of those who believe in her to be the original prime mover in control of all other creative or destructive gods. Some Hindus regard Devi as merely the wife of a number of the other gods. In some legends, Devi demonstrates her power in a number of violent and bloody ways.

In addition to these three primary titles, there are of course many secondary or lesser gods which Hindus may choose to worship. One such example is Krishna, considered by many to be a reincarnation of Vishnu, and about whom many legendary tales and myths abound. Similarly, Rama is another popular god, also viewed by some as being another reincarnation of Vishnu.

Hindu scripture is contained is what are known as the Vedas and the Smriti. The Vedas, a document with four parts, were developed over a period of about 500 years, and is considered by Hindus as revealed infallible knowledge. The Rig-veda consists of hymns to an assortment of gods; the Yajur-veda deals with ritual sacrifice; the Sama-veda contains more hymns; and the Atharva-veda describes some magical spells. In addition to the Vedas, two other texts are of importance to Hindus: the Brahmanas, dealing with priestly rituals; and the Upanishads, dealing with questions about everyday existence and the nature of the universe. For example, one chapter of the Upanishads, called the Bhagavad-Gita (which is credited to Krishna), outlines several routes to religious fulfillment, through knowledge, action, and devotion on the part of the individual Hindu. The Smriti, which is more commonly studied by ordinary Hindus than the Vedas, is of much later date (around 300 to 0 BCE), and primarily includes two heroic family stories or fables, several dozen cautionary tales of secondary importance, and a number of chapters on sacred laws.

With respect to supernatural beliefs, it might be said that Hinduism is more concerned with how people behave than with what they believe. In general, Hindus traditionally believe that the universe is contained within a sphere, layered like an onion, with India in the middle. This can be compared to astrologers, who place earth at the center of the cosmos, or Chinese concepts which place China at the center of the universe; the translation of the Chinese characters for the word "China" is the "Central Kingdom." With respect to existential opinion, Hindus believe that both time and life are cyclic, and that the soul, being separable from the body, appears in successive reincarnations, each modified by the accumulation of quality of life (or karma) of all the previous embodiments. In particular, the majority of Hindus follow a path of renunciation of earthly rewards as outlined in the Upanishads, while a minority follow a more worldly path according to guidelines contained in the Vedas.

Hindus are reminded of their faith by a variety of dietary laws, rites of passage, requirements to show reverence for animals in general and sacred cows in particular, and by remnants of a rather rigid class system, perpetuated by strict control of marriage alliances. They also consider the river Ganges to be holy, especially around Varansi, formerly known as Benares. Despite its seriously polluted condition, many Hindus still drink and bathe in this river for religious reasons. For centuries, they were allocated into their relative positions in society by an ancient and powerful caste system, which cast each person into a lifelong and inescapable situation. This system placed the *brahmans* or preachers at the top, followed in succession by the *kshatrya* or warrior class, the *vaisha* or merchant class, the *shudras* or servant class, and the *harijan* or untouchable class at the bottom. It was argued that, if each person knew his or her position, they would not be troubled with feelings of ambition to improve their lot, but rather learn how to live in the role in which life had cast them. Although it still prevails to some extent, and more so in rural than in urban areas, it is not clear how this system can still be justified, having regard to the International Declaration of Human Rights. In fact, the Constitution of India as a modern secular state expressly forbids discrimination on the basis of caste.

As a footnote, the modern Hare Krishna movement can be viewed as an offshoot of Hinduism proper. Devotees of this particular order are encumbered with over 60 rules governing thoughts and actions, arising out of the Vedic Scriptures. Renunciation of all worldly goods and pleasures is a key feature of their commitment to the order. Collecting financial donations to sustain their activities is also high on their list of priorities. Sikhism is also related to Hinduism, but is separately described in Section 2.3.9 later.

For further reading, the following titles are suggested:

1. *Arrow of the Blue Skinned God* [Blank 1993]
2. *Hinduism* [Renou 1962]

2.3.6 ISLAM

Islam originated around the 6th century CE in a part of the world formerly called Persia, and now covering parts of Iran, Iraq, Turkey, and other countries in the Middle East. It is strictly a monotheistic religion, based on the concept of a single all-powerful indivisible supreme being, called Allah. Although its general beginnings are to be found in Judaic roots, it is specifically founded on the basic teachings of a prophet called Muhammad (also spelled Mohammad, Muhammed, and Mohammed), who asserted at age 40 that Allah (i.e. God) spoke to him through Gabriel, an angel of revelation. Muhammad was an Arab merchant, who had commercial contacts with both Christians and Jews in that time and place.

The revelations of Allah to Muhammad are presented in the Koran, a book consisting of 114 chapters. Practitioners of Islam are called Muslims, and they believe the Koran to be infallible, just as other religions believe their holy books to be infallible. They also believe that their religion is the original one (despite the historical fact of predecessors) and that it is the religion of the natural universe, because according to them nature obeys God's laws. They say that this is self-evident in the order which they see in the universe (see Section 2.2.6.3 for further discussion of order in the universe). They believe that mankind's primary purpose is to serve Allah or God, and that this is achieved by serving mankind properly, in a moral and charitable manner. They also believe that God has sent or has permitted a number of entirely human prophets to live among men and women on earth, to give them guidance in moral and spiritual matters. Muslims also subscribe to the belief in a final day of judgment for all people, and indeed, for all nations as well, with the appropriate rewards and punishments common to most other religions: heaven for some, mostly Muslims, and hell for the rest.

Islam has a number of reminders to keep its ideals in front of its adherents. The word itself means submission to God. Prayer, fasting, dietary laws, a strict moral code, and a special dress code are some elements intended for daily practice, whereas a public acknowledgment of faith and a pilgrimage to Mecca, located in what is now Saudi Arabia, is expected to be made at least once in the lifetime of each Muslim. Certain things are strictly off-limits for Muslims, such as the consumption of pig-meat or alcohol in any form. Men are required to carry a small dagger, for personal protection and for use in certain religious rites. Among themselves, Muslims practice moderation in most things, but their attitude to those outside their religion is often one of bigotry, occasionally erupting into barbaric violence, euphemistically called Jihads or "Holy Wars." These are ostensibly wars to defend the Muslim faith, but there are parts of the Koran which are referred to as the "sword verses" which some of the more fanatical adherents, such as the recently discredited Taliban in Afghanistan, use to justify violent aggression against those with whom they disagree.

The Muslim calendar dates from the time Muhammad left Mecca for Medina, where he gathered strength and resources to spread his new religion over much of the then-known world by force. Islamic Law is derived from the Koran and the Sunna, both being tempered by individual judgement and community standards. The original composite body of Islam is split into two main (and competing) branches: Sunnites and Shiites, each with a separate territorial influence. For example, the Shiites are predominent in modern Iran. The modern practice of Islamic Law (enforced by a politically powerful clergy) is a mixture of secular and religious principles, and embraces aspects of practice ranging all the way from rationalism to mysticism. Sufism is an offshoot of Islam, and emphasizes direct union of the individual soul with Allah. It is practiced by a small group of Islamic mystics, who believe that *theirs* is the one and only true religion. This sect utilizes a variety of bodily functions to experience unity with their God, one of which involves lengthy twirling of the entire physical body by devotees; they are popularly known as the "Whirling Dervishes."

For further reading, the following titles are suggested:

1. *Islam* [Williams 1962]
2. *From Islam to Secular Humanism* [Sohail 2001]

2.3.7 JUDAISM

Judaism is one of the world's oldest continuous religions; its adherents are called Jews. It was allegedly initiated by a man called Abraham, whose descendants, the Hebrews, settled for some centuries in what is now called Egypt, until they were apparently freed from slavery by Moses, in events alluded to in Exodus in the Bible. This event involved a hasty crossing of the Red Sea and is still recalled in a Jewish celebration called the *Passover*. Later, these people developed into a number of tribes in Canaan at the eastern end of the Mediterranean Sea. Three kings (Saul, David, and Solomon) developed a theocratic state, later divided by civil war into Israel and Judah.

Judaism is as much a way of life and a tradition as it is a religion. Although not monolithic, because of the large number of prophets, it is monotheistic, in that Jews believe that there is one god who created the universe, provides for it, and governs over it. The basic Jewish view is that "God is One" in contrast to the "Trinity" of the Christian faith. Religious Jews so revere their god that they do not pronounce his (or its) name. While Jews are not expected to know all the attributes of their god, they should be aware of his apparently strong requirement for sound moral behavior and charitable actions among adherents. Jews further believe that their god actually revealed to their ancestors his divine will and purpose for humanity, in the form of commandments by which humans should conduct themselves. Although the commandments were allegedly inscribed in tablets of stone, their location, if they still exist, is unknown today. The Jews believe that their god's intelligence gives purpose to every event in the universe and therefore a cosmological meaning to every activity in life.

A fundamental tenet of Judaism is the belief that one God exists and that there is a specific covenant or contract between that God and the Jews, creating a sort of corporate priesthood, in which they agreed to recognize that he is the first and final lawmaker, in exchange for which God should view them in a special light or favor, as the "chosen" people. In this manner, they can see a direct relationship between behavior and destiny. If they obey God's laws, they will reap the benefits. They believe in an afterlife, and in the application of God's justice in that next life, by which virtue in this life will be rewarded, and sin punished.

Jews also believed (and some still do believe) that a savior or messiah was going to come at some unspecified time in the future, to restore them to some former position of power and security. This belief helps one to understand the apparent ready acceptance by part of the population in that time and place of the person claiming to be Jesus Christ; such a claim would be viewed with suspicion today.

Although Judaism has a messianic tradition, Jews do not accept that Jesus Christ was *the* messiah, as Christians claim, apparently because they feel that he did not fulfil any messianic prediction. It is more difficult to understand why God, if such exists, should have chosen such a small group as the Jews to receive his special benefits, when there were, at that same time, many other much larger and more politically powerful clans or races on which such munificence could have been bestowed. It could be that these other groups were unknown to the early Jews, and therefore were not included in their legends and history.

Judaism is filled with many reminders of the faith, in the form of special rituals, dress and head coverings, prayers, strict dietary laws, biblical studies, circumcision of male babies, requirements for marriage, family relationships, festivals and holy days scheduled throughout the year, and urging to assist fellow Jews who may be in need of help. The religious authorities will accept converts into the order, although there seems to be no great trend in this connection. Their most holy book is called the Torah, which means approximately "instructions," as revealed in the first five books (the Pentateuch) of the Old Testament portion of the modern Bible. All Jews are encouraged to study the Torah, to understand how it relates to their way of life and vice versa. There were originally over 600 commandments allegedly given to Moses by God (for some obscure reason numbered by the sum of the days of the year and the bones of the body) but these have been edited down to about a few dozen in modern times. There are two main streams in modern Judaism, namely those who believe in *naturalism* where the term God represents worthy human ideals without any notion of the Jews being a "chosen" people, and *revelation* where the existence of the traditional fearful God of the Bible is uppermost, and his/her/its existence therefore does not have to be proven. In Judaism, the world is not God; God is *in* the world. Many of the better known leaders of Jewry (such as Saadia in the 8th century and Maimonides in the 11th century CE) have been regarded as serious philosophers by some and by others as religious mystics.

The strict dietary laws, which may seem foreign to non Jews, have primarily three objectives: to promote healthy eating and cooking habits, to curb natural appetites towards over-eating and drinking, and to set Jews apart from other denominations. Of the many historical or legendary events which Jews celebrate, some of the better known include *Passover* mentioned earlier, *Rosh Hashanah* or New Year, and *Yom Kippur* or the Day of Atonement, involving fasting and prayers. Jewish philosophy asserts that although humans have free will and are therefore responsible for their actions, their omnipotent God will ultimately judge each human being. Jewish tradition also has its own answers to the conundrums of evil, suffering, life after death, the value of prayer, and many of the other religious problems which beset believers of every denomination.

The Jews as a people have suffered (and are indeed still suffering) greatly at the hands of others throughout their lengthy history, which stretches from biblical references to Moses through to the destruction of their First Temple in 589 BCE and their Second Temple in 70 CE by the Romans, and culminating in the establishment of the State of Israel by the United Nations General Assembly in the 20th century CE. Given a lengthy experience of *diaspora*, or the scattering of Jewish populations throughout the world, that establishment was an event of profound religious and political significance to all Jews, as well as to other middle eastern tribes and nations who also have long-standing claims to the same territories.

For further reading, the following titles are suggested:

1. *Judaism* [Hertzberg 1962]
2. *Eight Questions about Judaism* [Prager 1975]

2.3.8 SHINTOISM

This religion is native to Japan and essentially restricted to the Japanese people, at home and abroad. The word *Shinto* literally means the Way of the Gods. The origins of the religion are largely mythical, in that those who follow Shinto believe that the entire world was once peopled by gods at every level and in every quarter, and that god-like spirits were extant in every part of nature. Part of the myth involves the mistaken belief that the Japanese people have always occupied the Japanese Islands from the beginning of creation; this is simply not true, as the origins of the people appear to be found largely elsewhere in Asia and the Pacific Islands. The original myths, continued in rituals of nature and ancestor worship, were formalized to create the Shinto religion around 600 CE, when elements of Chinese culture, such as Buddhism and Confucianism, began to pervade Japanese culture at a significant rate.

With the adoption by Japan of the Chinese system for writing, the history of Japan in general and Shinto myths in particular began to be expressed in written form. In the 8th century CE, a major book about Shinto origins called the Kogo-shui was produced, followed in the 10th century by another one about Shinto traditions called the Engi-shiki, containing formal prayers and outlines for rites. Over many years, these rituals were raised to a highly refined level by the Japanese Court, as its members believed that they were the direct descendants of the original Shinto gods.

Court practices were later disseminated to the populace, resulting in essentially two modifed forms of Shinto being widely practiced throughout the country by the 12th century CE. One form involved individual sectarian rituals in the home; the other involved state or community rituals in public; both forms involved the use of shrines to house religious relics and regalia. This situation was further complicated by the clearer separation of worship of original Shinto deities and Buddhist characters up to the 14th century.

The succeeding 300 years saw a decline of interest in Shinto, owing to pressures from other religions, new and old. It was revived by intellectuals in a fairly pure form in the 18th century, and with state support and some attempts at rationalization of its mythical origins (particularly those dealing with ancestor worship), continued to be of importance right up to the end of the Second World War, at which time the western concept of separation of church and state was imposed on Japan by order of General Douglas MacArthur, who was in charge of the American Occupation Authority in 1946. State Shintoism was then abandoned, the Bureau of Religion closed, and the Emperor stripped of his unprovable claim to being directly descended from the gods. Sectarian Shintoism continued in more or less unadulterated form through the private practices of five main groups: the traditional, the Confucian, the faith healing, the purification, and the mountain worship sects. Approximately 80,000 public Shinto shrines throughout Japan are now maintained by voluntary public subscriptions supervised by a number of Shrine Associations; of these, one of the most important is the Grand Imperial Shrine at Ise, 350 km south of Tokyo.

Shinto ritual involves precise construction of the shrines, placement within each shrine of some revered object to represent embodiment of the supernatural powers or spirits, stylized approaches to the shrines made by priests, hand clapping to attract the attention of the gods, presentation of offerings of food and clothing to the gods, readings of norito (or prayers) from the sacred books, the giving of thanks to ancestors for guidance, and appropriate reverent physical withdrawal at the end of the ceremonies. Shinto practice is very much involved with the observations of festivals of many sorts, to mark the passage of the seasons through each year and of persons through their life-time journeys.

For further reading, the following title is suggested:

1. *Shinto* [Hartz 1997]

2.3.9 SIKHISM

Sikhism might be considered to be an extreme monotheistic form of polytheistic Hinduism (described in Section 2.3.5), mostly practiced by people in the northwest Indian region of the Punjab, but also in some urban centers in North America. Although its followers assert the existence of a single true and personal god, it adopts some of the elements of Hinduism, such as reincarnation and the effect of one's present life on future lives, while rejecting others, such as the priesthood and the caste system.

The religion was founded by a man called Guru (or Teacher) Nanak about 500 years ago. He was the first of a series of Sikh Prophets, the fourth of which (Ram Da) founded the Holy Sikh Golden Temple at Amritsar. The fifth (Arjun) is recorded as the developer of the Sikh holy book, called the *Adi Granth*, at the start of the 17th century CE. The tenth and last Guru, Govind Singh who lived toward the end of the 17th century, is credited with re-introducing aspects of the caste system, as well as introducing the turban as a required form of head-dress for Sikh males, who do not cut their hair. These turbans are usually made of light cotton material, and can be colored to suit the preferences of the wearer. Around the beginning of the 18th century, Sikhism became a powerful military as well as a religious force in northern Indian affairs. Some have described it as a military theocracy. For about a century, the Sikhs prospered under British rule and developed a world renowned reputation as soldiers, up until 1947, when the Punjab was divided between Pakistan and India. It was later reinstated in 1966, although border disputes continue to this day.

During a form of baptism, Sikh males add the name Singh (or Lion) to their given name, and thereafter resolve to observe what are called the 5 Ks: they do not cut their body hair (*kes*) which is why they wear head turbans as mentioned above; they wear special undershorts (*kacch*) for chastity; they carry a special comb (*khanga*) and a dagger (*khanda*); and they wear a charm bracelet (*kara*). As with Hinduism, Sikhism is very much bound up with politics and the daily lives of the people in the regions where it predominates. It advocates belief in a personal god and requires adherents to seriously contemplate the name of that god on a regular daily basis.

For further reading, the following title is suggested:

1. *The Study of Sikhism* [McLeod 1984]

2.3.10 ZOROASTRIANISM

This religion, like many others, is of minor significance to western minds. It is included in this compilation primarily for two reasons: it has some characteristics which it shares or contrasts with other religions, and to omit it would render the list substantially incomplete. The religion was invented around the 6th century BCE by a man called Zarathustra (modernized to *Zoroaster*) in what was then known as Persia, and now called Iran.

Zarathustra was about 30 years old when he crystalized his thoughts about religion, later incorporated into a book of psalms, called the Gathas. His personal story is remarkably similar to that of Moses of biblical fame, in that he had a vision, allegedly met his god in the clouds, received some directions from this god, and was thus convinced that he had been given insight into the one true religion. One might compare his development with a number of other mystics who appeared on the scene about the same time in history and at a similar point in their own lives: Buddha, Jina, Confucius, and later, Christ, among others.

In essence, Zoroastrianism is a monotheistic religion, but it shows traces of polytheistic paganism. The primary god of Zoroaster was named Ahura Mazda. A feature of this religion involves ethical dualism, which takes place in the human heart and involves two main spirits: Spenta Mainyu (the good spirit) representing truth, health, power and so on, and Angra Mainyu (the bad spirit) representing falsehood, evil, doubt, and so on.

Zoroastrianism also introduces or at least fosters the concept of free will, as it asserts that all humans can and must choose one or other spirit to guide them from time to time as they pass through life, and will be judged on their choice, leading to heaven for some and hell for the rest. Like many lesser religions, Zoroastrianism is beset by all sorts of mythology and legend, much of it in the form of imaginative embellishment of possible history. The religion also has a number of ceremonies associated with it, such as the preservation of holy fires and the ritual disposal of corpses. Zoroastrians do not bury their dead: they believe that the soul is taken to a narrow bridge where eternal judgement is passed on the quality of the life just concluded. They leave the physical corpses of deceased persons in open stone towers to be stripped of flesh by vultures. Although most modern Zoroastrians live in Iran, many live in India, where they are known as the Parsis, literally those from Persia.

For further reading, the following title is suggested:

1. *Zoroastrianism—an Introduction* [Clark 1998]

CHAPTER 2.4

NON-THEISTIC SYSTEMS

2.4.1 INTRODUCTION

In the previous chapter, all the religions described involve belief in one or more supernatural gods, each allegedly endowed with more or less mystical powers of one sort or another. It might be observed that every one of these religions was started by human beings, either in person or alleged through myth. There is no religion anywhere in the world that was started by a god, and for obvious reasons.

In this chapter, a number of additional religions are mentioned, none of which involve gods or deities. These non-theistic religions involve reverence for the ideals embodied in the thinking of some person of historical note, or they adopt certain ways of perceiving life and its opportunities and set-backs without reference to supernatural powers. However, they do still involve some sort of practices, creeds or sets of beliefs, which makes them fall under the rubric of religion.

For further reading, the following titles are suggested:

1. *Man's Religions* [Noss 1974]
2. *History of Religion* [Tokarov 1989]

2.4.2 BUDDHISM

The word *buddha* means "enlightened one." The first enlightened one was a man named Siddharta Gautama who apparently lived in the Nepal region of India about 500 years BCE. This makes him a contemporary of Confucious in China. Gautama was the son of a rich prince, who desired that he marry and become a warrior; Gautama had other ideas, and so left home to seek enlightenment. During his impoverished travels, he came to realize that suffering was a common feature of human life, and that in meditation a way might be found to arrive at truth. When he was about 30 years of age, and after considerable study, reflection, and subsequent rejection of several religions including Hinduism, he experienced what he considered to be enlightenment while meditating in the shade of a small tree one afternoon. Over a period of about 5 years, he gathered together a few followers who referred to him as Gautama Buddha or more simply—The Buddha. He established some small monasteries along the Ganges River, returned to visit his family, and then embarked on his life's work of spreading his particular brand of salvation (or soteriology) until his death at about age 80.

Like so many other major religious figures, such as Christ and Confucious, Gautama Buddha did not write down any of his own thoughts on his enlightenment. This task was left to his subsequent students, many of whom were idealists and who, like their Christian counterparts, might not have recorded thoughts and events with the accuracy of a scientist or historian. Also, the majority of these scribes and disciples were not contemporaries of Gautama. However, a clear picture of the central Buddhist philosophy emerges from the work of these followers. Gautama's enlightenment involved realization of four related truths: life consists of suffering; suffering is caused by ignorance; ignorance can be overcome; the method to overcome ignorance is to correctly follow a path having eight correct elements. The elements comprise correct action, contemplation, effort, intention, livelihood, opinion, speech, and thought.

Buddhists regard one's existence or being as a constantly changing conglomerate of one's physical body, plus perceptions, emotions, and consciousness, as well as a unique element called karma, which is an amalgam of actions and their consequences. Karma is something like the Christian concept of the soul of a person; to use a biblical phrase: as ye sow, so shall ye reap. Karma is also alleged to be a determinant of species and other aspects of good or bad fortune both in this life and in lives to come. One may return (through reincarnation) as a person, an animal, a god, or whatever, depending on the accumulation of karma over the generations. Buddhism places little importance on gods and accompanying prayers and sacrifices; it asserts that salvation or buddha is only of value to humans, and the objective of Buddhists is to achieve nirvana or a state of bliss in which the normal pleasures and pains of flesh and brain are overcome. Theoretically, nirvana may be achieved in one lifetime, but most Buddhists think that it will take several lifetimes to achieve proper "emptiness." One would be indeed lucky to be living the life in which it occurred.

Buddhism promotes kindness and compassion, and demotes lust and hatred. The religion is arranged into two major subdivisions: *Mahayana* and *Hinayana*, meaning the Great Vehicle and the Lesser Vehicle respectively. In Mahayana, the Buddha is considered to be (and is worshipped as being) God-like—transcendent, immanent, and so on, although Gautama Buddha did not consider himself to be a god. In this school of thought, it is possible for a person to become adhisattva, that is, one who has achieved enlightenment but voluntarily forgoes nirvana in order to help less enlightened beings. In Hinayana (also called Theravada or the Way of the Elders), the Buddha is considered to be no more than a perfectly enlightended human being, a perfect teacher of perfect knowledge and wisdom.

Buddhist scripture is contained in three major books, called the Tri-Pitaka. One (the *Sutra*) deals with dialogues between Buddha and other people, a second (the *Vinaya*) details monastic conduct, and the third (the *Abhidharma*) comprises some discussions about metaphysics and philosophy. These are generally held to reflect the ideals of the Buddha. There are several other texts (or *Sutra*) of later dates which are also of importance to followers of this religion, as they interpret many aspects of this faith. Buddhism accomodates both communal monastic and individual lay worship. Strictly speaking, theravada buddhists are not worshipping Buddha but rather paying homage to the tenets of Buddhism in general.

In any religion having a history extending over 2500 years, there are going to be many branches, sects, and interpretations; Buddhism is no exception. *Tantric* Buddhism (also known as Vajrayana or the Diamond Vehicle) involves a degree of mysticism using mandalas, mantras, and other sacraments. *Zen* Buddhism involves profound and extended meditation and the consideration of koans (or mental puzzles) under the direction of masters, all intended to lead towards personal enlightenment. *Tibetan* Buddhism involves the concept that the leaders of its monasteries are reincarnations of bodhisattvas; the over-all theocratic leader is the Dalai Lama or God-King. It is reported that some of these leaders have exhibited considerable disregard for Buddhist principles in their approach to secular government and the related rights of their citizens.

There are also many other forms of Buddhism which one might identify for study, if space permitted or necessity required. However, the foregoing information is probably sufficient to give readers some knowledge of and feeling for the main aspects of this interesting oriental religion.

For further reading, the following title is suggested:

1. *Buddhism* [Gard 1962]

2.4.3 CONFUCIANISM

This school of thought is named for an ancient Chinese philosopher named Confucius. He apparently lived in Shantung

Province in China about 500 years BCE (thus being a contemporary of Gautama Buddha), and it is known that he was married and had a family. He was an educated man by then current standards, and as such became an itinerant preacher of ideals and morals appropriate to the times. His primary instructional technique was that of example, although he was well into middle life before he was appointed to any significant public office and could then literally practice what he had been preaching.

He himself did not commit much of his own philosophy to paper; what we now know of his life and thoughts we owe to his contemporary and subsequent students, who consolidated his teachings into what are now called the Five Classics and the Four Books. The *Classics* are compendia of history, poetry, divination, and right conduct, some of which predate Confucius' own lifetime; the *Books* contain the collected sayings of Confucius and one of his greatest students, Meng Tzu (also known as Mencius). The main teachings of Confucius were in the realm of secular politics, morals, and ideals, and not in what we would now refer to as religion. He believed in a benign and paternalistic form of government, whereas Mencius is credited by some as being one of the originators of the concept of democracy.

From its beginning, Confucianism grew steadily for about six or seven hundred years, but then began to be overtaken by Buddhism. It had regained some popularity by the year 1200 CE, but carried with it some aspects of Buddhism and Taoism (see Sections 2.4.2 & 5 respectively). There developed two major schools of Confucian thought: the *nature* school and the *thought* school. The first contends that there are only two forces in nature: a general universal law and the substance of which things are made; the second contends that everything exists in the mind. Although it is not correctly called a religion, Confucianism philosophy is widespread throughout the Far East. It still forms the basis of much of Chinese social life, and it managed to weather some particularly rough storms during the Civil War of 1911 and the Cultural Revolution during the 1960s. It is now, however, of less importance in a political sense than it was in former times, although there are signs of a revival of interest in Confucian teachings in elementary schools in China and elsewhere. Confucianism is primarily concerned with what might be called humanitarianism—good conduct such as faithfulness and decorum, proper relationships based on honesty and kindness, and practical wisdom of every type. An aspect of spirituality is to be found in Confucianism regarding recommendations for reverence for one's parents and anscestors, both living and dead. Confucianist philosophy is embodied in a number of penetrating aphorisms or popular sayings. One which is attributed to it is the negative admonition: "Do not do unto others that which you would not have done to yourself." This is also the basic rule of humanism, as well as a number of religions, although it usually appears in its positive form: "Do unto others that which you would have them do unto you."

For further reading, the following title is suggested:

1. *The Analects of Confucius* [Leys1997]

2.4.4 JAINISM

This religion, while of minor significance to western minds in terms of its beliefs, its practices, and its following, is included in this review of world religions as an example of the extremes to which belief can be stretched. It is a religion of denial, appealing primarily to the ascetic mind. Jainism was founded in the 6th century BCE in Northern India by a man called Mahavira, also known as Jnatiputra, and more popularly as Jina, from which the word Jainism derives. Jina means a conqueror or hero. He was a contemporary of Guru Nanak, the founder of Sikhism, and his early private life and religious awakenings were not unlike that of Nanak. The basic beliefs of Jainism are similar to Buddhism in several respects, most notably in that Jina claimed to have found enlightenment after a 12 year search.

The general objective of Jainism is to free the soul from karma (the effects of past actions), and that the way to do this is by rigorous abstention from virtually all of life's so-called distractions and allegedly polluting influences. Killing or eating any living thing, whether plant or animal, is forbidden; true Jainists should therefore only eat food that has been prepared by others, a feature that critics say raises some difficult ideological questions. Lying, stealing, ownership of possessions, sexual or other improper conduct is shunned. Moderation in all and austerity in most things is practised and revered. No images or idols are worshipped. Some Jainists, usually monks, go naked and shun all possessions; others, usually laity, wear a simple white robe and own sufficient objects to conduct their lives adequately. Because of their aversion to killing of any kind, Jainists tend to be in business rather than in agriculture, a choice that has been of distinct financial benefit to them as a group, and that has given them power out of proportion to their numbers in Indian society.

For further reading, the following title is suggested:

1. *An Encyclopedia of Jainism* [Nahar 1988]

2.4.5 TAOISM

Taoism originated in north central China, during the Chou dynasty, which commenced about the 11th century BCE and extended as far as the 3rd century BCE. Taoism is generally derived from writings attributed to one Li Po-yang, more popularly called Lao Tzu, a Chinese name that can be translated to mean approximately the "Old Man" or "Old Guy" and to another later mystic named Chuang Tzu. Legend has it that Lao Tzu was a contemporary of Confucius around the 6th century, that he was employed by the Chou rulers as an historian, and that he wrote a book called the *Tao Te Ching*, or *The Way of Life*. It is more likely that the book is actually a compilation of the work of several unknown mystical authors, in which, through a series of poems, they endeavored to explain their understanding of life and the place of humankind in the forces of the universe. These forces are in general compensating opposites held in tension, such as positives and negatives, male and female, right and wrong, and so on. Chuang Tzu lived during the 4th century BCE, and also left a compendium of writings on his observations about life which have been incorporated into Taoism.

Mystics in every part of the world allege perception of a reality or a state beyond their own bodies and minds. This ultimate form of this state appears to be beyond description in words or pictures. It is immanent, ineffable, and it involves realization of the all-encompassing unity of nature. It cannot be achieved on an intellectual basis, nor can it be attained by discussion. Theistic religions call this state Knowledge of God; Taosim calls it The Way, and it involves contemplation of such things as energy, darkness, emptiness, equity, and humanity, among others. It is alleged that one may, through a regime of strict moral conduct, learn The Way; however The Way cannot be taught. The techniques used to learn The Way involve study of life, intensive meditation, correct posture, and control of the breath.

As stated, it is not possible to adequately describe The Way in words. To use a Taoist aphorism: "Knowers don't speak—speakers don't know." Furthermore, this author has no personal experience of The Way, although glimpses of the fundamental unity of nature have dimly penetrated his humanist consciousness from time to time. The closest that one might come to getting an intellectual grasp of the concept is to consider how useful a bowl is, not because of the material from which it is made or the beauty of its shape, but because of the empty space that it encloses and which can be used for practical purposes. At one and the same time, the bowl is acting and yet not acting. Or consider water naturally flowing in a small creek or stream, taking the paths that open to it, responding to texture, temperature, slope, and the natural pull of gravity, without pretension. The water is doing what it can do and has to do, while at the same time, it is really doing nothing. It is changing in shape, but not in form; it is unyielding, in that it may not be compressed nor expanded. However, space in a bowl or water in a stream is impersonal; The Way is personal. This is not to say that a bowl or water in a stream has no personality, but that it is not aware of its being or its virtue, though such exist. Awareness of virtue is a key element in knowing The Way; perfect morality is also of critical importance. Thus total freedom from social restraint may be achieved along The Way. But the Tao is by definition endless.

Compared to Buddhism or Confucianism, Taoism has always had a relatively small following, stemming partly from the difficulty of the literary form of the *Tao Te Ching*, which veiled much of its wisdom from the illiterate mass of the people, and partly from the extraordinary difficulty of fully attaining The Way through the rigorous practices necessary to achieve that end. It is, by it very nature, not readily open to the general public, although some popular forms of the regime may include the worship of any one of a number of personal gods.

For further reading, the following title is suggested:

1. *The Taoist Way* [McNaughton 1973]

CHAPTER 2.5

OTHER SYSTEMS

2.5.1 INTRODUCTION

In this chapter, a review is made of other points of view that do not admit elements of religious faith, although faith of a different type is often involved. It is debatable whether or not such non-belief can really be classified as a system of belief, although non-believers can be systematic in their approach to developing arguments to support their points of view. In this respect, the process itself represents a system of belief based on knowledge of a sort.

Indeed, one might go further and say that conclusions reached as the result of such systematic investigation, reflection, and rationalization have greater reason to be classified as a system of belief compared to the wholesale and uncritical adoption of predigested opinion that characterizes so many of the so-called organized religions. An approximate parallel may be drawn by comparing the rational and coherent *metric* system of measurement to the largely incoherent *imperial* system, which is not so much a system as a collection of rules of thumb and "old wives' tales." Non-belief often involves some rational thought and argument; theistic belief usually involves a fair number of "old wives' tales."

There follow sections on mythology, witchcraft, meditation, and some other cosmic views. Bodily health regimes such as aroma therapy, homeopathy, rolfing, healing touch, yoga and tai-chi are not discussed. Neither are more esoteric systems, such as *voo-doo-ism* (which involves the appearance of zombies or the "living dead"), *breatharianism* (which involves claims to live on air alone), *raelianism* (which alleges that humans are alien clones), *obeah* (which involves Caribbean sorcery), *fire-worship* (which is self evident) and the use of *crystals* or *pyramids* of every kind, each with alleged magical powers, among a number of other beliefs, such as the possibility of miracles.

2.5.2 ASTROLOGY

The craft of astrology has a very long history. Indeed, its very length permits its supporters to claim that there therefore must be something to it. Its origins are shrouded in mystery, but probably stem from pre-historic interest in various activities and events observed in the heavens by primitive humans. Its history certainly goes back several thousands of years to the early civilizations of Babylon and Chaldea. The earliest known written texts on the topic date from around 1600 BCE. The science of astronomy has some parallels in its roots, having developed in the same general region and about the same time as astrology. However, the fundamental difference between the two is that astronomy deals with predicting the behavior of celestial bodies, whereas astrology deals with the attempt to predict the behavior of human beings. While modern astronomy has a near perfect record in this regard, modern astrology can make no such claim. Some statistical studies show its success rate to be as low as 11% while others show that astrological prediction of outcomes in general is no better than pure chance. Predictions made by astrologers are called *horoscopes* and they are said to be *erected* or *cast*.

It is not easy to give a simple explanation of astrology because over the course of centuries, it has accumulated a large accretion of modifications without a corresponding deletion of earlier and perhaps discredited beliefs. However, it may be said that it basically involves a view of the cosmos which puts the earth at the center of the various manifestations of celestial bodies which appear to encircle the earth, each on a curved crystalline membrane somewhat like the layers of a transparent onion. Specifically, the path of the sun as it appears to circle the earth each year is called the plane of the *ecliptic*. A broad band, centered on the ecliptic and extending to eight or nine degrees either side of it is called the *zodiac*. The orbits of the moon and all the well-known planets (except Pluto, which follows a different orbital plane) fall within the zodiac. Some astrological systems use different bases, and there are other obvious problems, such as when one tries to locate the ecliptic in arctic or antarctic regions of the planet.

The full ecliptic circle is divided into 12 sectors of approximately 30° each, called the *houses* of the planets. Each house has a name and thus gives rise to the so-called *signs* of the zodiac. The signs are called in order of their location on the zodiac and relative to specific constellations of stars: *Aries* (the Ram), *Taurus* (the Bull), *Gemini* (the Twins), *Cancer* (the Crab), *Leo* (the Lion), *Libra* (the Balance), *Virgo* (the Virgin), *Scorpio* (the Scorpion), *Sagittarius* (the Archer), *Capricorn* (the Goat), *Aquarius* (the Water Bearer), and *Pisces* (the Fish). The position of the signs on the ecliptic starts with Aries at the spring vernal equinox, and proceeds in order towards the east. Each sign is alleged to be indicative of some human characteristic, such as temperament, mentality, creativity, professional aptitude, sexual attitude, and so on.

There are three subdivisions of the signs. First, the *polarities*, where each house is alternatively given a positive or negative value. Secondly, the *modes*, where each house is assigned into one of three groups of cardinal, fixed, or mutable signs. Thirdly, the *elements*, where each house is allocated one each of fire, air, water, or earth. All of the subdivisions start with *Aries* being *positive, cardinal*, and *fire*, and continuing in order around the zodiac.

So far so good, but now some complications appear. First, there are astrologers who assert that the eastern extremity of Aries is always coincidental with the vernal equinox, regardless of the position of their namesake constellations; these are classified as *tropical* astrologers. Other astrologers maintain that the houses are always coincident with the constellations for which they are named; these are referred to as *sidereal* astrologers. Horoscopes cast by either school can therefore differ from one another. Despite the foregoing description of the principles of astrology, the craft has some insurmountable defects. For example, it is based on the Ptolemaic belief, formerly held by many, that the Earth is at the center of the solar system, indeed of the Universe. We now know that the Earth is a very minor planet in a system of several in various orbits around a common star, which we call the Sun. It is a star of average characteristics located on one outer arm of one of a billion galaxies. The center of the Universe, assuming that there can even be such a point in space and time, is without question a long, long way away from planet Earth.

Secondly, astrology takes no account of the gravitational phenomenon of rotational precession, which causes the axis of the earth to swing or oscillate through a predictable arc over a period of about 26,000 years. One effect of this has been to shift the star constellations away from the positions they would have held about four thousand years ago, when astrology was being first formulated, to where they appear in the skies today. This shift naturally throws the relationships between the various constellations and their astrological "houses" significantly out of synchronisation. No allowance appears yet to have been made by astrologers to adjust for these fatal discrepancies, yet logically, all data based on such incorrect premises must themselves also be incorrect.

Thirdly, there are more than 300 billion stars in those portions of the universe observable from earth. New technology such as radio telescopes and other imaging process suggests the existence of many more. We have as yet no certain way of knowing how many more there may be beyond our ken. One might wonder, though, why only a few planets and stars selected by astrologers to be influential in affecting our lives continue to be taken into account.

Fourthly, while it is not clear just exactly in what way the celestial bodies influence the lives of humans, it does seem clear that it cannot be gravitational, for at least two reasons. First, the proximity of human beings to the mass of the earth and to the earthly objects, such as buildings and furniture around them, far outweighs and over-rides whatever minuscule amounts of energy in whatever form (such as neutrinos) might be emanating from the stars and planets. Secondly, light which we are only now seeing may have come over thousands of light-years from stars long since dead and gone, so even if the electro-magnetic energy may affect us in some unexplained way, the missing objects themselves certainly cannot continue to do so.

In reading horoscopes printed in the daily press, the general predictions contained within any one of the astrological houses (or signs) will approximately fit everyone, regardless of their birth-dates. The reason is three-fold: most are written in very general terms; they make generally positive assertions (about "love" or "success" or "personal relationships") which most people like to think could apply to themselves, and most include ambiguous wording (such as "could" or "may") involving a number of possibilities and leaving a number of openings for doubt. In one famous experiment a researcher offered to send free horoscopes to anyone who responded by sending their name and date and place of birth to a magazine advertisement. In response to a questionnaire sent to each of about 150 respondents, 94% said that they easily recognized themselves from the horoscope cast; and 90% of their friends agreed. What none of the participants knew was that they had all been given the same identical horoscope, one which had been prepared for one of the worst mass murderers in France, which described him as a warm and loving person, a right-thinking middle class citizen, proud of his home, and so on.

For further reading, the following title is suggested:

1. *Astrology: True or False?* [Culver 1988]

2.5.3 FALUN GONG

Falun Gong is not a true religion. It might better be described as a life-stance or a practice with some transcendent or spiritual overtones. It was created around 1992 by a charismatic man in his forties named Li Hongzhi in northern China. It was rapidly developed into a world wide movement by Li and adherents to the practice. Li apparently had an unremarkable upbringing, with no more than high school education and, prior to his involvement with Falun Gong, had held relatively unimportant positions in military and police units as a musician. His only known incursion into metaphysics involved a brief encounter with qigong (chee-gong), an exercise and breathing regime not unlike tai-chi and popular with tens of thousands of other people in China in the mid-1980's. "Qi" is alleged to be a sort of vital life force, and "gong" is the method or attempt to acquire qi; the qi-gong movement was barely tolerated by the Chinese government.

The word "falun" means a wheel. The word "gong" has been explained above as a means to acquisition. The wheel in falun gong is not an actual physical entity, but rather a metaphysical notion of a life force, vaguely involving yin and yang (i.e., good and bad, right and wrong, male and female, black and white, etc.) and an alternating system of rotation amounting to perpetual motion. The object of the falun gong practice is to reach what one might call one's true essence in this life, through right exercise, right thought, and right living. Mr. Li drew on virtually all of the ancient (and often suppressed) ways of oriental wisdom, such as Buddhism, Taoism, Confucianism, to produce his new and updated vision of the sure way to truth, compassion, forbearance and enlightenment.

In contrast to many Western religions, falun gong asserts that people are basically good. Human essence is created at a level higher than the purely physical dimension, where much of the "bad" stuff happens. According to Mr. Li, the falun wheel is symbolically inserted into the practitioner's abdomen, where it simultaneously absorbs cosmic energy and releases it, with allegedly beneficial results. Meditation helps to enhance the effects of the falun. Mr. Li also makes so-called "law bodies" available to practitioners (as long as they remain practitioners); these appear to be similar in function to what western believers would call "guardian angels." By cultivating their "xinxing" or true nature, practitioners can enhance their general well-being, partly through the involvement in beneficial physical exercise, and partly through teachings which encourage them to have less concern for the strictly material things of life. Interest in politics is discouraged, and participants are encouraged to live law-abiding productive lives.

As a matter of practical fact, falun gong does not appear to be a cult in any strict sense. There are no dues to pay, no memberships required, no initiation ceremonies, no clergy or sacred buildings, and no gods to worship. People seem to be free to join or leave as and when they wish. Instructional literature is plentiful, modestly priced, and even available free of charge over the InterNet. To get involved, one only has to show up at a gathering of other like-minded people. The only down side seems to be that there is an expectation that practitioners will believe what Mr. Li believes, such as the possibility that we are living in what might be called "end-times."

To conclude, although a well-organized world-wide movement developed out of the early days in Northern China, leading to membership in China alone estimated by 1999 at about 100 million people, a campaign of repression by the Chinese government began to reduce that number. In 1997, Mr. Li left China to take up residence in the United States. His whereabouts at the time of this writing are largely unknown to his followers, although he does show up unannounced at gatherings in Australia, Canada, and elsewhere from time to time. Towards the end of 1999, the chief falun gong organizers apparently misjudged the determination of the Communist Government of China under President Jiang Zemin to stamp out any movement which threatened its power. The ensuing crackdown and banishment virtually destroyed the movement in that country. Membership in falun gong is now estimated at around 2 million in China; it is not known what the world-wide membership may be.

For further reading, the following title is suggested

1. *The Power of the Wheel* [Adams 2000]

2.5.4 FENG SHUI

Feng shui is an ancient form of Chinese astrology, the origins of which are lost in antiquity, but the main features of which appear to be attributed to specific (though often legendary) individuals. The word "feng" means *wind* and "shui" means *water*, and the proper combination of these two elements is intended to direct practitioners towards happiness and success. The theory is the attempt to unify heaven (gods and spirits), earth (the natural order), man (human minds and ghosts), and matter (trees, rocks, mountains, etc.) using an alleged supreme cosmological force called "taiji" so that "qi," the so-called life force, will flow propitiously. The practice is to attempt to bring about the most harmonious relationship between the orientation and location of the spaces in which people live, work, and play, and the objects which they place in these spaces.

There are various forms of the art, loosely organized into seven main traditions each focusing on various elements such as stars, entrances, mountains, and so on. There are two broad classifications: *exterior* feng shui, concerned with choosing the most propitious sites for buildings and outdoor activities, and *interior* feng shui, dealing with enclosed spaces and events inside buildings. The primary piece of equipment used by all practitioners is a small magnetic compass. When used by professional feng shui masters, this may be secured in the center of a circular board upon which appropriate astrological characters are concentrically engraved, as well as indications for the various cardinal points of the compass.

The task of the feng shui master is first, to determine the center of qi energy for any specific space, and secondly, to arrange the features of and objects within that space according to traditional feng shui rules to enhance the qi. In this, the master would be guided by reference to various elements in the particular feng shui tradition being utilized. He may refer to the cardinal points of the compass, to the orientation of specific astronomical star configurations such Ursa Major (the Great Bear or Big Dipper) as well as various dragons, tigers, and birds having special significance. Curiously, Ursa Major, which is in fact a *seven* star system, is called the "Nine Stars" system; the two additional stars are entirely imaginary but are said to have influence on the others. Each star is assigned special positive or negative feng shui significance. The "Nine Stars" system is also used in conjunction with other aids, such as the "Eight Entrances" and the corresponding "Bagua." The bagua is a complex matrix of eight mystical trigrams (three-lined symbols) each representing particular aspects or combinations of natural forces and relationships between family members. The master takes into account aspects of water, fire, color, and light, as well as architectural features such as doors, windows, beams, and stairs. To minimize problems or enhance qi, the master will also use furniture, drapes, paintings, sculptures, mirrors, chimes, and other objects (such as swords) or artifacts (such as coins) in very specific ways.

To give a few simple examples, it is considered bad feng shui to have the front and back door of an apartment directly opposite each other; good feng shui would require that such direct opposition be interrupted. Good feng shui would not have windows located in a north-facing wall, though this rule may not apply in countries south of the equator. Bad feng shui would be to place one's bed opposite the bedroom door, where the leading edge of the door might take on the character of a knife edge pointing towards the bed. Good feng shui would avoid having a large tree directly opposite to the main entrance to a building. Bad feng shui would be to have the main staircase in a two-storey house ending opposite or close to the main front door. There are also rules governing the most beneficial number of rooms to have in a residence, and the proper placement of various articles of furniture, sculpture, and works of art in each room. And so on . . .

If one were to remove the superstitious or non-provable elements from feng shui, there is little in the system that any good school of architecture or interior design would not as efficiently teach, with just as effective results.

For further reading, the following title is suggested:

1. *Feng Shui for Today* [Lau1996]

2.5.5 MEDITATION

In recent years, an increasing number of people have become interested in a large variety of meditation and reflection techniques, originally developed as features of certain eastern religions, but now allegedly adapted to suit the western mind and life style. An entire industry appears to have been developed, based on the process. The techniques are presented by various leaders (usually called gurus) as being entirely free of religious content, but as shall be explained, this is not necessarily the case. Despite many variations, the basic process is similar in every case.

The meditation technique is simple; it involves utilizing a *mantra*, which is a single meaningless sound (such as "OM") or focusing on an object, such as a lit candle. One can select a mantra by oneself or be given one by a guru. Mantras selected by gurus come from a stock of about 20, allegedly chosen to suit one's personality, although any one-syllable meaningless sound will suffice. The mantra is memorized, and then repeated silently inside the head for two 20 minute periods each day, once before breakfast and again before supper. To meditate, one should wear loose clothing, sit upright in a firm but comfortable chair, with both feet flat on the floor, hands folded lightly in one's lap, and be located in a cool, quiet and slightly darkened room.

During recitation of the mantra or the act of focusing on the candle, if thoughts intrude, they are simply ignored, and attention is refocused. During these meditation sessions, there is a pleasant feeling of remoteness, of relaxation, and the breath rate, pulse rate, and blood pressure all appear to drop to lower than normal levels. One emerges from the meditative state with a feeling of well-being, and with one's senses more acutely tuned to the world for a while.

In the experience of this author, though, religion regrettably got in the way of this experiment with the mind. The mantra which I was given (and for which I had to pay) I later discovered was the name of a Hindu God. Admittedly, the word was indeed a meaningless sound to me at that time, as I did not know the names of many Hindu gods, and I mastered the meditation technique well enough by using it. However, the duplicity in the mind of the guru who, on the pretext of teaching me a relaxation technique advertised as non-religious, did in fact implant in my mind the name of an imaginary god and the instruction to repeat it twice a day for 20 minutes at each time, was and still is in my opinion unconscionable, and indeed tantamount to fraud.

For my part, I promised not to reveal the mantra which was given to me, and I have not done so, not because I fear any retribution of any sort if I were to do so, but rather because I believe, as a moral humanist, that a promise made should be a promise kept, even to those in whom trust is sometimes misplaced. If, in the light of later evidence, it turns out that such a promise would not have been made if full disclosure had been required or possible, then there may be some question as to what extent such promises should be kept. To what extent do we owe a duty of self-imposed faithfulness to those who are deliberately unfaithful to us? It is an interesting question, and one that I do not propose to answer here.

For further reading, the following title is suggested:

1. *Transcendental Meditation* [Maharishi 1963]

2.5.6 MYTHOLOGY

The borderline between religion and mythology is indistinct in many cases. Some religions embody considerable mythology, while some mythology has given rise to religion. One distinction which might be made between these two is that *religious* affairs or events are usually believed by some to have actually occurred at some moment or period in the past, whereas *mythological* affairs and events are not necessarily accepted as being so historically factual or accurate. Mythology is usually utilized to make some underlying point about humankind, its place in the universe, its internal political organization, and its external relationships with nature. Mythology is universally found in human societies, and represents attempts to explain the unjustifiable or to justify the inexplicable. Origins, destinies, gods, devils, angels, natural phenomena, life and death, as well as hopes and fears for the past and the future, all these are to be found in the innumerable mythical tales perpetuated in all societies. Myths generally deal with some central or fundamental aspects or concepts of any particular society at some given point in time; they are generally of importance to the people involved. They frequently describe larger-than-life events of excessive or perverted sexuality, incredible brutality, religious or racial significance, or extraordinary serenity and beauty.

To give some scale to the extent to which myths pervade our society, it may be noted in passing that the modern names of the primary celestial bodies in our immediate solar system have their origins in mythical gods: Sun, Moon, Mars, Mercury, Jupiter, Venus, and Saturn. In French, the words for the days of the week still show that direct connection. The word for Moon is lune and the word for *Monday* is Lundi. *Tuesday* is Mardi; *Wednesday* is Mercredi; *Thursday* is Jeudi, and *Friday* is Vendredi. In English, the names for the days of our week have been further modified. *Sunday* is the day of the Sun-god and *Monday* is still Moon-day. *Tuesday* is derived from Tiwaz, the Scandinavian sky-god; *Wednesday* is derived from Woden, the German god of wisdom; *Thursday* is derived from Thor, the Greek god of War or Thunder. *Friday* is derived from Freya or Frigg, a Scandinavian earth-goddess; and *Saturday* commemorates the God Saturn.

Religious myths are often utilized to convey some sacred belief or enhance some moral precept. However, myths seldom involve scientific truths, facts, methodologies, or accuracy. In general, myths deal with control of mankind. They explain how and why people should believe that things are the way the myths say they are. They tend to simplify the poorly understood complexities of nature by describing them in the form of highly embellished parables. If one were to believe most mythological structures, the universe has a chief executive officer, usually called God or the Great Spirit or some other overall grand title, whose task is to oversee a number of divisions or departments, each one headed up by a junior but more specialized branch god, such as the God of War, or the God of Fertility, or the God of Agriculture, and so on, just like some grand universal federal state. In turn, each God has emissaries in human, animal, or mythical form, endowed with magical powers and equipment, and sent into the world to do the delegated departmental business and to report on progress. It is impossible to list all the myths which abound in the world today; they are literally innumerable.

However, mention of a few might give the reader a flavor of the kinds of things which one finds in some of the great mythological tales of the world, and spark his or her interest to read some more about this interesting element in man's accumulation of follies. To begin with, there are some contrasts. For example, when a Christian dies, it is believed that, if good, his or her soul rises *above* the earth, towards the light, but when a Hindu dies, it is believed that, if good, his or her soul sinks *below* the earth, towards the light. Then there are some similarities. For example, the ancient Greeks thought that the earth was supported on a tortoise; the ancient Hindus thought that the universe was created out of a tortoise; the ancient Chinese thought that the feet of a tortoise were used to fix the cardinal points of the compass. Then there are separations. For example, Christians believe that God is all-loving, all-knowing, and all-powerful, which poses some difficulites for them with respect to the existence of evil. Zoroastrians neatly solve this problem by dividing good and evil equally between God and the Devil—God is all-good and the Devil (God bless him!) is all-bad. Zoroastrians also believe that the Devil causes death by involving the body, so that while the corpse of an ordinary human sinner is a very dangerous thing to them, and necessitates careful handling, the corpse of a dead priest is extremely dangerous, representing as it does the direct triumph of the Devil over one of God's special people.

Like the Greeks, Hindus, and Christians, the Chinese also believed in an assortment of myths. The greatest Chinese myth or legend involves a series of delightful tales about a magic and immortal monkey, loosely based on the character and activities of a Buddhist scholar who traveled from China to India and back again, around the 5th century CE. "Monkey" not only had many powers, but also had many admirable qualities, such as a puckish sense of humor, limitless bravery sometimes bordering on stupidity, and unerring judgement although he was not unfamiliar with the human foibles of excessive eating and drinking on occasion. Although "Monkey" went through enormous difficulties and also went to a lot of trouble to sort things out for the Chinese, they still had the most confusing assortment of gods of every rank and purpose, with myths attached to all, and with powers granted to the emperors to change it all, anyway.

In Japan, the present-day Emperor is still considered by many to be the direct descendent of Izanagi, who was one of the original dozen of earthly Gods, created by what they considered to be the five fundamental heavenly Gods. According to the myth, Izanagi and his sister Izanami, after some incestuous activity to produce off-spring, created the Japanese Islands with drops of sea water from the end of a magic spear, a myth with obvious phallic symbolism.

All peoples in all places and at all times have invented and circulated myths. Zulus in Africa, Maya in South America, Pueblo in Central America, Aborigines in Australia, Maori in New Zealand, Celts, Tibetans, Turks, Nazis, Vikings, everyone from the Arctic to the Antarctic, from the Dead Sea to the High Andes. Unfortunately, constraints of time and space permit no further extensive presentation of this topic in this book, although mention should be made of the distinction between harmless mythology and myths which cause pain and suffering.

Some myths can be extremely harmful on occasion: consider the mythical wisdom that "lightening never strikes in the same place twice" despite the fact that lightning has been observed to do just that. Other myths, offered as religious dogma, can be equally harmful. For example, if a person chooses to believe that the Pope is the infallible earthly representative of an omnipotent heavenly god, because he and some others say so, then there is no real harm in that, other than minor damage to that person's own credibility and judgement. However, if holding such beliefs causes that person to act to impinge or infringe on the rights of others who do not believe that particular myth, then a very great deal of harm is done, as in the case of the anti-abortion movement, which is actively supported as a matter of policy by the Roman Catholic Church of which the Pope is the head. Similarly, if a person wants to believe that the Emperor of Japan is a direct descendent of the original Sun God, there is no particular harm in holding that mythical belief. However, if as a result of holding that belief, that person then engages in activities which are dangerous to fellow humans, such as waging war at the behest and in the name of the Emperor and the Sun God, as happened in the middle of the 20th century, then there is very great harm in the belief. Many such cases abound, ranging all the way from adherents of black Haitian Voo-Doo cults through to members of white supremacist organizations like the Ku Klux Klan and the Aryan Nations.

An example of harmless mythology or superstition originates in Thailand, where it is considered unlucky for a pregnant woman to hammer nails into walls. The belief is that such action will result in the birth of an ugly child. Apart from the fact that there are no statistics on the number of pregnant women who have indeed hammered nails into walls and then given birth to ugly children, it is also unlikely that women in such a condition would be much inclined to perform such an act in any event. And who is to judge that any new-born baby is ugly, anyway? Even though the origins of the superstition are no longer discernable, the belief is still wide-spread. Another curious ritual is the belief held by some that, when making up a bed, the opening in the pillow case should not face the doorway, to avoid bad luck. If it faces away from the door and no bad luck comes, or vice versa on both counts, that is regarded as proof of the claim. If it faces away and bad luck does come, or vice versa, the luck, good or bad, cannot be attributed to the pillow case. It is more likely that the superstition of not walking under ladders probably has more of a rational basis than unprovable rituals involving making up beds.

Many other examples of harmless myths are to be found in connection with the curative values of certain plants and herbs. While there is some evidence to support medical claims in this regard, there are also innumerable absurd and nonsensical assertions made about the beneficial attributes of eating, drinking, and bathing in extracts from various plants or animals, claims that simply do not stand up under any test of science or experience. To give only one of many examples, it was believed by many that when the mandrake plant is pulled from the ground, its roots scream out in pain. Common sense suggests the obvious test for such a claim: pull and listen. But those who choose to believe such nonsense seldom see any need to test their assertions.

The same general observations can be made about those who place their hopes in plaster casts of saints, strings of beads, incense pots, burning candles, or other hopefully protective devices or regalia. For example, during the Second World War, some oriental warriors believed that a band of cloth, blessed by their priests and wrapped around their bodies, would stop bullets. When they found out how weak the blessing was, it was too late, as they had been shot. Science has since produced another type of cloth called *Keflar*© which will stop bullets, from which bullet-proof jackets can be made, and in which one can place considerable faith. It comes with something better than a blessing; it comes with a written money-back guarantee. If the cloth doesn't work, at least you can try to get your money back, after you get your health back, although your faith in bullet-proof technology may still be somewhat shaken.

A more recent instance of equally harmful mythology concerns a troop of 700 Ugandan Acholi tribesmen, sent into battle after being anointed with so-called bullet-proof oil, prepared by their resident witch-doctor and applied to their bodies. Unfortunately, the message about the protection did not get through to the government troops being attacked by the tribesmen, with the result that about 100 of the tribesmen were machine-gunned to death. Pessimists and non-believers would comment that the 15% of the total tribal force that were killed by the bullets were just unfortunate to be hit; optimists, mythologists, and other believers would comment that the protective oil appeared to be 85% effective.

A classic example of modern mythology which proved to be extremely harmful was contained in the elements of racial superiority in the Nazi Party policies and practices in Germany in the early part of the last century (1933-1945). That particular mythology virtually engulfed an entire nation into the mistaken belief that they belonged to a race superior to the rest of the world in general and to the Jewish people in particular, with disastrous consequences, not only for their victims, but ultimately for the German nation itself. These recent Japanese and German mythologies, combined with other mythologies regarding the superiority of Eastern (meaning communist) or Western (meaning capitalist) political and economic systems, have in the space of the last century alone engulfed much of the planet in the most incredible amount of merciless blood-letting ever seen in the entire history of humankind, namely two World Wars, the Korean War, the War in Vietnam, and ongoing religious and territorial problems in various pasts of the Middle East, to mention a few of the larger conflicts.

Regrettably, there are people in the world today who still seek to revive and continue with such debased, bigoted, racial, religious, political, and economic mythology. It is a serious situation for all of humankind, as some of the protagonists of new mythology still mistakenly suggest that a nuclear war can be fought and won with residual benefits which might be statistically and marginally better for the winner than for the loser. The winners would only be killed 10 times over, whereas the losers would be killed 20 times over! There are minds at work in several world capitals that allege that they can comprehend such idiotic mythology; they have to, because their military livelihoods depend on it. It need hardly be said that *none* of them are humanists, because no self-respecting humanist could or would subscribe to such mythological nonsense, or to such means for the wholesale destruction of life on earth.

For further reading, the following title is suggested:

1. *Mythology—An Illustrated Encyclopedia* [Cavendish 1980]

2.5.7 WITCHCRAFT

In general, sorcerers, wizards, and similar mystics represent themselves as having power and dominion over the Devil, as well as control over human action and direction. They claim to have special bodies of mystical knowledge or experiences, to be able to divine probable outcomes of actions by examining various propitious portents, to be able to cast spells by incantation, and to work a few miracles now and then, when so inclined. They have been traditionally involved with establishing, developing, and continuing superstitious beliefs in such things as the powers of alchemy, astrology, and occultism of various forms. Such people play on the credibility of the others who are deluded by facile demonstrations of apparently supernatural powers and tales of demonic punishments and rewards, but which in reality often involve misrepresentation, sleight-of-hand, diversion of attention, and usually a considerable amount of wishful thinking on the part of the observers.

In contrast, those who claim to be witches consider themselves to be servants of the Devil or of a deity they call Wicca, from whom they allegedly derive their magical powers to affect numerous natural phenomena, such as the weather and agriculture, as well as human health, wealth, and relationships. Many of them, and those who believe in them, consider that they have power to vanish and reappear at will, to fly through the air, to move through time, and to cast or remove spells of varying intensity and benefit. Modern scholars of the subject believe that witchcraft is the residual of an earlier pagan form of religion, having emphasis on aspects of human fertility. It is interesting to note that magic incantations made by such practitioners have absolutely no effect on non-believers, just as astrological predictions are proven to be only coincidentally correct, for those few that do in fact ever come to pass. If one does not believe in ghosts, one will never see a ghost.

Although most witches over the centuries have been female, it is interesting to note many have been male, most notably Moses, of biblical fame, who was considered to be a witch by the Egyptians of his day, because he swore allegiance to a god other than the current crop of Egyptian gods of that period. In general, witches have been persecuted throughout history, but with increasing ferocity and depravity by supporters of the Christian faith, who saw and still see in superstitious witchcraft a major threat to their own superstitious beliefs. Some of the tests used to establish proof of witchcraft were as nonsensical as the belief in it itself. For example, to determine if a person was a witch or not, he or she was immersed in a tub of water. To sink (and possibly drown) proved innocence; to float (and possibly survive) proved that the Devil was looking after that person, so they were removed from the water and executed, if possible in the most excruciatingly painful and prolonged manner. And the greatest joy of all for the executioners was the knowledge that they were doing the Lord's work, complete with biblical mandate, because in Exodus 22:18, it states that sorcerers shall not be permitted to live.

Witchcraft is still widespread in the modern world, playing a large role especially in countries of the Third World, where so-called witch doctors still attempt to intercede with good spirits and naughty devils on behalf of a gullible (but paying) clientele.

It is part of human nature to hope (and indeed plan) for the best, while having to make do with (and indeed accept) the worst that life has to offer from time to time. For many, witchcraft fills this need.

For further reading, the following title is suggested:

1. *The Occult Source Book* [Drury 1978]

EPILOGUE

E.1 INTRODUCTION

What then are we to make of all of the foregoing information and opinion? If the main objective of humanism is to discover the true place of mankind in nature, then those who would be humanists should make a reasonable, impartial, and unbiased investigation of the thoughts, ideas, and experiences which have been held to be valuable by mankind over the centuries. Then, by examining those values, humanists could determine what they may or ought to achieve or to avoid in the impartial light of purely secular knowledge, avoiding any leap of faith at any point. Humanists can foster adoption of the highest possible benefits to all of humankind here right now in this-earthly world.

> "What religion? What race? What nationality? Today, these questions are considered logical. By 2001, it will occur that these questions are absurd, meaningless, illogical, anti-evolutionary."

So said Buckminster.Fuller in 1970. Regrettably, 2001 is past us now, and divisive religions, races, and nationalities remain. In this concluding chapter, some *difficulties* that humanist investigators may encounter are mentioned, some *concerns* that this author has felt are articulated, and some *suggestions* are left with patient readers to aid them to formulate ideas for themselves, and perhaps to realize Fuller's interesting prognosis in the foreseeable future.

E.2 SOME DIFFICULTIES

In making the attempt to reach enlightenment or at least understanding, one can read books that present views clearly favorable or in opposition to humanist philosophy and values (see endnotes and bibliography for details). For example, Bertrand Russell [1985] gives an unequivocal view of the reasons for his non-belief, and Corliss Lamont [1982] enthusiastically enunciates the philosophy of humanism in his book having that title. Similarly, one can read books that present the opposite view; for example, Hartley Grattan [1968] presents forceful opinion and argument against the humanist view. However, when one starts, in good faith, to read a book by Roy Varghese [1984] with the title *"Intellectuals Speak Out About God"* to discover that only the arguments of intellectuals already sympathetic to the idea of the existence of God are included, but none opposed, one must surely question the motives of the editors of such publications. One would think that the presentation of balancing views by non-believing intellectuals would give such a book more credibility, as the reader would then be able to directly compare the strengths of the various arguments, and judge for him or her self the relative merits of each view. As with most things in life, though, we must take the world as we find it. The humanist's obligation to himself or herself is to become exposed to a sufficiently wide and diverse range of opinion, so that his or her own views are reinforced by cogent argument and not by uncritical acceptance of predigested dogma. Such advice extends to the contents of this book and to the biased views of this author.

To compound the complexities, what are we to make of the views of say, Alan Watts [1972] who, holding degrees of both master and doctor of divinity and after practicing as an Anglican priest in California for many years, asserted that to hold any specific religious views was to commit intellectual suicide. And what of renowned theologian Paul Tillich [1960] asking the question "What is the meaning of life?" without asking and answering the logically anterior question "Does life have to have a particular meaning?" And what of Michael Goulder [1983] who, after 30 years of intensive work as a theological scholar, ordained minister, and missionary preacher in England, Hong Kong, and elsewhere, came to the conclusion that he had made a mistake, and that atheism was the correct intellectual position to hold, based on the evidence, although there might still be room for a church of some sort in human affairs. One could read the works of Dan Barker [1992] who also realized, after 20 years of pushing Christianity as a Pentecostalist preacher, that based on the evidence, he had made a mistake and that humanism was the correct intellectual position to hold. Or professors George Wells [1982] and Earl Doherty [1999] who both implied in separate books about the disputed historical existence of the person known as Jesus Christ, that much of the scripture in the New Testament amounts to little more than legend. Charles Templeton [1996], a Canadian colleague of the TV evangelist Billy Graham for about 20 years, came to the conclusion that what he had been preaching had too many problems in it, that he no longer believed in it, and so he abandoned it to become a writer on agnostic topics.

These complexities make it all the more difficult for the ordinary untutored lay person to come to some reasonable conclusions about life and religion, if the so-called experts in the field are presenting such conflicting thoughts. If God or gods truly exist, there should be no need for oral or verbal arguments to prove such existence. It should simply be obvious to all, like the existence of a thing, such as a tree, or an idea, such as a mathematical equation, or a feeling, such as love. The sheer magnitude of the number of arguments that have been developed to prove such existence itself militates against such belief. The sheer size of religious organizations promoting varieties of religious belief does not present a foundation for such belief. There is simply no evidence or proof of such existence, beyond a conviction in the minds of some die-hard believers. To the rational mind, such conviction is not enough.

E.3 SOME CONCERNS

It would be naive to think that every right-thinking person will be immediately converted to humanism at the first personal encounter with a dedicated humanist, or by attending one humanist meeting, or on a first reading of some humanist literature, such as publicity pamphlets or books such as this one. It would also be a mistake to believe that the truths and advantages of humanism are so clear, so self-evident, and so rational, that people will just naturally gravitate towards the cause upon a first exposure to these verities. Experience proves otherwise. Many people who appear to be well educated, widely traveled, and otherwise realistic in their views and outlook still actually or apparently subscribe to all sorts of spiritual beliefs, for social, psychological, economic, and other reasons or excuses. There are a number of reasons for this apparent resistance, and so the topic is therefore worthy of some study.

For example, many people simply do not know that there are alternatives to their own type of religious belief; they have literally never seriously considered that possibility. Whatever fleeting thoughts they may have entertained from time to time have been promptly squelched by parents, peers, priests, and other vested interests. Many of those who are aware of the possibility of alternatives are at a loss to know how one can abandon belief without substituting something else. They might be inclined towards humanism if they knew more about it, but they are understandably fearful of letting go the old and comfortable ways. While this may be a groundless fear, it is none the less disturbing to those who quaver on the brink between belief and skepticism. The proper humanist response to those who hold such doubts might be to compare religious thoughts to weeds in a garden. When we remove weeds to let desired plants grow, we do not replace the weeds with more weeds; we just get rid of the weeds. It is the same with religious thoughts; we just let them go, and turn our attention to more fruitful things.

As it is becoming clear that religious belief can lead to a number of psychoses, arising from guilt, doubt, and stress, humanists should examine ways to give more help to free those who still hold such beliefs from such bonds. One task for the humanist is to reassure people that there is absolutely no risk whatsoever in adopting humanism, and that at worst, they will experience a few temporary, minor, and manageable feelings of loss and perhaps aimlessness for a short while, followed by increasingly positive feelings of relief, certainty, and joy at the loss of feelings of guilt and fear. Another task for humanists is to spread the word about humanist values. The great majority of the general public simply do not know about humanism. A minority of the public who have at least heard about humanism have little knowledge of its ideals, aims, or philosophy, for two main reasons: one, there is not a great deal of popular literature available on the subject, and two, they are discouraged from studying humanism by restrictions and false publicity spread about by religious organizations who view it as a threat to their own self-appointed mandates.

It is a well-founded fear for such organizations, as statistics show an overall decline in religious affiliation, from about 2% of the world's population in the year 1900 to more than 20% in the year 2000. Fewer people still are aware that there is a world-wide organizational pattern of humanist associations and regional chapters already established in most major cities, to which they can become formally attached or with which they can become informally affiliated. In essence these barriers constitute a public relations problem which so far has been poorly handled by the humanist movement, primarily for budgetary reasons. It costs money to advertise.

The primary concern, however, is not with what the individual person chooses to believe or not believe; each is as entitled to his or her own beliefs as anyone else. The primary concern is undoubtedly with the organization of religion into big business by the establishment of churches of every stripe, shade, and hue. The main objective of these organizations appears to be the raising of financial fortunes through the imposition of dogmatic nonsense and false promises of forlorn hopes on adherents on one hand, while on the other hand financing the pursuit of restraints of many repressive and anti-social kinds on adherents and non-adherents alike, through pressure on weak-minded politicians at every level of government. That is one of the problems facing society in general and humanism in particular. The members of humanist associations in company with their colleagues and sympathizers around the world must therefore do what they can to bring about change, within the confines of the legal, democratic, and educational processes available to them.

To be successful in this task, humanists must convince an optimum number of other human beings of the strength of the humanist intellectual stance. This critical number is not yet known, and some thought might be given to research by sociologists to attempt to determine it. Once it has been established, and then achieved, a form of momentum will tend to carry the message out in ever widening circles to the rest of society. The next task is then to place humanists in positions of political power, to ensure that a broad and democratic humanist education is made available to all, but especially to the young people throughout the world. In the meantime, it is necessary that all humanists encourage other individuals whom they know to have sympathetic views to join existing humanist groups or to start new ones. Active membership and adequate funding are the primary keys to success in any organization, as a study of any religious group confirms. The most effective counterbalance to organized religion will be organized humanism.

The seriousness and urgency of the situation can be best understood by realizing that there is a definite purpose expressed by the leaders of the 35 million fundamentalist Christians in the United States. One of their leaders, during an interview on a nationally televised broadcast, categorically stated that, if they gain power, no secular humanist would be permitted to hold any public office in the United States. Former President George Bush is on record as saying that atheists should not be considered as citizens. Such statements indicate a level of intolerance, bigotry, and political purpose that the humanist movement ignores at its peril.

A review of the preceding chapters of this book makes it clear that there are many different schools of religious thought and human belief. They may all be wrong, but they cannot all be right. Indeed, if any one of them is right, then the others must be wrong, because of the generally opposing, conflicting, and exclusive views which they take and hold. It is of course not necessary to decide which one is right or wrong, as the question is never raised for discussion, certainly not by these groups themselves. The followers of each (including humanists) think that their views are the correct ones. It is therefore up to the reader to form his or her own opinion about the rightness, wrongness, or worth of any of these dogmas.

Most religions claim to have only the best interests of the human condition at heart. Few religions make the claim that its beliefs or its adherents are inherently harmful to the rest of humanity, provided the rest of humanity is prepared to adopt and adapt to the creed and style of the specific religion. Yet the record clearly shows that most of the strife in the world, both in history and at present, stems from differences in religious belief or tradition, and the attempts by one group or another to impose its parochial or supernatural views on its neighbors.

If there is any doubt in the mind of the reader that religion is not harmful, consider a few examples from recent years. Christians have slaughtered Muslims in Beirut; Muslims slaughtered Jews in Israel; Sikhs slaughtered Hindus in Pakistan; Hindus slaughtered Sikhs in the Punjab; Protestants slaughtered Catholics in Northern Ireland, Catholics slaughtered Protestants in Eire; Jews slaughtered Palestinians in North Africa; Dutch Reformed Christians slaughtered Blacks in South Africa; Shiites slaughtered high-jacked air passengers in India; the Ayatollah of Iran and the rulers of Iraq have between them slaughtered 300,000 people in a Holy War, and the President of the United States of America talked of biblical Armageddon in the name of

Christianity. This list could unfortunately be extended at much greater length, as the events of September 11, 2001 have sadly shown.

In contrast, not one death anywhere in the entire world can be attributed to the modern humanist movement with respect to opposition to its ideals. It is a profound contrast. Perhaps it is time for the people of the world to consider adoption of the more kindly, tolerant, non-religious humanist approach to the solution of its problems.

E.4 SOME SUGGESTIONS

The realm of ideas, articulated by Pierre Teilhard in his invention and use of the word "noosphere," to add to the earthly concepts of lithosphere, biosphere, and atmosphere, are now accepted as having aspects of reality by many existentialists, atheists, agnostics, humanists, and others who do not hold traditional religious beliefs. The development of the InterNet is a concrete example of the Teilhard "realm." Using the InterNet, humanists are in the position to improve the quality of life for everyone, through the inexpensive and broad dissemination of ideas about education and caring, and not through force or dogma. The age of strict materialism and mechanism may be declining, and a new age of understanding of the real nature of humankind may soon be ushered in. Informed people do not now consider humankind to be nothing more than atoms interacting, like the parts of a machine. To continue to say that the lives of those who do not believe in a supernatural God are therefore machine-like and bereft of moral standards is drivel. The quality of life may be intangible, but it is nevertheless real.

It is possible to believe and accept that the living cell is, in the final analysis, simply the most complex of all systems yet evolved, synergetically possessing more value than the structural, mechanical, chemical, or electrical properties of which it consists, and the human animal to which these cells give rise, simply but equally synergetically the most complex of all animals, in so far as we know. The cumulative effect of all these machine-like attributes could certainly give rise to beings such as man and the other animals, having non-material characteristics that may be described as emotional or psychological for lack of more descriptive words. Certainly, there are still many unanswered questions about living processes which are not now understood, but the humanist is prepared to live with such uncertainty for the time being, to go about his or her daily life with some equanimity, but ready to rise to the challenge of seeking more answers to life's many marvelous mysteries.

With respect to our universal origins, one can say that if the universe has always existed, it is also plausible to believe that life in the universe has always existed. We just cannot prove it at this point in our development; in fact, we may never prove it conclusively. But we should be cautious about holding such unsubstantiated beliefs, for the reasons given in an earlier section of this book. Nevertheless, there long has been and still is a great deal of pernicious nonsense being spread about by religious apologists regarding the start of life. Stories which debunk the so-called primordial soup from which life on earth allegedly sprang abound in the theological literature, and yet, if an infinite life force is universally pervasive (as it appears to be) and if the correct chemical, physical, electrical and other conditions prevailed at some point in time on earth, then life as we know it would start on earth (as it obviously did) and probably has done so in other forms that we do not know elsewhere in the universe.

With respect to morality, the root of the problem of good and evil lies in the fact that both concepts exist only in the human mind (as shown in Chapter 1.4) and have nothing to do with gods that do not exist. When the external environment of heaven and earth is placed uppermost in the human mind as it undeniably is in our society which is founded on the Christian/Judaic and more recently Islamic heritage, then the tendency in society at large is towards theism; conversely, if it could be placed below human interest in itself, as it should be in a rational society, the tendency would be towards atheism. The task for humanism is refocus the attention and priorities of humankind at the proper level of interest in the development of humankind. It is a difficult task. Although the opportunities for humanism are undoubtedly great, there is still a general lack of knowledge of and therefore uninformed distaste for humanist ideals in homes, schools, universities, and colleges, and particularly in churches, temples, mosques, and synagogues, as well as in the workplace and throughout society in general.

With respect to the objectives of humanism, there is nothing threatening in humanism to anyone or anything except those with vested interests in the prolongation of religion. Steps should be taken by humanists to insist on the teaching of humanistic values in the public school system, to encourage the placement of books by humanist authors in the public libraries, to hasten the reduction of religious influence in society at large, and to bring about the corresponding abandonment of public manifestations of religion at periods of celebration of good fortune or mourning in the event of misfortune, so that children would grow up knowing that rational and respectable alternatives to so-called revealed religion exist.

In an earlier section, this book endeavored to put man in his proper place in the universe. It now concludes by putting the idea of imaginary gods in their proper place in the minds of humans, namely, the imagination. It will remain to be seen how history treats religion in future. The German philosopher Friedrich Nietzsche described Christianity as "the immortal blemish of mankind"; it might be more accurate to describe religion in general as a mortal blemish, mortal because it is conceivable (though not imminent) that all religious notions will one day be abandoned and die out, and a blemish because of the false hopes and misery which these ideas and practices have caused and still cause untold millions of people throughout the length and breadth of human history and geography.

To end on a positive note, though, humanists might well remember the pragmatic advice of William James, who said that "ideas become true just in so far as they help us to get into satisfactory relations with the other parts of our experience." There is therefore no need to get hung up on worries about the origins or future fate of the universe, about the wrath and vengeance of jealous gods, or about the astonishing claims of parasitical mystics, mendacious magicians, and others quoting from revealed scripture. It is time for humanists to get the true, reassuring, and happy message about the dependability of human experience out to the people of the world. For humanists, the heavens may be indeed empty of gods, but their minds can and should be full of knowledge and love, coupled to optimism, for time and common sense are on their side.

Appendices and Bibliography

APPENDICES

A.1 GLOSSARY

In discussions about philosophy and religion, technical terms having special meanings are often used, as well as many common words to which more refined or accurate meanings have to be ascribed. For convenience of the reader, many such special words, encountered in this book and elsewhere, are alphabetically listed below with simplified explanations. The meanings of most other words in this book will be clear from the contexts in which they used.

1. List of Words

Angel: an imaginary spiritual guide, messenger, or attendant; placed into any one of nine ranks.
Animism: belief that all animate and inanimate objects have some kind of magical spirit in them.
Armageddon: the alleged final battle between the forces of good and evil. The name derives from a mountain in Israel.
Awe: treatment of a sacred object or place with feelings of profound reverence, coupled to the notion that blessings or harm may flow as a result of various attitudes or actions.
Blasphemy: to speak irreverently or impiously about things held sacred by some, such as gods; to represent oneself as a god or God.
Bliss: the alleged joy of heaven; pure enlightenment.
Catechism: elementary instruction in the principles of Christianity.

Chrism: an anointment, an unguent, a salve oil.
Christ: one who has been anointed with consecrated oil.
Consecrate: to declare sacred, by an appropriate clergyman.
Cosmogony: a theory of the origin of the universe.
Cosmology: a branch of philosophy dealing with the origin and general structure of the universe.
Deist: one who believes gods exist, but that they are not concerned with human affairs.
Deity: having the character or rank of a supreme being.
Dialectic: pertaining to the nature of logical argumentation, such as one finds in formal teaching/learning transactions.
Didactic: pertaining to authoritative instruction, such as occurs in bible study courses.
Divination: the attempt to predict, either directly or through an intermediary, the intentions of a god or a spirit.
Empirical: derived from or guided by experience or experiment, not necessarily with the use of science or theory.
Epistemology: philosophical investigation of theories of the origin, nature, methods, and limits of knowledge and belief.
Fetishism: thought processes intended to imbue objects with magical powers
Heuristic: to point out; to indicate; to encourage learning.
Idolatry: the process of worshiping icons, idols, or images, that may or may not represent deities.
Immanent: taking place in the mind, and having no effect outside of it.
Ineffable: an inexpressible, unspeakable idea or sensation.
Laic, Lay: secular; not belonging to or connected with a profession, especially a religious order.
Manna: believed by some to be a type of universal supernatural energy or occult power, silent but all-pervasive.
Metaphysics: a branch of philosophy dealing with first principles. It considers the relationship of mind and body.
Miracle: an occurrence which allegedly surpasses the known laws of nature.

Mythology: a body of traditional or legendary stories.
Nirvana: a state of bliss, free of pain, allegedly achieved through repeated reincarnations of the soul.
Ontology: the science of being; metaphysical investigation of the nature of being.
Pious: showing a dutiful spirit of reverence for God.
Pragmatism: a system of thought which places emphasis on practical consequences and values.
Primordial: original, elementary, a beginning.
Rapturing: alleged transportation by God of the souls of the saved from earth to heaven at an unspecified end time.
Ritual: a system of religious observances or procedures, the meaning of much of which has been often forgotten.
Sacrament: a visible act intended to confer divine grace on persons entitled to receive such blessing.
Shunning: excommunication and ostracization (banishment) of individuals from religious sects or cults because of real or alleged transgressions against set rules of conduct or belief.
Soul: regarded by some as an entity of unspecified form, distinct from the physical aspects of mind and body.
Spirit: the alleged vital essence of living human beings, mediating between the body and its soul; semantically associated with the breath. All humans allegedly *have* spirits; angels, demons, devils, elves, etc. allegedly *are* spirits.
Teleology: the study of evidence of design or purpose in nature, based on the erroneous belief that apparent order in the universe implies an orderer, such as God.
Theogony: study of the origin of gods.
Theology: study of attributes of gods and their relationship to the universe.
Veneration: to be worthy of reverence; involving the worship of sacred things, such as a plant or an animal, or sacred concepts or ideas, such as the soul of a saint, because of their imaginary spiritual powers.

2. A Note about Dates

The current "Gregorian Calendar" was developed (by Pope Gregory) from an earlier "Julian Calendar" (established by Julius Caesar) in 46 BCE. In the Gregorian system, dates are given as being either BC (for *Before Christ*) or AD (for *Anno Domini*—the Year of our Lord). Cleopatra was Queen of Egypt in 30 BC (and thus would have been a contemporary of Jesus Christ, if such ever existed.); America was discovered in 1492 AD. Dates in this book are secularly characterized as being either CE (for *Current* or *Common* Era) or BCE.(Before the *Current* or *Common* Era). America was discovered in 1492 CE; Cleopatra was Queen in 30 BCE. It can also be noted that other cultures (such as the Chinese) have their own calendars distinct from those above.

A.2 HUMANIST ASSOCIATIONS

Similar to the views mentioned in Section 1.2.3 *Authorities*, many people not only do not know of any humanist *authors*, they also have no idea of the number of *associations* which already exist to cater to the needs of atheists, agnostics, humanists, and other free-thinkers. The purpose of this section of the book is likewise to close this gap in information, by listing the names and addresses of some of the many national and international organizations that readers can contact for support and to support, and to meet and exchange views with like-minded people of all abilities, ages, colors, enthusiasms, ethnic origins, nationalities, races, and so on.

Most of these bodies hold regular meetings in local chapters, organize annual conferences, publish newsletters or magazines, and generally put forward the non-believer's cause to government and to the public at large. Once each year, an international conference on topics of interest to humanists is organized in a different major world capital.

In the United States, there are humanist chapters in about 25 states and contacts for the American Humanist Association in each of the remaining 25 states. In Canada, there are chapters in about 5 provinces with contacts for the Humanist Association of Canada in the remaining 5 provinces. The current and correct addresses for all of these chapters and contacts can be obtained from each national association office respectively. Many of them also have Internet addresses and e-mail facilities.

1. List of Selected Associations

Alliance of Secular Humanist Societies, PO Box 664, Amherst, New York. 14226-0664 USA

American Humanist Association, 7 Harwood Drive, PO Box 146, Amherst, New York. 14226

Atheist Center, Benz Circle, Vijayawada, 520 006, India

British Humanist Association, 13 Prince of Wales Terrace, London. W8 5PG, England

Council for Democratic and Secular Humanism, PO Box 5, Central Park Station, Buffalo, New York. 14215

Freedom from Religion Foundation, PO Box 750, Madison, Wisconsin. 53701 USA

Humanist Association of Canada, PO Box 3736, Station C, Ottawa, Ontario, K1Y 4J8, Canada

International Humanist and Ethical Union, 47 Theobald's Road, London WC1X 8SP, England

Apart from the associations listed above, there are of course many others, in countries such as Argentina, Australia, Denmark, France, Holland, Germany, Ireland, Japan, Korea, Malaysia, New Zealand, the Philippines, Scotland, Singapore, and elsewhere, for which addresses may be obtained through the International Union. The reason that their postal addresses are not listed here is that, because there are so many of them, they are more likely to change than the addresses of the major national and international associations given above, all of which were correct at the time of this publication.

2. InterNet Addresses

1. *Humanist Association of Canada*
   www.humanists.net/hic
2. *International Humanist & Ethical Union*
   www.iheu.org
3. *American Humanist Association*
   www.humanist.net
4. *Freedom from Religion Foundation*
   www.ffrf.org
5. *Alliance of Secular Humanist Societies*
   www.secularhumanist.org/ashs/

A.3 HUMANIST PUBLICATIONS

To complete the introduction to sources of information about humanist activities and affairs given in Section A.2, mention should be made of the enormous range of literature that is available either free of charge or by subscription to interested readers. Almost every humanist organization publishes a newsletter, a monthly journal, a quarterly periodical, or an annual report of some sort.

1. Newspapers and Magazines

Some examples of current magazine-style publications available at a nominal subscription rate would include "The Humanist," published bi-monthly by the American Humanist Association, "Humanist in Canada," published quarterly by the Humanist Association of Canada, "International Humanist," also published quarterly by the International Humanist and Ethical Union, "The Humanist Newsletter," published monthly by the British Humanist Association, and "Free Enquiry." The Australian Council of Humanist Associations publishes a quarterly magazine titled "The Australian Humanist" and each of the five Australian Humanist Societies publishes either a monthly or bi-monthly magazine of its own. The New Zealand Humanist Information Service also publishes topical material. The Freedom From Religion Foundation publishes a monthly newspaper generally concerned with issues related to the separation of church and state. Addresses for each of these Associations, Councils, and Services are listed below or in Appendix A.2 *Associations.*

2. Books and Audio-Visuals

Readers preferring to acquire lengthier books on humanism and related topics may refer to the *Bibliography*. The following publishers also offer a wide range of appropriate hard and soft cover material; some also produce audio and video tapes. Subscribe, read, learn, discuss, exchange, and enjoy.

American Atheist Press, PO Box 2117, Austin, Texas 78768, USA
Canadian Humanist Publications, PO Box 3769, Station C, Ottawa, Ontario. K1Y 4J8
Freedom From Religion Foundation, Inc., PO Box 750, Madison, Wisconsin 53701, USA
Free Inquiry, PO Box 5, Buffalo, New York, 14215 USA
The Humanist Press, PO Box 146, Amherst, New York 14226, USA
Prometheus Books, Inc., 700 East Amherst Street, Buffalo, New York 14215, USA
Rationalist Press Association, 88 Islington High Street, London, N1 8EW, ENGLAND
The Skeptical Inquirer, PO Box 703, Amherst, New York. 14228, USA

A.4 CHAPTER FORMATION

1. Introduction

If there are no humanist organizations in the area where the reader resides, he or she can start a local group or chapter, with or without the assistance of the larger national bodies. The technique is simple and is explained below. The main thing about starting a humanist group is just to go ahead and do it, and not to worry that it might not work, or that there will be problems, or that people won't come or won't pay, or that there may be some adverse reaction. There are difficulties with any enterprise involving humans, but that should not deter people from doing what they know is right and worthwhile. The two main elements involved in any local humanist chapter or group are more or less as listed in the following section: *establish* it, and *operate* it. The two main issues will be *people* and *money*—both need careful handling.

2. Chapter Establishment

A Chapter can be (and many have been) formed by following the suggestions outlined below:

1. Discuss the possibility of establishing a local group or chapter with one or two like-minded friends.
2. Review the possibility that such groups may already exist, such as in local universities, colleges, community centers, or in connection with the local branch of the Unitarian Church (if such exists), with a view to consolidating and not duplicating existing opportunities.
3. Contact the national Humanist Association in your own country (see Appendix A.2) for names of members in your region. If none is listed, the International Humanist and Ethical Union may be able to help.
4. Hold a few meetings in a private home or office, until there are about 8 or 10 interested members.
5. Collect about $100 US (or its local equivalent) in donations from the informal group, and appoint a president, a secretary, and a treasurer, to put together a membership mailing list and a simple program.
6. Rent a post office box and telephone service, and get stationary printed, to establish permanent communication links. When

funds permit, get a phone-answering and fax machine, and arrange for InterNet and e-mail communication.

7. Decide on the classifications of membership and the annual dues relative to each classification. Membership categories might include Individual, Family, Student, Retired, Honorary, and Associate (for those who are unemployed or otherwise disadvantaged).

8. Delegate one member to extend publicity for the meetings, by sending notices to local newspapers, preparing announcements for free community service spots on local radio and TV stations, and by preparing simple notices for posting on local bulletin boards in libraries, laundromats, and work-place notice boards.

9. Delegate one member to secure a suitable monthly meeting place, by renting a room in a community center, school, museum, or private building. If possible, hold each meeting at the same place. Obviously, avoid using church halls, and avoid any situation involving some sort of obligation to the landlord, other than simple payment of rent.

10. Delegate one member to keep the membership lists up-to-date and to develop a phoning committee to keep members in touch. As membership grows, delegate one member to develop, print, and circulate a newsletter.

11. The executive board as a whole should decide on a suitable themes for the program of meetings. Delegate a couple of members to coordinate the program of activities.

12. No matter what day of the week is chosen for meetings, it is not possible to satisfy everyone every month. One solution is to hold meetings on different days of the week, such as a Sunday afternoon in one month, and a Wednesday evening the following month, and perhaps one or two social gatherings per year for a picnic or a casual dinner.

13. It is good (some say necessary) practice to take up a collection at each meeting to cover at least the costs of the room and equipment rental, and to pay or otherwise host

the guest speaker, if necessary. Such costs should not come out of membership fees; most people will willingly contribute a reasonable amount. There is also the positive psychological factor of paying for something of value.
14. Delegate one member to keep the Association archival records of incorporation, affiliation, executive meetings, financial affairs, publicity, correspondence, etc.
15. Form a non-profit society (using legal aid or assistance from a lawyer member) and get it registered as such with local government, making any necessary adjustments to the Executive Board. There are significant financial benefits to such official registration. Apply to the appropriate government revenue department for tax-exempt status as a non-profit society. Take special care to select a truly representative name or title for the group, such as a local urban or rural geographical region.

3. Chapter Operation

The Operation involves selection of topics for discussion, speakers, and activities.

1. Topics for discussion at the regular monthly meetings can include anything of interest to the membership, such as explanation of the basic humanist ideals, the humanist manifestos, social issues such as the constitution, abortion, ecology, ethics, euthanasia, capital punishment, gun control, library collections, marriage, morality, prayer in schools, separation of church and state, sex education, skepticism, and suicide, to name only a few. Talks can be developed on humanism in art, in music, in history, in literature, in politics, and in government. Topics can be presented using discussion leaders, small group sessions, video or cassette tapes, films, field trips, and even amateur dramatic skits for fun and a change of pace. Participation by and involvement of the listening audience is to be

encouraged; humanists as a group tend to be lively, gregarious, well-informed, and out-spoken, so plenty of time and opportunity for assertion, rebuttal, and questions should be allowed at every meeting.

2. Take care to invite reasonably talented and knowledgeable speakers to give *informed* views on the selected program topics. Many universities and colleges have speaker's bureaus, through which lecturers can be often secured for little or no charge, to talk on a given subject; many professional associations (such as legal, medical, or social) can provide speakers to talk on issues of public interest and concern, such as public transit, senior's issues, child care, or health facilities. The program leader or chairperson should be fairly comfortable and skilled at leading such meetings, as they can become quite boisterous at times, and at other times, things may not go too smoothly, if speakers come late, or audio-visual equipment breaks down, or an argument develops. It is always wise to have a back-up plan (such as a video) ready in the event of failure.

3. Group activities can include giving support to peace marches, fair parades, abortion services and clinics, and public service ventures, such as hospital and prison visits. There are also many other public opportunities to get some free publicity for the humanist movement. Simple banners can be made, tee-shirts produced with the humanist logo, and inexpensive flyers and lapel buttons can be printed for handing out to the public. A small table stall to distribute humanist information can be set up at almost any public function, such as a fete or picnic for a national holiday, while display boards can be assembled and then located in the lobbies of local libraries or school buildings, with permission. Letters to the editors of local newspapers is probably the least expensive way to get good public coverage at short notice.

Individual activities can include development of talks for presentation to the members at their monthly meetings, preparation of humanist book-title lists, printing of humanist greetings cards, manufacture of humanist lapel pins, organization of specific aspects of publicity, or arranging simple social events, such as informal pot-luck dinners for the members, where members bring a favorite dish of food to share with others.

4. The main thing is to *get on with it*—it will more than likely work out just fine!

4. Brief History

As a footnote to all of the foregoing information, humanism as we now know it in North America grew out of the humanist movement in Europe, reaching back to about the 16th Century CE. In the United States, it had its beginnings with some of the deists involved in composing the Declaration of Independence, and much later, with John Dietrich in 1916 in the Unitarian Church in Minneapolis. By 1924, Dietrich and a colleague named Curtiss Reese had formed the nucleus of the new movement, leading to the publication of a magazine called "The New Humanist" by students at the University of Chicago in 1927. The first humanist society in the USA appears to have been established by a man named Theodore Curtiss Abell in Hollywood, California, on 13 January 1929; the first Humanist Manifesto was published in 1933 and the first Humanist National Assembly was held in New York City on 10 October 1934. The American Humanist Association was incorporated in 1941, the International Humanist and Ethical Union was founded in 1952 in Holland, and the Humanist Association of Canada was incorporated in 1966. The first edition of the AHA "Humanist" magazine was published in 1942, and the first edition of the HAC "Humanist in Canada" magazine was published in 1967. There are now approximately 60 million humanists world-wide, of whom about one third are active members of hundreds of humanist associations in about 35 countries. New groups are being formed with increasing frequency and existing groups are being enlarged with increasing rapidity all over the world. For readers interested in this aspect of the humanist movement, there is a wealth of information available from national associations.

BIBLIOGRAPHIES

B.1 REFERENCES IN PART ONE

This section lists titles actually mentioned or to which **direct reference** was made for **Part One** of the book

Alper, Matthew. *The "God" Part of the Brain.* Rogue Press, New York. 2000
Baigent, Michael et al. *Holy Blood and Holy Grail.* Corgi Books, London, 1986
Beckwith, Burnham P. *The Decline of U.S. Religious Faith.* Beckwith Publications, CA 1985
Bromley, David G. *Falling from the Faith.* Sage Publications, CA. 1988
Caplovitz, S. *The Religious Drop-Outs.* Sage Publications, CA. 1977
Duncan, Alastair R.C. *Moral Philosophy.* CBC Publications, Toronto. 1965
Fuller, R. Buckminster. *I seem to be a Verb.* Bantam Books, New York. 1970
Gagne, Robert M. *The Conditions of Learning.* Holt, Rinehart, and Winston, Inc. N.Y. 1970
Gaylor, Annie L. (Ed) *Women without Superstition.* FFRF Press, Madison, WI 1997
Greely, R.E. (Ed.) *The Best of Humanism,* Prometheus Books, New York. 1988
Gould, Stephen Jay. *This View of Life.* New Zealand "Humanist," Winter 1986

Hayes, Judith. *In God We Trust: But Which One?* FFRF Press, Madison WI. 1996

Hendricks, Willian D. *Exit Interviews.* Moody Press, Chicago. 1993

Hume, D. *An Enquiry Concerning the Principle of Morals.* Open Court, Chicago. 1995

Huxley, Julian. *The Humanist Frame.* Harper and Brothers, New York. 1962

Knight Margaret. *Morals without Religion.* National Secular Society, London. 1983

Kurtz, Paul. *The New Skepticism.* Prometheus Books. Buffalo, New York. 1992

Lamont, Corliss. *The Philosophy of Humanism.* Frederick Ungar Publishing Co., N.Y. 1982

Lecky, William. *A History of European Morals.* Longmans Green, London. 1911 (Vols I & II)

Mackie, J.L. *Ethics: Inventing Right & Wrong.* Penguin Books, London, UK 1990

Neill, A.S. *Summerhill—A Radical Approach to Child Rearing* Hart Publishing Co., N.Y. 1960

Piaget, Jean. *The Construction of Reality in the Child.* Ballantyne Books, New York. 1971.

Rooney, Andrew A. *And More by Andy Rooney.* Antheum Press, New York. 1982 (p. 203)

Smith, George A. *Atheism: The Case Against God.* Prometheus Books, Buffalo, NY. 1989

Smith, Warren Allen. *Celebrities in Hell,* Barricade Books, New Jersey. 2002

Smoker, Barbara. *Humanism.* The National Secular Society, London. 1984

Stein, Gordon (Ed.) *The Encyclopedia of Unbelief.* Prometheus Books, Buffalo. 1985

Strem, George G. *Agnosticism is Also Faith.* Libra Books, San Diego, California. 1986

Wilson, Edwin H. *The Genesis of a Humanist Manifesto.* Humanist Press, New York. 1995

Wilson, John. *Moral Thinking.* Heinemann Educational Books. London. 1973

Winell, Marlene *Leaving the Fold.* New Harbinger Publications, Oakland, CA 1994

B.2 REFERENCES IN PART TWO

This section lists titles actually mentioned or to which **direct reference** was made for **Part Two** of the book

Adams, I. and Galati, R. *The Power of the Wheel: Falun Gong.* Stoddart Publishing, Toronto. 2000

Amanat, Abbas. *Resurrection and Renewal.* Cornell University Press, Ithica. 1989

Aristotle. *Nicomachean Ethics* (Trans. T. Irwin) Hackett Publishing, Indiana. 1985

Baha'u'llah (excerpts) *The Reality of Man.* Baha'i Publishing Trust, Wilmette. Illinois. 1969

Barker, Dan. *Losing Faith in Faith.* Freedom from Religion Foundation, Inc., Madison. 1992

2 Blank, Jonah. *Arrow of the Blue Skinned God.* Image-Doubleday, New York. 1993

Brantl, George. (Ed.) *Catholicism.* George Braziller, Inc., New York, 1962

Cavendish, Richard. (Ed.) *Mythology—An Illustrated Encyclopedia.* Rizzoli Publishers, NY 1980

Clark, Peter. *Zoroastrianism.* Sussex Academic Press, Portland, OR. 1998

Cook, Michael. *The Koran—a Very Short Introduction.* Oxford University Press, U.K. 2000

Culver, Roger B. and Ianna, Philip A. *Astrology: True or False?* Prometheus Books, Buffalo. 1988

Dancy, Jonathan. *Introduction to Contemporary Epistemology.* Basil Blackwell, Oxford. 1989

Doherty, Earl. *The Jesus Puzzle.* Canadian Humanist Publications, Ottawa. 1999

Drury, N. & Tillert, G. *The Occult Source Book.* Routledge & Kegan Paul, Ltd., London. 1978

Dunstan, J. Leslie. (Ed.) *Protestantism*. George Braziller, Inc., New York, 1962

Feather, Norman T. *Values in Education and Society*. Free Press, New York, 1975)

Fuller, R. Buckminster. *Critical Path*. St. Martins Press, New York. 1981

Gagné, Robert M. *The Conditions of Learning*. Holt, Rinehart, Winston, Inc., New York. 1970

Gard, Richard A. (Ed.) *Buddhism*. George Braziller, Inc., New York. 1962

Goulder, Michael and Hick, John. *Why Believe in God?* SCM Press, Ltd., London. 1983

Grattan, Hartley C. (Ed.) *The Critique of Humanism*. Books for Libraries Press, New York. 1968

Green, Ruth H. *The Born Again Skeptic's Guide to the Bible* FFRF Press, Madison, WI. 1992

Harris, Bill. *The Good Luck Book*. Ottenheimer Publications, Baltimore, MD. 1996

Hartz, Paula R. *Shinto*. Facts on File Publishers, New York. 1997

Hawkin, Stephen W. *A Brief History of Time* Bantam Books, New York.1988

Hertzberg, Arthur. (Ed.) *Judaism*. George Braziller, Inc., New York, 1962

Jung, Carl G. *Modern Man in Search of a Soul*. Harcourt Brace & World, New York. 1933

Knight, Margaret. *Christianity: the Debit Account*. National Secular Society, London. 1975

Lau, Kwan. *Feng Shui for Today*. Tengu Books, New York. 1996

Leys, Simon. *The Analects of Confucius*. W.W. Norton & Co., New York. 1997

Maharishi Mahesh Yogi *Transcendental Meditation*. Signet Books, New Jersey. 1963

Maslow, A.H. *A Theory of Human Motivation*. Pyschological Review, Vol. 50, Page 370. 1943

Mcleod, W.H. *The Study of Sikhism—Textual Sources*. Manchester University Press, U.K. 1984

McNaughton, William. *The Taoist Vision*. Ann Arbor Paperbacks, Michigan. 1973

Meyer, P. & Levesque, C. *Honore-Timothee Lempfrit (Trail Journal)*. Galleon Press, WA. 1985

Momen, Moojan. *The Phenomenon of Religion*. One World Press, Oxford. 1999

Nabokov, Peter (Ed.) *Native American Testimony*. Thomas Y. Crowall, New York.1978

Nahar, P.C. & Ghosh, K.C. *An Encyclopedia of Jainism*. Sri Satguru Publications, Delhi. 1988

Noss, John B. *Man's Religions*. Macmillan Publishing Co., Inc., New York. 1974

O'Brien, J. and Martin, P. *The State of Religion Atlas*. Simon & Schuster, New York. 1993

Prager D, & Telkushkin, J. *Eight Questions About Judaism*. Tze Ulmad Press, New York. 1975

Renou, Luois. (Ed.) *Hinduism*. George Braziller, Inc., New York, 1962

Revised Standard Version. *The Holy Bible*. Thomas Nelson & Sons. New York. 1953

Robinson, Richard. *An Atheist's Values*. Clarendon Press, Oxford. 1964

Rokeach, M. *The Nature of Human Values*. Free Press, New York, 1973

Ross, Nancy W. *Three Ways of Asian Wisdom*. *Clarion* Books, Simon & Schuster, Inc., NY 1966

Russell, Bertrand. *Why I am Not a Christian*. Simon & Schuster, Inc., New York. 1957

Scriven, Michael. *Primary Philosophy*. McGraw-Hill, New York. 1966

Secaucus, N.J. *Proverbs from around the World*. (N. Gleason, Ed.) Carol Publishing Group, 1992

Shulma Albert M. *The Religious Heritage of America*. A.S Barnes & Co., Inc., New York. 1981

Sohail, K. *From Islam to Secular Humanism*. Abbey Field Publishers, Toronto. 2001

Stein, Gordon (Ed.) *The Encyclopedia of Unbelief.* Prometheus Books, Buffalo. 1985

Stenger, Victor. *Not by Design.* Prometheus Books, Buffalo, NY. 1988

Templeton, Charles. *Farewell to God.* McClelland & Stewart, Toronto. 1996

Teilhard, Pierre. *The Phenomenon of Man.* Fontana Books, William Collins & Son, London. 1955

Tillich, Paul. "Lost Dimensions in Religion" *Adventures of the Mind.* A. Knopf, New York. 1960

Tokarev, Sergei. *History of Religion* Progress Publishers, Moscow, 1989

Watters, Wendell W. *Deadly Doctrine: Christian God-talk.* Prometheus Books, Buffalo. 1988

Watts, Alan. *The Book—On the Taboo Against Knowing Who You Are.* Random, NY. 1972

Wells, George A. *The Historical Evidence for Jesus.* Prometheus Books, Buffalo. 1982

Williams, John A. (Ed.) *Islam.* George Braziller, Inc., New York, 1962

Varghese, Roy Abraham. *Intellectuals Speak Out about God.* Regnery Gateway, Chicago. 1984

Young, Willard A. *Fallacies of Creationism.* Detselig Enterprises, Calgary. 1985

B.3 REFERENCES IN GENERAL

In addition to the foregoing, there are many other publications which influenced the thoughts of the author before and during the preparation of this work. This section is in two parts, relative to the two parts of the book.

A. Background to Part One.

American Humanist Association. *Statement of Principles.* Buffalo, New York. 2000

Ayer, A.J. *The Problem of Knowledge*. Penguin Books, London, UK. 1966

Blackham, H.J. *Objections to Humanism* Penguin Books, London. UK 1965

Blanshard, Paul. *Classics of Free Thought*. Prometheus Books, Buffalo, 1977

Buckman, Robert. *Can We Be Good Without God?* Penguin Books, Toronto. 2000

Dawkins, Richard. *The Blind Watchmaker*. Penguin Books, London. UK 1991

Durant, Will. *The Story of Philosophy*. Simon & Schuster, Inc., New York. 1953

Ehrenfeld, David W. *The Arrogance of Humanism*. Oxford University Press, New York. 1978

Ericson, Edward L. *The Humanist Way*. Continuum Publishing Company, New York. 1988

Flew, A.(Ed.) *Hume: Enquiry Concerning Human Understanding*. Open Court, Chicago. 1996

Hawton, Hector. *The Humanist Revolution*. Pemberton Books, London. 1963

Humanist Association of Canada *Statement of Principles*. H.A.C, Ottawa. 1974

Hutcheon, Pat Duffy. *The Road to Reason* Canadian Humanist Publications, Ottawa. 2001

Hutcheon, Pat Duffy. *Leaving the Cave*. Wilfred Laurier University Press, Ontario. 1996

Hume, David. *Writings on Religion* (A: Flew, Ed.) Open Court, Chicago. 1992

James, William. *Pragmatism*. New American Library, New York. 1974

Kant, Immanuel. *Critique of Pure Reason* (Kemp-Smith Trans.) St. Martin's Press, N.Y. 1965

Knight, Margaret. *Humanist Anthology*. Pemberton Publishing Co., Ltd., London. 1961

Kurtz, Paul W. *In Defense of Secular Humanism*. Prometheus Books, Buffalo. 1983

Kurtz, Paul W. (Ed.) *Moral Problems in Contemporary Society* Prentice-Hall, Inc., NY. 1969

Kurtz, Paul W. (Ed.) *The Humanist Alternative*. Prometheus Books, Inc., Buffalo. 1973

Kurtz, Paul W. *The Transcendental Temptation*. Prometheus Books, Buffalo. 1986

Larue, Gerald A. *Freethought Across the Centuries*. Humanist Press, New York. 1996

Lonergan, Bernard J.F. *Insight—A Study of Human Understanding* Longmans, London, 1957.

MacIntyre, Alisdair *A Short History of Ethics*. Macmillan Publishing Co., New York. 1966

Neilson, Kai. *Philosophy and Atheism*. Prometheus Books, Buffalo. 1986

Rogers, Carl. *On Becoming a Person*. Houghton-Miflin, Inc., Boston. 1961

Russell, Bertrand. *Skeptical Essays*. Unwin Paperbacks, London. UK 1985

Schiller, Ferdinand C.S. *Humanism—Philosophical Essays*. Macmillan Company, N.Y. 1903

Sher, George. *Moral Philosophy: Selected Readings*. Harcourt Brace Johanovich, Inc., NY. 1987

Smith, Peter & Jones, O.R. *The Philosophy of Mind*. Cambridge University Press, UK. 1987

Watson, Gary. *Free Will*. Oxford University Press, UK 1990

B. Background to Part Two

Angeles, Peter. *Critiques of God*. Prometheus Books, New York. 1976

Bedoyere, M. de la, et al. *Objections to Roman Catholicism*. Penguin Books, London. 1964

Berkeley, George. *The Principles of Human Knowledge (1710)*. William Collins, London. 1975

Blackham, H.J. (Ed.) *Reality, Man and Existence*. Bantam Books, New York. 1965

Burtchaell, James Tunstead. *The Dying of the Light*. Eerdmans Publishing, Michigan. 1998

Davies, Paul. *The Mind of God*. Simon & Schuster, New York. 1992

Donyo, Victor (Ed.) *Mark Twain: Selected Writings*. Prometheus Books, Buffalo, 1995

Fromm, Erich. *You Shall Be As Gods*. Holt, Rinehart, Wilson, Inc., New York. 1966

Funk & Wagnalls. *New Encyclopedia*. Dun and Bradstreet Corporation, New York. 1983

James, William. *Pragmatism*. New American Library, New York. 1974

Martin, Michael. *The Case Against Christianity*. Temple University Press, Philadelphia. 1991

Nelms, Randel. *Gospel Fictions*. Prometheus Books, Buffalo, NY 1989

Newberg, Andrew et al. *NewsWeek* (p.52) "Religion and the Brain." May 7, 2001

Santayana, George. *Reason in Religion*. Dover Publications, Inc., New York. 1982

Tzu Lao. *The Way of Life*. (Trans. R.B. Blakney) New American Library, New York. 1955

Yallop, David. *In God's Name*. Jonathan Cape, London. 1984

INDEX

Aboriginal 167
Abortion 54,85
Adam & Eve 91
Adultery 79
Agnosticism 40,91
Allah 179
Animism 167
Angels 141
Apostasy:
    in general 94
    characteristics 97
Apostates 21,37,99
Armageddon 225
Arguments, theistic:
    design 156
    first cause 154
    moral 158
    natural laws 156
    ontological 160
    teleological 156
Ark of Covenant 79
Ark, Noah's 163
Aristotle 63,117
Astrology 140,178,200,206
Astronomy 200
Associations 22,236

Atheism 36,99,224
Authors, Authorities:
    Asimov, Isaac 99
    Barker, Dan 99,221
    Barrington, Dennis 47
    Beckwith, B.P. 97
    Bradlaugh, Charles 99
    Bromley, D.G 97
    Burns, Robert 77
    Bush, George, Sr. 224
    Calvin, John 175
    Caplovitz,S. 98
    Dawkins, Richard 108
    Descartes, Rene 62
    Doherty, Earl. 221
    France, Anatole 165
    Flynn, Tom 35
    Fuller, Buckminster 120,219
    George, Chief Dan 168
    Grattan, H. 220
    Gould, Stephen Jay 82,108
    Goulder, M. 221
    Haldeman, Julius 100
    Hendricks, W.D. 97
    Hook, Sydney 35
    Hume, David 46

Authors (continued)
   Huxley, T.H. 40
   Ingersoll, Robert 41,100
   James, William 228
   Kant, Immanuel 84,161
   Kurtz, Paul 35,47,72
   Lamont, Corliss 33,72,220
   MacArthur, Douglas 186
   Maslow, Abraham 116
   Moore, G.E. 161
   Nader, Ralph 150
   Nasrim, Taslima 100
   Nietzsche, F. 228
   Paine, Thomas 100
   Pfalzner, Paul 135
   Richler, Mordecai 72,100
   Russell, Bertrand: 36,135,151,159
   Sagan, Carl 100
   Scriven, Michael 136
   Seattle, Chief 169
   Shaw, Bernard G. 101
   Stanton, Elizabeth 100
   Stenger, Victor 108
   Teilhard, P. 226
   Templeton, C.101,221
   Toscaro, Roy 152
   Turner, Ted. 101
   Twain, Mark 77
   Varghese, R. 220
   Voltaire 22
   Watts, Alan 220
   Wells, G.A. 221

Bab, The 170
Bagua 207

Baha'i 170
Baha'u'llah 170
Baptism 16,187
Behavior 78,109
Beliefs: 60,132,139,142, 143,148,171,182,211
Bhagavad-Gita 178
Bible 168
Bible, translations 124
Biblical references: 61,79,80,124,159,217
Bigotry 28
Birth, accident 16
Birth, virgin 139
Black holes 128
Boy's Brigade 18
Brain states 96,137,162
Buddha 191
Buddhism 191
   Hinayana 192
   Mahyana 192
   Tantric 193
   Zen 193

Calendars 181,236
Calvin, John 175
Capital punishment 53
Cartesian 62
Caste system 179,187
Celibacy 152
Ceremony 64,70
Child development 88
Christ:
   crusade for 119
   evidence for 171

Christianity:
    and sin 91
    doxies 173
    Eucharist 172
    fundamentalist 224
    subdivisions of 176
    Trinity 172
Church:
    Protestant 175
    reformation of 175
    Rites 174
    Roman Catholic 173
Communications 119
Commandments 183
Confucianism 193
Constitutions 138,152,179
Cosmic theories:
    in general 126
    Big Bang 126
    Creationist 129
    Oscillation 127
    Steady State 127
    Thermodynamics 129
Councils, church 174
Covenant, Jewish 182
Creed 60,134
Cults 213
Cultural mosaic 30

Dalai Lama 193
Dark matter 64,130
Dates 236
Days of week 210
Deacon 17
Dead, arise from 172
Death 51
Death penalty
Decalogue 78
DEEDS 33
Definitions:
    apostasy 95
    belief 133,148
    humanism 33,34,42
    human beings 115
    learning 92
    religion 133,135
    secular 43,85
    sin 90
    value 117
Democratic 33
Dervishes, whirling 181
Devi 177
Devil 212,216
Diaspora, Jewish 184
Disasters 139,159
Divorce 86
DNA 55
Do unto others . . . 27,195
Dreams 148
Drugs 138
Duty 89,209

Earth 64,152
Education 23,68,88,224
Eroticism 57
Ethical 32
Euthanasia 53
Evangelicalism 176
Evil 159,227
Evolution 63,108

Eye of needle 124
Experience 18, 41, 82, 144, 161, 229

Faith 135, 136, 141, 142
Faith, leap of 86
Fallacies 151
Falun Gong 204
Fanaticism 142
Fear 151
Feng Shui 206
Fetus 56
Five Ks 187
Fraud 209
Free thinkers 60, 177
Funerals 66, 70

Gautama, Siddharta 191
Gender 69
Ghosts, holy 139
Glossary 233
God:
   acts of 67
   and creation
   and humor 139
   attributes of 39, 43, 79, 142
   belief in 38, 149
   existence of:
     22, 43, 154, 160, 162
   in mythologies 211
   jealous 80
   kingdom of 171
   laws of 152, 156
   proofs 154
Good 117, 149, 159, 204, 207, 227

Good life 106
Gora 40
Govind, Singh 187
Grammar 160
Graphics 121
Great Spirit 167, 211
Gurus 187

Halley's comet 51, 140
Happiness 117
Heaven 150, 229
Hebrews 182
Hell 165
Henry VIII 176
Hinduism 177
Holy books:
   Adi Granth 187
   Bible 125
   Classics 194
   Gathas
   Kogo-shui 185
   Koran (Q'ran) 180
   Pentateuch 183
   Smriti 177
   Torah 183
   Tri-Pitaka 192
   Vedas 177
   Upanishads 178
Homosexuality 58
Horoscopes 203
Humanism:
   and crime 110
   and politics 29, 67, 109
   as religion 31, 44
   essence of 106
   method of 30

objectives 228
  philosophy of
  precepts of 27
  principles 28,32
  purpose 30,108
  secular 43
  tasks for 146,223,227
  technique 30
Humanist:
  activities 69,110
  associations 36,236
  authorities 70 et seq
  chapters 23,239-244
  heroes 13
  history 244
  leaders 32
  logo 48
  manifestos 102-105
  personalities 72,73
  philosophy 28
  publications 75,238
  qualifications
  religious 43,44
Human rights 56
Humans 115

I Ching 77
IHEU 32,44
Internet 226
Intolerance 61
Islam 179

Jainism 195
Jihad (Holy War) 181
Jesus 37,171
Jews 20,93,181

Judaism 181
Judgements 83

Karma 192,195
Killing 54,196,216
Knowledge 27,136
Koans 193
Krishna 177
Krishna, Hare 179

Language 120,123,125
Lao Tzu 196
Laws, dietary 31,178,
  180,183
Li, Hongzhi 204
Lies 89
Life, life 50
Life stance 28
Literacy 125,147
Logical positivists 43
Love 28
Luther, Martin 175

Magnetism 128
Mahavira 195
Mantra 208
Marriage 65,70
Materialist 62
Measurements 199
Meditation 208
Melting pot 30
Mencius 194
Messiah 171,183
Mistakes 63
Miracles 121,139
Monist 62

Monkey tales 212
Morals, elements 80,81
Morality 58,77,83,109
Moses 78,184,217
Muhammad 180
Muslim 180
Mythology 209
Myths:
    German 215
    Japan 212,213
    Orient 214
    Thai 213
    Uganda 215
Mystics 181

Nanak, Guru 187
Nature 34,167
Naturalism 157
Nazi Party 215
Needs 115,132,169
Noosphere 226
Numerical 122

Occult 140
Old wives tales 163,199
Ought 81,83

Pascal's wager 41
Passover 184
Place Names:
    Benares 178
    Canada 54,121,146,239
    China 55,178,212, 196,204
    France 71
    Europe 110
    Ganges 178
    Glasgow 16
    India 40,177, 189,195,
    Ireland 138
    Japan 185
    Mecca 181
    Nepal 191
    Norway 65
    Persia 179,188
    Scotland 16
    United States 54,147,239
    Vancouver 21
    Vancouver Island 121
    Vatican 174
    Vijayawada 40
    (see also Myths)
Politics 29,67,109
Pope 174,213
Populations 146,223
Pornography 57
Pragmatism 59
Prayers 31,38,67,186
Presbyterian 18
Promises 209
Prophets 180,187
Proverbs 163
Puritanism 176
Purpose 108

Qi 204
Quantum physics 152

Rama 177
Reason 59,60
Reformation 176

Reincarnation 192
Religion:
    as big business 223
    as sport 17
    communal 173
    comparative 21
    non theistic 190
    reason for 151
    theistic 166
Religiosity 96
Religious:
    adherents 146,181
    denominations 98,143,176
    dietary laws 178,180,185
    paid holidays 42
    strife 225
Right & Wrong 88,90
Rights of passage 64,178
Roles 89
Rosh Hashanah 184

Saints, various 161,164,174
Santa Claus 16
Sasquatch 39
Saudi Arabia 180
Scientific method 59,107,141
Semantics 162
Sex, Sexuality 57
Science 59,141
Shiites 181
Shintoism 185
Shiva 177
Sikhism 187
Singh 187
Sin, sinners 90,91
Skepticism 45,107

Slaughter 225
Souls 62,120,145,150,211
Soup, primordial 130
Spirituality 16,62,176
Sufism 181
Suicide 53
Sunday school 17,19
Sunna 181
Sunnites 181
Superstitions 140
Supremacy, Act of 176
Sutra 193
Sword verses 181
Symbolism 47

Taliban 181
Taoism 134,196
Tao Te Ching 196
Ten Commandments 78
Testaments, old & new 172
Thinking, lateral
Thirteen 163
Time 155
Tithes 31
Tooth Fairy 16
Trinity 172
Triskaidecaphobia 163
Trobriand Island 169
Truth, revealed 60
Truths 191
Turbans 187

Unitarianism 176
Universe: 51,64,108,
    130,155,202, 227

Values 86,89,117
Verbal 123
Virgin Mary 138,175
Vishnu 177

War 20,186,214,215
Wars, holy 181
Way, The 197
Weeds 222
Wicca 216
Witchcraft 216,217
Wizards 216
World Trade Center 142

Yom Kippur 184

Zarathustra 189
Zodiac 201
Zoroastriansim 189,212
Zygote 55